Stalking in Children and Adults

Stalking in Children and Adults
The Primitive Bond

Joseph T. McCann, PsyD, JD

American Psychological Association, Washington, DC

Published by
American Psychological Association
750 First Street, NE
Washington, DC 20002

Copies may be ordered from
APA Order Department
P.O. Box 92984
Washington, DC 20090-2984

In the U.K., Europe, Africa, and the Middle East,
copies may be ordered from
American Psychological Association
3 Henrietta Street
Covent Garden, London
WC2E 8LU England

Typeset in Minion by Innovation Publication Services

Printer: Edwards Brothers, Inc., Ann Arbor, Michigan
Cover Designer: Naylor Design, Washington, DC
Editorial Production Service: Innovation Publication Services

The opinions and statements published are the responsibility of the authors, and such opinions and statements do not necessarily represent the policies of the APA.

Library of Congress Cataloging-in-Publication Data

McCann, Joseph T.
   Stalking in children and adolescents : the primitive bond / Joseph T. McCann.
      p. cm
   Includes bibliographical references and index.
   ISBN 1-55798-744-0 (alk. paper)
      1. Stalkers. 2. Stalking. 3. Stalking victims. 4. Attachment behavior in children. 5. Children—Mental health. I. American Psychological Association. II. Title.
   RJ507.A77 M385 2001
   618.92'8582—dc21   00-051062

British Library Cataloguing-in-Publication Data
A CIP record is available from the British Library.

Printed in the United States of America
First Edition

To my daughter, Ava Christina.
May health, love, and happiness
surround you always.

Contents

Foreword

W. H. Auden once wrote, "If equal affections cannot be, let the more loving one be me." The yearning of unrequited love—ubiquitous throughout great literature and studied most recently in the psychopathologically motivated behavior of stalking—now moves into the shadows of childhood and adolescence in this important book by Joseph T. McCann.

Both a psychologist and attorney, Dr. McCann is a studious and creative explorer of the attachment pathologies and identity deformations that contribute to stalking by young people. Drawing on the contributions of researchers, including myself, in the field of adult stalking, he first carefully defines the problem and then convincingly argues with direct evidence and related research that stalking is a late childhood and adolescent aberration warranting our serious attention.

One of the most original contributions of Dr. McCann is his application of Eriksonian identity development to the problem of stalking. He accomplishes this new integration by showing how pathologies of early attachment can distort the identity formation of the child and its recapitulation in adolescence, establishing a behavioral predisposition to obsess, follow, and in some cases, aggressively bully another. This is an abnormal object-relational world, which reminds me of Michael Balint's "basic fault" (1969) and Masud Khan's "resourceless dependency" (1974). I am also personally indebted to Dr. McCann for applying and extending my concept of "narcissistic linking fantasies" to youthful stalkers. He contributes to this psychodynamic formulation by detailing and differentiating the emotions of envy and jealousy and their affectively charged relationship to these consciously idealized fantasies of destiny with another, often compensating for low self-esteem in the young stalker.

Dr. McCann continues his exploration of stalking by drawing on the childhood and adolescent sexual harassment research, dating violence research, and the fine work of Brian Spitzberg and William Cupach concerning "obsessive relational intrusions" among college students. He emphasizes the worrisome parallels between adult stalking violence data (typically 25%–35% of those who assault their target) and the high rates of criminal violence among teenagers. He also pays close attention to the young victims of stalking and their likely high rates of anxiety, depression, and trauma, which may be verified in future research. He gracefully interweaves empirical research with an empathic understanding of the fears and angers of adolescents caught in the *danse macabre* of stalking.

Dr. McCann, moreover, offers some answers to the vexing questions that he raises. Treatment interventions for both victims and perpetrators, community prevention models, and appropriate legal parameters of antistalking laws for minors are discussed and carefully weighed. Joint efforts between criminal justice and mental health professionals are recommended in clear-cut stalking cases, and the importance of a positive and secure bond to both family and school is a central aspect of prevention for kids at risk. *Stalking in Children and Adolescents: The Primitive Bond* is an empirically sound, theoretically rich, and evocative contribution to our understanding of obsession, stalking, and violent attachments in the youngest generation.

J. Reid Meloy, PhD
San Diego, CA

Preface

Whenever I have discussed the issue of stalking among children and adolescents with others, it has often raised an eyebrow or two. During the course of developing and writing this book, I have frequently discussed many of the observations and thoughts contained herein with others. Invariably, one question that people ask is, "Stalking in children? How often does that happen?" The answers to these and related questions are outlined in the chapters that follow. However, it is interesting to note that at each stage in researching and writing about an issue related to stalking among children and adolescents, I frequently came upon theoretical works or empirical data that supported many of the thoughts I had about stalking among young people.

Stalking among children and adolescents is a problem that I first observed in clinical settings in the early part of the 1990s when anti-stalking laws were being passed across the United States. Around the time that I was independently conducting legal research on these new laws, I was also encountering a number of cases in my hospital-based practice in which adolescents were being referred for behaviors that revealed an obsessive fixation or preoccupation with a former girlfriend, a peer, or a media figure. In many of these cases, the youths were exhibiting behavior that met the definition of stalking as outlined in anti-stalking laws. Therefore, it is almost by coincidence that my parallel experiences as a lawyer and clinical psychologist began to converge on the topic of stalking.

Throughout this book I present a number of case examples that portray the principles and dynamics of stalking cases involving children and adolescents. In some instances, I use cases that have been obtained from published accounts in court opinions or media reports. These cases are accessible to the public, and therefore I have not made any concerted effort to alter the information provided in these cases as it was presented in the sources that are referenced. In other instances, I have drawn on cases from my professional work as a clinical and forensic psychologist. To protect the privacy and confidentiality of those involved in these cases, I have changed identifying information or have modified slightly some of the material. However, in each case the basic principles and dynamics have been preserved, and I believe that the examples accurately represent the issues raised in each case.

As I have continued to research stalking, as well as other forms of interpersonal violence, I have been struck by the fact that there is virtually no empirical data on the issue of stalking among children and adolescents. In my reviews of existing data, I discovered evidence that stalking can develop at younger ages; however, this evidence is typically buried in other statistics or not discussed as representing the problem of stalking among young people. The most recent example of this trend occurred as I began writing this text.

I had recently obtained *Stalking and Domestic Violence: The Third Annual Report to Congress Under the Violence Against Women Act* (Violence Against Women Grants Office, 1998) and was reviewing some data on stalking. In 1994, the Violence Against Women Act (P.L. 103-322) was passed as part of the Violent Crime Control and Law Enforcement Act. A major impetus for this law was to impose criminal sanctions against individuals who perpetrate violence against women, including stalking. Furthermore, the Violence Against Women Act specifies that an annual report must be submitted to Congress by the U.S. Attorney General in which information is provided about the incidence of stalking and the effectiveness of anti-stalking legislation. This third annual report to Congress was submitted in July 1998 (Violence Against Women Grants Office, 1998). Contained within that report are data from a sample of 797 male and female stalking victims that reveal 12% were first stalked before they reached the age of 18. Because the report does not specify an age for the stalking perpetrators who targeted these younger stalking victims, it is not possible to discern how many victims younger than 18 were first stalked by an adult and how many were stalked by another youth. Nevertheless, these data suggest that nearly one in eight stalking victims is first victimized in childhood or adolescence.

Another recent study examined the problem of stalking by looking at a large sample of individuals who were referred to a forensic psychiatric clinic in Australia that specializes in the evaluation of stalking offenders. Mullen, Pathe, Purcell, and Stuart (1999) examined 145 stalkers who were referred for treatment, and their sample of stalking offenders represents one of the largest to be systematically studied. One noteworthy finding in this study was that the sample of stalking offenders ranged in age from 15 to 75 years. Although Mullen and his colleagues do not note the percentage of stalkers who were younger than 18, their data reveal that stalking is perpetrated by adolescents. Although it has been shown empirically that stalkers are generally older than other types of criminal offenders (Meloy, 1996; Meloy & Gothard, 1995; Mullen, et al., 1999), clinical, anecdotal, and empirical evidence also reveals that children and adolescents represent a small portion of stalking victims and perpetrators. As a result, several interesting questions can be formulated on the basis of this observation, including, (a) What can we learn about how stalking develops by studying young offenders? (b) Do stalking offenders manifest warning signs early in their life of a propensity to obsessionally follow someone? and (c) Are the dynamics of stalking different when the victim and/or perpetrator is a child or adolescent? This book attempts to answer some of these and other questions and to point out directions for further research.

Acknowledgments

There are several individuals who deserve recognition and thanks for supporting this and related projects that I have undertaken over the past several years. I thank Charles Patrick Ewing at the State University of New York at Buffalo School of Law for his valuable comments on earlier drafts of my papers on anti-stalking laws and children. He has been a close friend and colleague over the years, and he continues to provide support, encouragement, and guidance. In addition, I thank Frank Dyer and Pam Vrendenburgh for reading earlier drafts of the manuscript and offering valuable suggestions for strengthening the way in which the material is presented. Their efforts were beyond the call of duty and are greatly appreciated. I also acknowledge my colleagues at the Binghamton Psychiatric Center, including Alan Hochberg, Linda Huntley, and Connie Kinch, for their willingness to discuss challenging cases with me. I thank Jennifer Berryman, James Merry, Carol Kelly, and Margaret Dugan for their support and encouragement. In addition, Martha Mason provided valuable library support for my research; I value greatly the assistance that she has given willingly over the years.

At United Health Services Hospitals, I am grateful for the support of Faye Utyro and Les Major, as well as the research and library support provided by Cheryl Slocum.

In my work with youthful offenders, I have also encountered the support of numerous individuals who have each provided their own unique contribution. I thank Gary Cohen, Marshall Kuhns, M. George Feeney, Ruben Reyes, Lee Wynn, Eileen Cornell, Claudia Soriano, June Schroeder, and Mary Miller.

A special note of thanks goes to J. Reid Meloy, who made himself very accessible to provide important contributions to this book. In addition to his willingness to write a foreword, his innovative theoretical and empirical work provided a body of literature that made the challenging task of writing about stalking in young people a bit easier. He also provided advance copies of forthcoming papers and made suggestions for references that provided greater substance to several themes that are developed in this book. I am extremely grateful to him.

There have also been valuable contributions made by my attorney colleagues. Robert M. O'Leary and James F. Moran discussed emerging issues in stalking legislation from a criminal law perspective, and they each offered useful input on issues related to community support services for stalking victims. John Hogan provided valuable insights on issues pertaining to civil litigation in school settings, particularly with respect to cases involving sexual harassment. I am extremely grateful to him for his contributions.

I also thank James Garbarino and Irene Hanson Frieze for their very thoughtful and helpful comments on an early draft of the manuscript. As always, it was a pleasure to work with the staff at APA Books. Susan Reynolds was very supportive of the project and provided encouragement throughout the development and writing of the manuscript. In addition, Anne Woodworth and Peg Markow provided valuable suggestions and comments for improving the organization and clarity of the manuscript. I am indebted to them for their help in getting the book into its final form.

Finally, I thank my family for their love, encouragement, and support. My wife Michele has been my most avid supporter, as well as my most balanced and rational critic. I value her love, advice, and friendship more than words can express. In addition, my son Alexander and daughter Ava are sources of inspiration to learn more about our world and to try and make it a better and safer place. Above all, my family has provided me with the motivation to write this book as well as the insight to realize that there are more important things in life than working in front of a computer.

Introduction

On October 15, 1999, 21-year-old Liam Youens of Nashua, New Hampshire, ambushed 20-year-old Mary Boyer (Wolfe, 1999). When she had gotten into her vehicle after leaving her job at a dentist's office, he pulled his car up next to hers and shot her several times before shooting himself in a murder–suicide. The lethal attack was seemingly unprovoked and occurred without any warning, because there was no apparent relationship between the two, other than that they had gone to the same high school several years earlier. For several years, Mr. Youens had maintained an obsessive fixation on Ms. Boyer, who was unaware of his bizarre infatuation with her. According to information obtained in a follow-up investigation, Mr. Youens had maintained an Internet web page devoted to Ms. Boyer on which he posted pictures that he had taken of her and personal statements to the effect that he wanted to kill her and other students from their high school (Ritter & Cole, 1999; Trudell, 1999).

The motive behind Mr. Youens's lethal attack remains elusive; however, the case is more complex than one involving a murder–suicide perpetrated by one adult against another. The investigation of Mr. Youens's web site, personal writings, and home revealed that he had developed his obsessive preoccupation with Ms. Boyer in the eighth grade when they met each other briefly at a church youth camp (Trudell, 1999). Mr. Youens was described as a very quiet youth who rarely spoke to others, and throughout school he and Ms. Boyer saw each other only occasionally, had apparently never dated, and rarely spoke to one another. For several years, Mr. Youens stalked Ms. Boyer and maintained a private romantic interest in her (Wolfe, 1999). In his private writings, he stated that he once loved her but no longer did. He ambushed her in a lethal attack with no clear motive, although he had chronic feelings of loneliness, suicidal thoughts, and a wish to kill the former object of his long-standing romantic obsession.

This case illustrates that the social problem of stalking, although typically viewed as a problem in adult relationships, often has origins in childhood and adolescence. Mr. Youens's fixation began in the eighth grade, when he would have been about age 13, and it evolved into a pattern of stalking behavior that persisted throughout high school. Law enforcement agencies in this case focused on how the attack took place by turning their attention to the arsenal of guns Mr. Youens had in his possession, as well as the immediate situational triggers that prompted his attack (Ritter & Cole, 1999). However, the challenging questions raised by this case include the following: Why did Mr. Youens develop his fixation on Ms. Boyer at such a young age? Why did his fixation persist for years? How and why did he keep his obsession concealed from others, including his victim? Why did no one notice or intervene sooner? Why did his obsession turn violent? What steps could have been taken to prevent this tragedy?

The social problem of stalking has become the focus of increasing attention since 1990, when California became the first state to enact legislation that made stalking a crime (Saunders, 1998). Over the last decade, there has been a gradual increase in research on the prevalence, nature, and impact of stalking on its victims. Although most of the literature on stalking has focused on the problem in adult populations, there is emerging evidence that stalking is a significant problem among younger people. Various forms of obsessional harassment and interpersonal violence among children and adolescents, such as sexual harassment and bullying, have been the focus of attention. However, in cases of more persistent or pervasive harassment, stalking behaviors appear to be a significant problem among young people.

Although no large-scale studies have addressed the prevalence and nature of stalking in young people, it is important to examine this social problem in younger populations for several reasons. First, given the evidence that stalking is so prevalent in the general adult population, as shown by Tjaden (1997), efforts to understand the developmental antecedents and early risk factors of stalking and other forms of obsessional harassment may provide valuable insights into our understanding of the problem that will hopefully lead to better assessment, treatment, and prevention. Second, evidence of related forms of aggression in young people, such as sexual harassment, bullying, and dating violence, suggests that the problem of stalking may be as significant in young people as it is in adult populations. However, stalking only recently has become an important focus of behavioral science research; as a result, not much useful information on this problem in younger populations has appeared in the literature. Finally, there is an inherent conflict in identifying certain forms of behavior in children and adolescents as criminal or abnormal. This conflict ranges from the tendency to minimize rather severe forms of violence and aggression to, conversely, overpathologizing and inappropriately labeling certain types of harassing behavior by children or adolescents as stalking. Therefore, a serious and scholarly approach to analyzing the available theoretical literature and empirical data will help to avoid the risks of minimizing or overpathologizing problematic behavior in young people.

ABOUT THIS BOOK

The focus of this book is the social problem of stalking primarily as it occurs among children and adolescents. It is intended for mental health professionals, attorneys, judges, legislators, policymakers, educators, parents, and anyone who has an interest in protecting young people and making schools, neighborhoods, and communities safer. The hope is that professionals will obtain information about stalking that will be of use to them in their work providing mental health, legal, educational, and case management services to young stalking perpetrators and victims. The book is also intended to be helpful to parents and school officials who are looking for information on how to deal with situations in which a child or teenager is being stalked.

Stalking, as conceptualized by various researchers, is a disturbance in attachment in which there is a failure in the capacity of the stalker to grieve the loss of unattainable or former love objects or to tolerate separation (Kienlen, 1998; Meloy, 1996, 1998b). When focusing on this social problem among children and adolescents, various developmental issues must be considered, including emotional and social maturity factors; the level of cognitive development; and other differences that exist among children, adolescents, and adults. Therefore, this book seeks to integrate some principles of developmental psychology with what is currently known about stalking based on research from adult populations.

As a result, the subtitle of this book reflects the complexity and challenges of this task. The word *bond* has traditionally been used in psychology to refer to a binding, fastening, or uniting that takes place between two things. With respect to social settings or interpersonal relationships, a bond generally refers to a link or connection that exists between people. The word *bond* has also been used to describe a specific behavioral response that typically follows a person's exposure to a particular stimulus (English & English, 1958); in behavioral psychology, the term is often used to describe the strength of motivation that connects a behavioral response and a specific stimulus. The word *primitive*, on the other hand, conveys two relevant themes. This term generally means that something occurs earlier in time; it also has certain connotations in psychoanalytic literature as referring to some psychological phenomena, such as needs or motives, that are less mature, underdeveloped, or formed in the very early phases of human development. Therefore, the title of this book, *Stalking in Children and Adolescents: The Primitive Bond*, captures what I view as the essence of stalking and other forms of obsessional harassment in children and adolescents. More specifically, these terms reflect the notion that stalking in younger age groups is characterized by an immature attachment that arises early in a person's life and represents a deviation from the normal course of development of interpersonal attachments. In addition, these terms suggest that stalking in children and adolescents is a maladaptive and underdeveloped behavioral response to a specific environmental cue, namely another person.

To lay a foundation for understanding stalking, the initial focus of this book is on general aspects of the problem, followed by a discussion of whether children and adolescents actually engage in this form of harassment. If younger individuals engage in stalking, which evidence strongly indicates they do, then several questions emerge about the types of behaviors and psychological dynamics that characterize younger stalking offenders. The discussion then turns to potential causes and motivations, including developmental factors that contribute to the behavior. Other relevant issues include recognizing early manifestations of stalking behavior and the relationship between stalking and violence. In later chapters, practical assessment, treatment, and case management issues that are related to young stalking victims are reviewed, including management of stalking cases by mental health, criminal justice, and school officials.

In chapter 1, definitions of the term *stalking* are outlined with respect to its uses in legal and behavioral science settings as well as in everyday conversation. The different ways in which the word is used to describe harassing or threatening behavior are explained, with case examples used to illustrate important distinctions. In addition, a general overview of stalking research is provided, including data on prevalence rates, behavioral dynamics, and the impact of stalking on victims. Although most of this research is based on adult populations, a general review of the stalking literature provides a useful context for understanding the material presented in later discussions on stalking in younger individuals.

Chapter 2 examines the question of whether or not stalking occurs in children and adolescents. Although very limited data are available on the direct issue of stalking in these age groups, individual case reports and data on related forms of aggression, such as sexual harassment and dating violence, are reviewed. An analysis of these data reveals that stalking behaviors can be identified in children and adolescents and that these behaviors appear to represent a severe subtype of harassment in school-age children. A continuum model is proposed in which stalking is viewed as lying at the extreme end of harassing and intrusive behavior. Moreover, I argue that a continuum model serves to recognize severe forms of harassing behavior in younger individuals and reduces the likelihood of magnifying or overpathologizing some forms of harassment.

The nature of stalking behavior in children and adolescents is discussed in chapter 3. An overview of the various types of behaviors that young stalkers use to threaten and harass their victims is provided. Similarities and differences between adult and younger stalking offenders are also outlined. In addition, the issue of youthful fixations on public figures, which range from benign infatuation to more severe forms of obsessive preoccupation, are analyzed. I also review the types of psychological disturbances that are found in child and adolescent stalkers, including similarities and differences between older and younger stalking offenders.

Chapter 4 is more theoretical than other chapters in this book and reviews the various etiological theories that have been proposed for understanding stalking behavior. One of the theories that has received the most attention is the view of stalking as a disturbance in attachment. Developmental issues related to the formation of identity and social attachments over the life span are discussed, with particular attention given to Meloy's (1996, 1998b) psychodynamic model of stalking. It is argued that the way in which people develop attachments to others, a sense of identity, and strategies for managing intense feelings of anger, envy, and jealousy can affect a person's capacity to begin and end relationships adaptively. Moreover, these factors provide a useful theoretical model for understanding the development of stalking at younger ages.

Chapter 5 addresses the possible early manifestations of stalking behavior. While researching this book, I examined some of the literature on bullying in childhood and was struck by many of the parallels that existed in the way these two forms of harassment are defined and conceptualized. Therefore, I review some of the similarities between bullying and stalking. In addition, the early histories of adult stalking offenders reveal that some have developed pathological fixations on other people early in life and that stalking can manifest in the early stages of development when people normally begin to explore attachments outside the family. I also review other early risk factors for stalking later in life that have been suggested in the theoretical and empirical literature. By identifying valid risk factors, preventive programs might be designed to help reduce the incidence of stalking behavior as the person enters adulthood.

One of the most significant concerns in stalking cases is whether or not the offender poses a risk of violence to the victim. Although some research is available on the prevalence of violence among adults who stalk, there are limited data on violence among younger individuals who stalk. Chapter 6 reviews what is currently known about various risk factors for violence in stalking cases. The literature on violence risk assessment has improved our understanding of many aspects of the precipitants of violence. With respect to children and adolescents, however, this literature provides evidence of general factors that increase or decrease the potential for violence, without necessarily informing us of the risk factors that are specific to stalking in younger people. Moreover, personal safety advocates and private security personnel often set forth the proposition that violence can be predicted before it occurs, yet the empirical literature generally suggests that violence cannot be definitively predicted, even though general levels of approximate risk can be provided. These opposing views can be reconciled by discussing the differences between personal and professional prediction of violence. Chapter 6 reviews ways in which both of these approaches to violence and threat assessment can coexist and be viewed as valid in specific situations.

Chapter 7 addresses the impact of stalking on its victims, particularly with reference to the young stalking victim. Among the issues addressed are the unique problem of adults who stalk children or adolescents and how these cases are both similar to and different from cases of sexual offending against young people. Other issues addressed in this chapter are the psychological impact of stalking on victims and the various community and professional resources that are available to stalking victims and their families. I recommend a multidisciplinary approach to stalking cases that involves input from the victim; his or her family; and mental health, legal, and educational professionals to maximize the secure and safe management of stalking cases involving a child or adolescent victim.

Chapter 8 offers more specific recommendations for managing stalking cases. The school environment is one setting in which stalking is likely to be encountered, and suggestions are offered for writing policy, updating student handbooks, and educating staff about the social problem of stalking. In addition, mental health professionals, teachers, guidance counselors, and other professionals need to be trained to identify the manifestations of stalking and to make referrals to appropriate legal, community, and mental health agencies. Legal measures, such as the use of status offense laws and community diversion programs, are briefly reviewed as measures for intervening with the young stalking perpetrator. Personal protection measures are also discussed, including educating children and adolescents about effective ways to deal with stalking behavior and advising parents on how to protect their children but not reinforce unreasonable fears or create general feelings of paranoia.

Finally, chapter 9 discusses legal approaches to dealing with the problem of stalking in young people. More specifically, anti-stalking laws are discussed as they apply to the adjudication of young stalking offenders and the protection of young stalking victims. Although these laws appear to offer promise for protecting children and adolescents, their potential has not been realized, and more stringent protective measures for younger victims have not been implemented by most legislatures. Moreover, policy surrounding anti-stalking laws needs to encompass a number of factors, including developmental differences in the way young people and adults perceive threats. I also review the efficacy of protective orders and make recommendations for legislators and policy makers to improve legal protections for young stalking victims.

This book examines a social problem that has been recognized in clinical and forensic settings in which children and adolescents have been both the perpetrators and the victims of stalking behavior. Although empirical literature is lacking on this specific problem, anecdotal and clinical case evidence suggests that stalking is a problem among children and adolescents. Moreover, a review of related forms of harassment, such as bullying and sexual harassment, suggests that stalking is a subset of more severe forms of harassing behavior in younger individuals. It is my hope that this book not only provides a review of what is known about stalking behavior among children and adolescents but also offers useful suggestions for managing cases of this type as well as pointing out directions for further research.

Stalking in Children and Adults

1

What Is Stalking?

Two observations are often made about the relationship between popular media, such as movies or television shows, and the problems that society faces at any given time. One observation is that the content of movies and television programs often reflects many of the difficulties or social ills that exist. The other observation, of course, is that media portrayals of problems, such as violence or promiscuous sexuality, contribute to our social ills. With respect to the social problem of stalking, the media have provided both romanticized and tragic examples of stalking in a variety of contexts and across many age groups. Meloy (1998a), for instance, has stated that "a plethora of stalking films" have been released over the years (p. xix).

Society's concern about stalking seems to arise from a general uneasiness that many people feel about unprovoked attacks by strangers with mental illnesses, as well as violence by personal acquaintances (Farnham, James, & Cantrell, 2000). Despite these concerns, which seem to have intensified in recent years with highly publicized lethal attacks in schools and workplace settings, good evidence indicates that the social problem of stalking has been around for a long time. In fact, it has been suggested that some of William Shakespeare's sonnets, written centuries ago, are dominated by themes of romantic obsession that derived from an obsession he had with a woman that may have involved stalking (Skoler, 1998). Evidence of obsessional harassment and stalking behavior dating back so many years prompted Meloy (1998a) to write that "stalking is an old behavior, but a new crime" (p. xix).

This chapter offers some perspectives on why stalking has come to the forefront of public concern over personal safety and how stalking is defined in the law and behavioral sciences. By carefully distinguishing formal legal and scientific definitions from non-technical definitions of stalking that are used in everyday conversation, the reader will gain an appreciation for some of the complexities in how stalking is defined. The chapter then moves to a discussion of what is currently known about the prevalence of stalking in adults and the characteristics of stalking perpetrators, victims, and behaviors. Although this discussion focuses primarily on adults, it serves as a foundation for understanding the principles and analyses of stalking in children and adolescents that are provided in the remainder of this book.

RISING CONCERNS ABOUT STALKING

Our current fascination with and interest in stalking can be traced back to July 18, 1989, when the popular actress Rebecca Schaeffer, who co-starred in the television sitcom *My Sister Sam,* was shot and killed by obsessed fan Robert Bardo. This act of violence is significant because Mr. Bardo had maintained a long-standing psychotic obsession with Ms. Schaeffer over approximately two years (Gilligan, 1992; McAnaney, Curliss, & Abeyta-Price, 1993). During the course of his obsession, Mr. Bardo sent numerous letters to Ms. Schaeffer, in which he told her that he would harm her, and he followed her on numerous occasions. One time he was restrained by a security guard at the television studio where her program was being taped. Because of the persistent nature of his obsession, Mr. Bardo acted on his wishes to contact the actress by hiring a private detective who was able to locate Ms. Schaeffer's home address through California motor vehicle records. Mr. Bardo then went to Ms. Schaeffer's residence with a .357 magnum handgun to complete what he later described as a "mission" and fatally shot her.

What makes this particular incident significant is that it precipitated a wake of public outcry that resulted in legal action resulting in the enactment of the nation's first anti-stalking law in California in 1990 (Guy, 1993; Thomas, 1993). The law was passed in response to the need for protection of individuals from repetitive forms of harassment. By 1993, nearly every state in the country had passed some form of anti-stalking legislation, and the federal jurisdictions had also passed similar legislation that made stalking an illegal act (McCann, 1995). Only one or two states had not passed a specific anti-stalking law, yet those states relied on harassment or menacing statutes in their penal law to deal with stalking behavior. Today, anti-stalking laws exist in all state and federal jurisdictions, and many other countries, including Canada and England, have some form of anti-stalking legislation (Bradfield, 1998).

Although the murder of Rebecca Schaeffer was a major motivating factor for passing anti-stalking laws, recent history shows that there have been numerous cases predating her murder in which a famous person was stalked by an obsessed fan. In 1980, for example, the infamous case of John Hinkley, Jr. brought the problem of stalking to the forefront of awareness for Americans. Mr. Hinkley maintained an obsessive fixation on movie actress Jodie Foster; he had even made attempts to visit her while she was a student at Yale University and had also telephoned her but was rebuffed. Consequently, Mr. Hinkley made an assassination attempt on President Ronald Reagan in an effort to demonstrate to Ms. Foster the extent of his affections for her. The shooting death of John Lennon outside his New York City apartment in 1980 is yet another instance in which the social problem of stalking came to the foreground of media attention (Jones, 1992). Mark David Chapman pursued John Lennon and had approached the ex-Beatle for an autograph prior to the fatal shooting. One of the most vicious, non-fatal attacks that resulted from an obsessive individual pursuing a celebrity occurred when actress Theresa Saldana was repeatedly stabbed by Arthur Jackson, who was severely psychotic

(Markman & Labrecque, 1994). In 1982, Mr. Jackson acted on the numerous threats he had made to the actress over a very long period of time by following her and stabbing her on a public street. If not for the heroic acts of a nearby delivery man, Ms. Saldana would likely have been killed by her attacker.

Most recently, several celebrities have had their experiences with being stalked by an obsessive individual made public. David Letterman was repeatedly pursued by a delusional woman who claimed to be his wife, entered his residence on numerous occasions, and even stole his automobile. Other celebrities who have been the victims of stalking include Madonna, Steven Spielberg, Michael J. Fox, and Cher. In each case, a wide range of threats had been made against the celebrity, and the stalking raised significant fear in the person being stalked. It is also worth noting that in the cases involving Madonna and Steven Spielberg, anti-stalking laws were used successfully to prosecute and obtain convictions against the stalking perpetrator (Saunders, 1998).

Although there have been numerous cases in which stalking is directed toward a famous celebrity or an individual in a position of power, such as a politician, the murder of Rebecca Schaeffer stands as particularly significant because of the public attention that followed her death. Since that time, passage of anti-stalking laws has also been accompanied by a significant amount of attention in the behavioral sciences literature as well as popular media outlets. More specifically, research into the nature of stalking and the characteristics of those who engage in this form of behavior has shown that it is not a social problem confined only to celebrities, politicians, or others who are frequently in the public eye. Moreover, people who engage in stalking are not invariably individuals who are psychotic or have a severe mental illness; there are several instances in which obsessional harassment or stalking has been perpetrated by less severely disturbed individuals and against victims who are ordinary citizens in the community. Among the other settings in which stalking can occur are domestic disputes, intimate relationships that have soured, and interpersonal relationships that have developed in the workplace. In short, stalking has been found to be a social problem that cuts across a wide range of individuals.

One of the first scholarly studies on stalking and other forms of obsessive harassment was undertaken by Zona, Sharma, and Lane (1993). Their study is significant because it constituted an attempt to classify different types of stalking cases. These researchers analyzed the first 74 cases that came to the attention of the Threat Management Unit of the Los Angeles Police Department. Many of these cases were considered high profile because they involved individuals in the entertainment industry; however, others who had been stalking victims were not particularly well known. Three major types of stalking were identified: (a) erotomania, (b) love obsessional, and (c) simple obsessional. *Erotomania* is a mental disorder classified in the *Diagnostic and Statistical Manual of Mental Disorders-IV (DSM-IV)* as a delusional disorder subtype that is characterized by a belief that the person is passionately loved by another person, usually someone of higher social status (American Psychiatric Association, 1994). Such individuals often go to great lengths to approach the victim, who is believed to be in love with them, and law enforcement officials are sometimes required to intervene. *Love obsessional stalking* is characterized by individuals who maintain a fanatical love for the victim. The love obsessional type differs from erotomania in that the delusional beliefs in love obsessional following are usually one symptom of a more severe mental illness. Love obsessional followers typically have a primary psychiatric diagnosis, and at times their beliefs may not rise to the level of a belief that the victim is in love with them, but may involve the belief that the victim will grow to love them if given a proper chance. In general, love obsessional followers, such as Liam Youens who was described in the Introduction, are socially maladjusted and have a history of poor adjustment in intimate relationships (Zona, Palerea, & Lane, 1998). In *simple obsessional stalking,* a prior relationship exists between the victim and the person engaging in the stalking behavior. More specifically, the prior relationships vary in terms of intensity and the degree of involvement between the perpetrator and victim. In most cases in Zona et al.'s study, the relationships had soured, and the individual perceived that the victim had mistreated him or her in some way. As such, the stalking behavior constituted an effort to correct a perceived wrong or to seek revenge or retribution.

Since this initial study by Zona and his colleagues, several other studies on stalking and obsessional following have begun to appear in the literature. Although the details of specific research findings on stalking will be outlined in later chapters, it is worth noting that stalking represents a rather provocative and sometimes dangerous form of behavior that can be devastating for the victims involved and extremely challenging for those who attempt to intervene and manage such cases. Before examining the stalking literature in any detail, however, it is necessary to define what stalking is and what it is not.

WHAT STALKING IS

A clear discussion of any clinical issue depends on the adequate delineation and formulation of terms and concepts. With respect to stalking, there are a number of meanings that have been attached to the term, as well as other phrases that have been used to describe the phenomenon. Therefore, it is useful to examine the various ways in which the term has been defined, including less technical uses, legal definitions, and psychological approaches to formulating the concept. Each type of definition is important for outlining the issues to be discussed later in this book.

Nontechnical Definitions

Stalking as Predatory Aggression

According to *Webster's New World Dictionary* (Guralnick, 1987), the word *stalk* means "to walk in a stiff, haughty, or grim manner" or "to pursue or approach game, an enemy, etc. stealthily, as from cover" (p. 582). Thus, in everyday language use, *stalking* often refers to an act of secretly approaching or pursuing someone with the intent to capture or harm. The classic example is the wild animal that silently and secretly pursues its prey just prior to a kill. When applied to human relationships, this definition suggests that when one person stalks another, there is an intent to threaten or harm the other person.

Although this definition reflects the images typically evoked by the term *stalking*, it also reflects various types of aggressive actions as a prelude to violence. An example of this behavior is *predatory aggression,* which is similar to the action required to destroy prey as when land mammals "stalk their prey and attack with lethal strikes. . ." (Meloy, 1988, p. 213). Moreover, predatory violence is characterized by a lack of autonomic nervous system arousal and involves minimal emotional arousal, minimal perception of threat, and heightened sensory awareness of one's environment. The goals of predatory aggression are generally variable and can involve such motives as the gratification of hostile fantasy, reduction of threats to one's sense of self-control, satisfaction of self-centered needs, and relief from psychotic symptoms. As a result of these factors, predatory aggression involves planned and purposeful violence, when the aggression leads to violent acts (Meloy, 1988). Moreover, because the affective arousal in predatory violence is lacking, the perpetrator of predatory aggression is not bound by specific time constraints when carrying out behavior that satisfies one's goals and thus there is room for "private rituals" in which the aggressor engages in hidden or private actions that serve to reduce threat or heighten narcissistic wishes or needs. Overall, predatory aggression can be characterized as the callous, deliberate, and planned aggression that precedes violence in which the perpetrator maintains reality testing and victimizes others for gratification of self-centered needs. This form of aggression is associated with the psychopathic personality.

Stalking as a Preparatory Act of Aggression

Predatory aggression reflects the general nature of the stealth and focused predator that destroys its prey. What emerges from the informal meaning often attributed to the term *stalking* is an individual who consciously, intently, and secretly follows a plan of aggression, resulting in violence toward another in the same way that a wild animal stalks its prey prior to attack. Although this generalization is typically true, in a few cases of preparatory aggression, other forms of psychopathology may also be present, such as dissociative disturbances, delusions, or psychotic thinking.

In this way, stalking behavior may therefore encompass the preparatory acts of discrete violence that occur during the commission of a criminal act such as murder, sexual assault, or robbery. For instance, an adolescent or group of adolescents may watch and follow an elderly person for hours or days to learn that person's routine or schedule in preparation for the opportune time to commit a robbery. Or, a lonely teenager may monitor, follow, and stalk a group of classmates who have incessantly teased him as a prelude to the more violent act of killing them by opening fire with a weapon. Thus, such acts as lying in wait, hiding and then surprising the victim, and other tactics that increase the element of surprise are often thought to be a form of stalking. In short, preparatory behavior that precedes violence is sometimes incorrectly referred to as stalking.

An example of the confusion that can occur when preparatory acts of aggression are referred to as stalking is in the case of *Arizona v. Laird* (1996). In that case, the defendant was a 17-year-old young man who was tried as an adult and convicted of first-degree murder, kidnapping, burglary, theft, forgery, and robbery. One of several issues raised on appeal included the imposition of the death penalty. The court imposed the death penalty because it found evidence of particularly heinous, cruel, and depraved conduct during commission of the crime. Among the issues was a defense argument that the defendant's crime was the result of immaturity and impulsivity given his developmental level and that his age should be a mitigating factor. The Arizona Supreme Court decision noted that testimony by the victim's neighbors at trial indicated that the defendant had been "stalking" the victim on the day prior to the murder. Moreover, the evidence showed that the defendant broke into the victim's home and waited until morning to "ambush" the victim. It is significant that the facts of the case indicated that the motive for the crime was the defendant's wish to have a truck, even if he had to kill for it, and that there was no relationship between the defendant and the victim. Rather, the crime was motivated by a wish to steal the victim's truck. Also, expert testimony at trial noted that the defendant had antisocial, narcissistic, and borderline personality characteristics. As such, the facts reveal a crime of opportunity committed by a psychopathic adolescent.

The confusion in this case has to do with using the term *stalking* to describe the defendant's behavior prior to the crime. In fact, his actions were carried out in such a manner as to maximize the element of surprise. There was no evidence of repetitive following and no intent on the part of the defendant to instill fear in his victim as is required in formal legal definitions of stalking. Moreover, the youth was charged with several offenses, but not stalking. Therefore, his behavior during the commission of the crime was predatory in nature, but did not constitute stalking as it is legally defined or conceptualized in the behavioral science literature. Although included in a state appellate court decision, this case is an example of the colloquial use of the term *stalking*, but in fact the defendant's behavior is an example of predatory aggression, or preparatory activity as part of his modus operandi, but was not stalking in the legal sense. This distinction is important because for the purposes of this book, the legal and behavioral science definitions of stalking as outlined below is used.

These preparatory acts have been attributed to a small group of stalking offenders that have been identified as psychopathic or sociopathic stalkers (Cupach & Spitzberg, 1998). However, this narrowly defined form of stalking that has its basis in colloquial uses of the word should not necessarily be considered a form of stalking. Psychopathic stalking, as it has been called (McAnaney et al., 1993), is more appropriately conceptualized as a predatory form of aggression (Meloy, 1988) because the pursuit in these cases is motivated more by whether a victim meets certain criteria for victimization or attack; the psychopathic individual is not interested in developing or maintaining a relationship with the victim as is the case in true stalking or obsessional following. Although psychopathic individuals are not precluded from engaging in stalking, the limited attachment capacity of psychopathic individuals and the attachment needs that underlie stalking behavior make it less likely that psychopathic individuals will engage in stalking (Meloy, 1996). Moreover, the act of secretly following or pursuing a victim frequently takes place outside the awareness of the victim until the final act of aggression or violence. Thus, the victim does not experience a sense of fear or does not perceive a threat of harm as is often required in legal definitions of stalking. Therefore, predatory aggression is distinguished from legal definitions of stalking (as described below) or clinical terms such as obsessional following or harassment, in that it describes a unique form of pursuit that sometimes serves as a prelude to a violent act or crime. With predatory aggression, there is following and monitoring behavior that may occur, but there is generally no intent to create fear or anxiety in the victim and instead there is generally a wish to maximize the victim's surprise or to avoid detection during commission of the criminal act. In addition, predatory aggression is not based on an interest or desire to develop, maintain, or repair an interpersonal relationship, as is the case in stalking.

Legal Definitions

As noted earlier, California was the first state to pass an anti-stalking law. This statute became a model for other states, which soon followed and enacted their own version of such legislation. By 1993, 48 states had passed some form of anti-stalking legislation, and the federal government undertook an effort to design a model code for use throughout the United States (National Institute of Justice, 1993). Currently, there is some form of anti-stalking legislation in effect in each of the 50 states and in all federal jurisdictions (Bradfield, 1998).

The California statute, which encompasses the criteria found in most anti-stalking laws, provides the following definition of *stalking:*

> Any person who willfully, maliciously, and repeatedly follows or harasses another person and who makes a credible threat with the intent to place that person in reasonable fear of death or great bodily injury or to place that person in reasonable fear of the death or great bodily injury of his or her immediate family is guilty of the crime of stalking . . . (Cal. Penal Code §646.9(a), 1993).

This definition encompasses a number of factors that are found in most statutory descriptions of the offense. In particular, two chief elements found in anti-stalking laws are threat and criminal intent.

The Threat Requirement

Threatening behavior that constitutes stalking is defined in a variety of ways; however, the most common forms of threat are repeated following, harassment through repeated telephone calls or threatening letters, and threats against one's family members (McAnaney et al., 1993). Common forms of threatening behavior include such things as repeated trespassing on the person's property, displaying a weapon, vandalizing the victim's belongings, making threats of bodily harm, intimidating the person, and engaging in surveillance of the victim's actions. Indeed, the scope of stalking behaviors is broad. Anti-stalking laws also frequently require that the threatening behavior constitute a course of conduct, wherein there is more than one occurrence and in which there is a series of acts (at least two) over a period of time that show a uniform purpose of creating a credible threat to the victim. In order for threatening or harassing behavior to rise to the level of criminal stalking, there is generally a requirement that the threats are believable such that a reasonable person would feel threatened (National Institute of Justice, 1993).

The Criminal Intent Requirement

There is also an intent element that is a part of most anti-stalking laws, in which the course of the perpetrator's conduct must be purposeful, intentional, willful, or knowing (National Institute of Justice, 1993). This general provision requires that the perpetrator intend to cause fear in the victim, while the issue of whether the victim actually experiences threat or fear is not always required. Since the passage of anti-stalking legislation, there has been considerable academic debate over these statutes, such as their constitutionality (Gilligan, 1992; Guy, 1993; McAnaney et al., 1993; Thomas, 1993) and potential efficacy (Anderson, 1993). Among the various concerns raised about the efficacy of these laws include the fact that the seriousness and pervasiveness of psychopathology found in stalking perpetrators may result in more intense rage and anger over legal interventions, such as restraining orders or brief incarceration, that a victim can access through these laws.

Despite the advantages or limitations of these laws, it is important to recognize how the legal definition of stalking differs from the colloquial meaning attached to the term. As noted earlier, stalking is commonly associated with secretive, preparatory acts of violence that are often subsumed under the legal term of *lying in wait*. However, legally defined stalking is broader in scope, because lying in wait is only one form of threatening behavior that is possible under most anti-stalking laws. In addition, the stalking behaviors meant to be proscribed by statute are those that typically involve a more overt and visible threat, unlike predatory forms of aggression that imply a more secretive approach to the victim. That is, predatory acts such as lying in wait typically involve an intent on the part of the perpetrator to avoid detection and to heighten the element of surprise, whereas legally proscribed stalking necessarily involves an intent on the part of the perpetrator to induce fear and apprehension in the victim. Therefore, predatory aggression will rarely constitute a crime in and of itself and is more appropriately conceptualized as part of the modus operandi of criminal conduct. Legally defined stalking, on the other hand, is by definition criminal and involves a different set of behaviors that are carried out for different reasons than predatory stalking. More specifically, criminal stalking involves threats and repeated harassment that is meant to be not only made known to the victim, but also to evoke fear in the victim.

Behavioral Science Definitions

Obsessional Following

Because stalking constitutes an abnormal form of behavior, there have been recent efforts to examine the clinical characteristics of those individuals who engage in this behavior. In his comprehensive review of the literature on the subject, Meloy (1996) pointed out the limitations of the term *stalking*, including the sensationalistic connotation it has had in the popular media and the fact that it refers to legally defined criminal conduct. He offered the term *obsessional following* to refer to stalking, and he distinguishes it from the legal and non-technical ways in which *stalking* is used.

According to Meloy (1996), the term *obsessional following* is drawn from clinical studies on individuals who engage in stalking and "describes a person who engages in an abnormal or long-term pattern of threat or harassment directed toward a specific individual" (p. 148). Meloy also noted that the pattern of threat is abnormal and long-term when it involves "more than one overt act of unwanted pursuit of the victim that is perceived by the victim as being harassing" (p. 148). Most importantly, Meloy found that obsessional following is not a clinical diagnosis and refers instead to the behavior and intent of the perpetrator.

Meloy's definition of obsessional following bears many similarities to the legal definition of stalking. Both definitions incorporate notions of long-term, repetitive harassment that is directed toward a specific victim and that is perceived by the victim as threatening. In this way, both the legal definition of stalking and Meloy's definition of obsessional following differ from the colloquial use of the term in that the stalking behavior is intended to be known by the victim rather than a secretive lying in wait that might precede a crime such as murder or robbery. Obsessional following differs from legal definitions of stalking in that there is a greater focus on the abnormal nature of the behavior. In particular, Meloy emphasized the obsessional quality of the stalker's actions because they are typically associated with intense affect, persistent ideas about the object, and recurrent impulses to approach the victim. Obsessional following is thus conceptualized as a clinical disturbance of attachment that serves to describe the nature of the ambivalent and disturbed connection the follower has with his or her victim. Most importantly, obsessional following does not infer a specific diagnosis such as obsessive–compulsive disorder or compulsive personality disorder (Meloy, 1996). In later discussions, the nature of psychopathology encountered in child and adolescent obsessional followers is reviewed. It is worth repeating that stalking behavior represents a disturbance encompassing a range of psychological functions, including attachment, identity, thought content and cognitive processing, affect regulation, interpersonal relationships, and behavioral controls. A behavioral science approach to understanding the dynamics of stalking necessarily focuses on these various factors, not just on the behavior and the intent of the perpetrator, as is found in legal approaches to conceptualizing stalking.

Obsessive Relational Intrusion

Another concept in the behavioral science literature that is associated with stalking is *obsessive relational intrusion,* which has been outlined by Cupach and Spitzberg (1998) and defined as "repeated and unwanted pursuit and invasion of one's sense of physical or symbolic privacy by another person, either stranger or acquaintance, who desires and/or presumes an intimate relationship" (pp. 234–235). Several key components include the fact that the pursuer and object do not have mutual goals for a relationship, there is more than one instance of intrusion resulting in a pattern of harassment over time, and both psychological/symbolic and physical intrusions can occur. What makes the concept of obsessive relational intrusion very useful, particularly when discussing the problem of stalking among children and adolescents, is that it represents a continuum of intrusive or harassing behavior ranging from minor annoyances to extreme forms of threat of which stalking and menacing are severe types.

According to Cupach and Spitzberg's analysis, some intrusive behaviors are merely annoying, yet expected in the initial stages of spurned relationships, such as receiving unwanted notes or gifts from someone for a brief period of time. Milder forms of annoyance generally cease and are not pervasive or chronic. On the other hand, some relational intrusions cross a blurry boundary into more problematic behaviors that are persistent, obsessive, and maladaptive. As noted by Cupach and Spitzberg (1998), "it is precisely this aspect of pursuit—when intrusion becomes both unwanted and obsessive—that renders interaction between pursuer and object problematic" (p. 244). Thus, obsessive relational intrusions occur along a continuum of severity in which stalking is an extreme form that is unreasonable and implies some relational context between pursuer and victim. Also, obsessive relational intrusions that include stalking behavior are distinguished from predatory aggression or stalking in the colloquial sense in that there is some interpersonal relationship that exists or is desired between the pursuer and object.

Moreover, obsessive relational intrusion is particularly useful for conceptualizing the problem of stalking and obsessional following in children and adolescents. More specifically, there is a risk of overpathologizing relatively innocuous, and less severe forms of interpersonal intrusions in young people, such as sending "love letters" or making several attempts at pursuing a relationship, that are a normal part of childhood and adolescence. On the other hand, there is also a risk of minimizing severe forms of harassment, stalking, and menacing in young people by dismissing such behaviors as "puppy love," "childhood infatuation," "having a crush," or "kids being kids." Minimization of severe forms of obsessional harassment in young people may prevent appropriate measures from being taken at the earliest point in time. The manner in which Cupach and Spitzberg (1998) conceptualized general forms of relational intrusions along a continuum—which also provides for a subjective boundary between reasonable and unreasonable intrusions in relationships—is highly useful for addressing these issues in young people.

The Prevalence of Stalking in Adults

If media attention is any indication of the relative significance of a problem, then one would expect that stalking is an extremely rampant and pervasive social problem. Given the attention, and sometimes sensationalistic treatment of the issue, it would surprise no one to learn that stalking is indeed widespread in society. Unfortunately, media attention is not a very precise gauge of the true prevalence of a particular social issue. Moreover, the attention often generated on stalking in the popular media is a function of the popularity of the victim; when a celebrity or politician becomes the object of an obsessional follower, there is often a flood of news coverage on the incident. Thus, media attention tells us little about the true prevalence of stalking or obsessional following.

Because scientific knowledge about stalking is in its infancy, little is known about the true prevalence of the problem. Recently, the National Institute of Justice, in collaboration with the Centers for Disease Control and Prevention, undertook a comprehensive national survey of 8,000 women and 8,000 men on a broad range of issues that pertained to violence, including stalking (Tjaden, 1997). The researchers defined *stalking* as repetitive physical or visual proximity, unwanted communication, or verbal or written threats that were carried out on a number of occasions. According to the results of this study, 8% of women and 2% of men report having been stalked at some time in their lives. These figures roughly equate with about 1.4 million individuals being stalked each year (i.e., 1,000,000 women and 400,000 men) and a projected lifetime stalking victim rate of 8.2 million females and 2 million males in the United States. These numbers suggest that stalking is an extensive problem in our society.

There is evidence within the clinical literature that documents an increase in the prevalence of obsessional following as a problem in clinical and forensic settings. In a study of referrals to a forensic psychiatric clinic specializing in the evaluation of criminal offenders in New York City, Harmon, Rosner, and Owens (1995) found that the number of stalking perpetrators referred for evaluation tripled between 1987 and 1993. According to this study, stalking offenders accounted for 0.6% of referrals at the beginning of the study period, but they accounted for 1.7% of referrals six years later. Meloy (1996) interpreted this increase as reflecting an increase in stalking, but he noted that the passage of extensive anti-stalking legislation across the country during the period that Harmon and colleagues conducted their study could also account for the increase.

Although there has been significant attention given to adult perpetrators and victims of stalking, it does not necessarily follow that this social problem is confined only to adults. In fact, the behavioral science literature contains numerous examples of psychological disturbances, once believed to occur only in adults, that have been observed in children and adolescents such as sex offending (Barbaree, Marshall, & Hudson, 1993), malingering (McCann, 1998a), and homicide (Ewing, 1990). In short, many behavioral and criminal behaviors typically viewed as limited to adults are also observed in young people. More importantly, the adequate understanding of problem behaviors in children and adolescents does not involve the unqualified application of theories and empirical finding on adult populations to young people.

Although it has been only within the past four years that any attempts have been made to document the prevalence of stalking and obsessional following, there are a number of factors that are impediments to obtaining accurate estimates among children and adolescents. The most significant of these impediments has to do with the nature of how crimes are prosecuted in the juvenile justice system: youthful offenders proceed through a different court system than do adults. Typically, those young offenders who have been arrested for a crime are initially processed in the juvenile or family court system, unless their criminal behavior is so violent or egregious that they are transferred to adult status. Because juvenile courts often operate under more restricted access and juvenile court records are often expunged or sealed when a juvenile reaches the age of 18, there are inadequate data about the types of less violent crimes a juvenile commits, some of which may fall into the category of stalking. Therefore, access to juvenile court records can be difficult, making the determination of prevalence rates on certain types of juvenile crime more difficult.

Other possible reasons for the lack of accurate prevalence rates on stalking in juveniles may rest on the assumption that certain types of offenses associated with stalking are not particularly problematic among children and adolescents and that stalking or obsessional following do not occur in certain age groups. In fact, there may be a presumption that certain forms of violence and harassment are not found in younger age groups. In chapter 2, evidence is presented that demonstrates stalking occurs in children and adolescents. Also, data from studies on issues related to stalking in young people are presented, including studies of sexual harassment in schools, issuance of restraining orders against young offenders, and anecdotal case studies of stalking in children and adolescents. Although these sources do not provide clear data on the extent of stalking in young people, they circumvent some of the problems noted above with respect to obtaining complete information on offenses by young offenders that are adjudicated in the more confidential and restricted juvenile and family court system.

Before examining the problem of stalking in children and adolescents, it is useful to first have some general understanding of what is currently known about stalking. Toward this end, a brief overview of the literature on stalking among adult offenders and victims is provided as a context for addressing the problem among young people in later chapters.

CURRENT KNOWLEDGE ABOUT STALKING

There has been a significant amount of empirical research that has developed in the past several years on many aspects of stalking, such as the characteristics of people who engage in this criminal behavior, the types of behaviors that are used to stalk others, the effect of stalking on victims, and some of the dynamics as to why people stalk. The most succinct, yet comprehensive, survey of the research on stalking is provided by Meloy (1998a) in the introductory chapter of *The Psychology of Stalking*. All of the research reported in this chapter is based on adult samples, but it provides a very useful context for understanding the general nature of stalking.

Most individuals who engage in stalking are males, with percentages in various samples ranging from 66% to 90% of all offenders being male (Harmon, Rosner, & Owens, 1995; Kienlen, Birmingham, Solberg, O'Regan, & Meloy, 1997; Meloy & Gothard, 1995; Mullen & Pathe, 1994a; Zona et al., 1993). The empirical research also shows that stalking offenders are older than most criminal offenders, with an average age in the late 30s. This finding is relevant to the issue of stalking in children and adolescents because it raises the question of whether or not stalking is significant in younger people. As the next chapter illustrates, stalking does appear to occur with some frequency in younger ages, which must be reconciled with the empirical findings that stalking offenders tend to be older than the average criminal offender. It may be that children and adolescents who stalk constitute a subset of stalking offenders at the end of the age distribution of those who stalk or the distribution of stalking offenders may be bimodal; however, an alternative explanation may be that research has been confined to adult populations, and the issue of stalking in younger individuals has not received adequate attention thus far. At the present time, it is unclear which of these possibilities is most likely to represent the pervasiveness of stalking in young people.

Other demographic characteristics of stalking offenders that have been identified include the fact that these individuals tend to be unemployed or have unstable work histories (Kienlen et al., 1997; Meloy & Gothard, 1995; Mullen & Pathe, 1994a); they tend to be single and have a history of poor attachments (Harmon et al., 1995; Schwartz-Watts, Morgan, & Barnes, 1997); and they are often more intelligent and better educated than other criminal offenders, which may account for their skill at manipulating others (Kienlen et al., 1997; Meloy & Gothard, 1995; Meloy, Rivers, Siegel, Gothard, Naimark, & Nicolini, 2000). Another indication of poor adjustment in stalking offenders is the finding that they tend to have work histories that are not commensurate with their above-average intelligence and education (Kienlen et al, 1997; Mullen & Pathe, 1994a). Although some studies have found more stalking offenders to be White, it is unclear if these findings are due to the way research samples have been obtained. It has been pointed out that no data are currently available on whether or not stalking is more prevalent in a particular social or ethnic group (Meloy, 1998b).

Other demographic factors have been identified as having some impact on the development and maintenance of stalking behavior. For example, some individuals who stalk have a history of failed intimate relationships that constitutes a "courtship disorder" (Freund, Scher, & Hucker, 1983; Meloy, 1998b). More specifically, some stalking is precipitated by feelings of failure, isolation, and ineffectiveness while the offender is not in a relationship at the time of the stalking. In addition, immigration and cultural factors have been identified as creating a risk for stalking in some cases. More specifically, immigration to a new country may create feelings of loss and identity concerns that translate into a search for attachments that may become intense or are the result of misinterpretation of cues from people in the new culture that causes problems with acculturation (Meyers, 1998; Meyers & Meloy, 1994). For example, men from less permissive cultures may misinterpret a friendly smile from a woman as an indication that the two are destined to be together forever. As such, certain demographic factors such as current relationship status and immigration are factors that can be relevant in some stalking cases.

There is a wide range of mental disturbances that characterize stalking offenders, which strongly supports the notion that stalking is not a behavior observed in normal or psychologically healthy individuals who are otherwise experiencing a transient preoccupation or infatuation. Common diagnoses in stalking offenders include mood disturbances such as depression or bipolar disorder, substance abuse, schizophrenia, delusional disorder, and organic mental disorder (Harmon et al., 1995; Meloy & Gothard, 1995; Mullen & Pathe, 1994a; Schwartz-Watts et al., 1997). A major finding is that personality disorders are found in a majority of stalking offenders, particularly character disturbances with eccentric thought and behavior patterns or anxious and fearful attachments to others. Individuals with antisocial or psychopathic personality disturbances are less common among stalking offenders, compared to other criminal offenders because antisocial and psychopathic individuals are less concerned with repairing or maintaining attachments and instead remain in relationships only to get what they need and then move on to the next relationship. In addition, although individuals who stalk when they are psychotic are prone to be influenced by their delusions, most individuals are not actively psychotic at the time of stalking (Meloy, 1998b).

The three types of stalking perpetrators identified by Zona et al. (1993) have been the most useful for classifying offenders. Meloy (1996) has also reviewed several studies on stalking and found that victims of stalking tend to fall into one of three categories, namely prior sexual intimates, prior acquaintances, and strangers. The most common reasons for stalking to occur appear to be anger or hostility toward the victim and usually involve males stalking a prior intimate female partner. In short, the prototypic stalking case is one in which a courtship has failed; the stalking offender has a history of failed intimate relationships; and the obsessive pursuit represents a maladaptive effort to cope with feelings of anger, inadequacy, isolation, and loneliness. However, there are other motives and victim–perpetrator relationships that can define the stalking case. For instance, Harmon and colleagues (1995) used two dimensions to classify various types of obsessional harassment. One dimension was defined by the nature of attachment between victim and offender and consisted of either affectionate/amorous attachments or persecutory/angry ones. A second dimension defined the object of the offender's attention and included personal acquaintances, professional relationships, employment relationships, people in the media, and casual acquaintances. These researchers found that stalking offenders who engaged in their following behavior out of feelings of anger or persecution did so more in the context of professional or employment settings. The typical case would be the disgruntled employee who stalks his or her former supervisor after being terminated from a job. When stalking occurred out of affectionate or amorous motives, such as love for a particular person, these cases occurred fairly consistently across all types of victim–offender relationships.

The pursuit of a victim in stalking cases is not a one-time occurrence and the length of time spent pursuing the victim is typically measured in months and years (Meloy, 1998b). In one study, the average duration of obsession with a specific victim was about 10 to 11 years when the individual engaging in stalking had either erotomanic delusions or severe mental illness associated with the stalking (Zona et al., 1993). However, the amount of time actually spent pursuing or attempting to contact the victim may average between 5 and 19 months. A wide range of individual acts are used to harass and stalk others, including following, physically approaching, telephoning, letter writing, sending gifts or objects by mail, direct physical attacks, and property damage (Harmon et al., 1995; Mullen & Pathe, 1994a, 1994b).

A substantial body of theoretical literature has emerged that points to a severe disturbance in attachment as a major causal factor in stalking. Meloy (1989, 1996, 1999b) has developed a psychodynamic hypothesis that is designed to explain stalking behavior. He suggested that individuals who stalk have a narcissistic linking fantasy in which the victim is viewed as having a special, ideal, or unique relationship with the offender and that the two are destined to be with one another. When the offender experiences either sudden or continued rejection, he or she experiences shame and humiliation that cannot be accepted, and thus the offender defends with rage and hostility. These feelings of rage result in a wish to harm, control, or destroy the victim, resulting in obsessive pursuit that restores the offender's idealized fantasy of being linked or connected to the victim. This theoretical explanation has very important implications for our understanding of stalking in children and adolescents because recent research has demonstrated that disturbances in attachment, identity, and interpersonal coping are manifest throughout the early stages of life. Because the causal factors of attachment disturbance and narcissistic fantasy exist in children and adolescents, these factors may help to explain why children and adolescents develop patterns of stalking behavior.

Another critical issue in the research on stalking is whether or not stalking leads to violence and poses a serious risk to the safety of the victim. In a review of empirical research on stalking, Meloy (1996) found that the rate of violence is rather high among individuals who stalk, compared to other criminal offenders, with an average frequency of 25%–35% for violence in this population. The homicide rate in stalking cases is less than 2%, based on an average across all studies with adequate sample sizes, although two studies found rates of homicide to be 7% (Mullen & Pathe, 1994a) and 8% (Kienlen et al., 1997). Some studies have identified certain factors that may increase the risk for violence in stalking cases. More specifically, violence is most likely to occur in cases where there has been a prior intimate relationship between the perpetrator and victim, where there are more dangerous stalking behaviors present, and when the perpetrator has greater proximity to the victim (Meloy, Davis, & Lovette, in press; Palerea, Zona, Lane, & Langhinrichsen-Rohling, 1999). Although threats occur in at least half of stalking cases, most threats are not carried through, but a threat nevertheless raises the risk for violence in prior intimate cases.

There are several reasons why victims are pursued in stalking cases, including anger and resentment, sexual attraction, control, and idiosyncratic reasons in cases in which the stalking is driven by delusions. Meloy (1996) noted that anger and hostility, not sexuality, are the most common motivations for stalking, although victims often perceive control as the most common motivation.

There is a growing body of empirical research on the impact of stalking on victims. In a large national study on stalking, Tjaden (1997) found that one-third of stalking victims receive psychological treatment as a result of being stalked, 7% of stalking victims never return to work, many victims move away to escape the stalking behavior, and victims report feeling anxious, controlled, and frightened. Results from another study by D. M. Hall (1998) reveal that victims experience a number of changes as a result of being stalked, including changes in personality and an increase in self-protective behaviors. For instance, stalking victims, as a group, report being less friendly and outgoing as a result of being repeatedly harassed and there are higher levels of cautiousness, paranoia, and anxiety. Many female victims report being less trusting of men and there is often an expectation among many victims that the stalking will occur again even after a period during which it has stopped.

The demographic characteristics of stalking victims reveal that most victims are female, outnumbering male victims 3 to 1 (Harmon et al., 1995; Kienlen et al., 1997; Mullen & Pathe, 1994a; Tjaden, 1997; Zona et al., 1993). The age range of victims is quite broad; one study by Mullen and Pathe (1994a) included victims ranging in age from 14 to 50. D. M. Hall (1998) found that 3% of the victims in her sample were younger than 18. Stalking of children and adolescents has not been extensively studied; however, the data reveal that young people are victims of stalking and cases presented in later chapters will show that many perpetrator–victim age combinations are possible. Some young perpetrators stalk young victims, whereas others stalk adults; some adults stalk other adult victims, whereas others stalk children and adolescent victims.

CONCLUSION

The scholarly literature on stalking is just beginning to provide useful theoretical and empirical insights into the dynamics of stalking. A number of studies have used various typologies of perpetrators to understand the motives for why some people stalk and the clinical and demographic characteristics of those who stalk provide useful insights into the factors that describe and explain this puzzling behavior. Various psychological theories and concepts have been used to help explain the motivations and dynamics of why some people stalk others. These theories and concepts include attachment theory (Kienlen, 1998; Meloy, 1992), obsessive relational intrusions defined in communication theory (Cupach & Spitzberg, 1994; Spitzberg & Cupach, 1998), psychodynamic theory (Meloy, 1992, 1996), jealousy (Mullen & Pathe, 1994b), and cultural factors (Meyers, 1998).

In subsequent chapters, these and other principles and theories are discussed as they relate to the issue of stalking in children and adolescents. Other topics such as bullying, developmental psychopathology, and child abuse and neglect are also relevant to understanding the serious social problem of stalking. However, before we explore the many issues surrounding stalking in younger people, it is first necessary to examine if stalking occurs in children and adolescents, and if it does, to examine the extent of the problem in this age group.

2

Stalking as a Problem in Young People

E mpirical research has only recently begun to expand and address many of the most relevant issues in stalking because stalking has been defined as a crime within the past 10 years. Much of the attention has focused on the demographic characteristics of stalking offenders and victims, as well as the dynamics of stalking such as the factors associated with risk for violence, the forms of psychopathology that sometimes motivate stalkers, and the ways in which offenders stalk their victims. It is not surprising that most of the literature has focused almost entirely on adult stalking offenders. However, an interesting question that begs an answer is whether or not children and adolescents engage in stalking.

This chapter seeks to provide an answer to this question by examining anecdotal case reports and studies documenting stalking or related forms of obsessional harassment in children and adolescents. After looking at the evidence for stalking in young people, I explore the prevalence of this problem among young people. A number of factors interfere with establishing adequate prevalence rates of stalking in younger populations, including the manner in which juvenile offenders are adjudicated and the incorrect presumption by some individuals that stalking is a behavior that is confined only to adults. In fact, the evidence presented in this chapter supports the conclusion that children and adolescents engage in stalking. However, it remains unclear how children and adolescents who stalk differ from adults who stalk.

To lay an adequate foundation for discussing the problem of stalking in children and adolescents, I address three critical questions. The first section of this chapter explores in greater detail evidence that illustrates children and adolescents engage in stalking. This discussion focuses primarily on the presentation of anecdotal evidence and clinical case material that documents stalking in children and adolescents. The second section seeks an answer to the following question: If stalking occurs in children and adolescents, then how pervasive is the problem? Toward this end, studies on high school and college students are reviewed to gain some sense of the extent to which stalking occurs in younger populations. Research on related forms of obsessive harassment in young people is reviewed, including sexual harassment, dating violence, and sexual aggression. As this evidence shows, stalking may be a significant subset of other forms of obsessional harassment for which detailed prevalence data are available. Finally, the third section outlines some important considerations that must be taken into account when conceptualizing the problem of stalking in children and adolescents. In particular, some developmental issues used to define childhood and adolescence as periods of development are discussed as they bear on the manifestation of stalking in young people. The intent of this latter discussion is to raise awareness of the risks posed by identifying stalking in young people so as not to inappropriately criminalize or mislabel various obsessive forms of behavior in younger age groups.

EVIDENCE THAT STALKING OCCURS IN CHILDREN AND ADOLESCENTS

A number of stalking cases involving children and adolescents have been reported in various sources, including media reports and published case studies. Based on the anecdotal evidence provided by these cases, it appears that a variety of contexts and dynamics characterize the phenomenon of stalking in young people. In one well-publicized media report of stalking by a child, a 9-year-old boy from Hastings, Michigan, was accused of violating the state's anti-stalking law ("9-year-old," 1996). According to the parents of the 10-year-old girl who was the object of his stalking behavior, the boy had made about 200 telephone calls to the girl's home over several months. The need for legal action arose after the girl received a message several days before Valentine's Day in which the boy said, "I want to be your lover." Additionally, the two children's families once lived across the street from one another, and the boy and girl both went to the same elementary school. Although the boy's attorney minimized the sexual nature of the boy's telephone messages, the youth was petitioned in juvenile court to answer the stalking charges. He was subsequently placed into counseling for 6 months, and charges against him were eventually dropped.

Another case was reported by Snow (1998) in which a 10-year-old boy in Albuquerque, New Mexico, had a complaint brought against him in domestic violence court. The complaint made an allegation that he had stalked an 11-year-old girl. It was reported that the boy had a crush on the girl and assaulted her, threatened her by telephone, broke windows in her house, and vandalized the family's car. These behaviors apparently occurred in response to the girl's rejection of the boy's romantic interests.

Aside from these reports in the media, there are also individual case studies in the professional literature that provide evidence of stalking in adolescent populations. A case of pure erotomania has been documented (Urbach, Khalily, & Mitchell, 1992). *Erotomania,* as defined by the *DSM-IV,* is a delusional disturbance in which the person falsely believes that he or she is loved by another person and that person is typically someone of higher status (American Psychiatric Association, 1994). This case involved a 13-year-old girl who maintained an erotomanic fixation on a teacher and later on a physician. She engaged in repetitive following and inappropriate communications that were motivated by her delusional beliefs. The girl developed an erotic fixation on a teacher that she had encountered in the school cafeteria. This fixation evolved into an elaborate delusional system in which the girl believed that the female teacher loved her as a wife, and the student later began reciprocating by writing love letters to the teacher. These letters were turned over to school administrators. When the teacher who was the object of the girl's delusional system was scheduled to leave the school and work elsewhere, the girl began exhibiting suicidal behavior and symptoms of depression. This rejection by the teacher was an instance of what Meloy (1997) called a "dramatic moment," in which the risk for violence may be greatest in stalking cases when the pursuer experiences either a direct or indirect rejection such as an issuance of a restraining order or other attempt to prevent approach by a stalker. While hospitalized for suicidal gestures following the perceived rejection and abandonment by the object of the student's erotomanic delusions, the girl transferred her fixation onto a physician who was treating her. In addition, the girl later assaulted another inpatient who was believed to be reporting back to staff about the girl. In many ways, this case of erotomania in early adolescence has many features of stalking that occurs in adult erotomanic subtypes of stalking. There was a pattern of repetitive harassing, letter writing, threats toward third parties who were viewed as interfering with access to the romantic object, and repetitive unwanted sexual advances. Moreover, the obsessive harassment was severe enough to warrant inpatient psychiatric treatment, which indicates that this case was more than just an instance of teenage infatuation that went awry.

In another set of case studies of stalking in adolescents, McCann (1998c) presented two additional examples of obsessional following that represent the love obsessional and simple obsessional subtypes of stalking that were identified by Zona, Sharma, and Lane (1993) and discussed previously in chapter 1. One case of love obsessional stalking involved a teenager with a serious psychotic disorder in which he maintained a delusional belief that he could communicate with the girls in his class through broadcasting his thoughts. He had very poor interpersonal skills, was socially isolated, and did not relate well to peers. Over a period of several weeks, he wrote sexually explicit letters to several girls in his class, which became increasingly more bizarre; the girls viewed these letters as intrusive and threatening. This youth believed that the letters were a means through which he could have a romantic and sexual relationship with a young woman solely through writing these letters, much like the belief of love obsessional followers with a mental illness who frequently pursue unattainable people portrayed in the media through letter writing. The second case discussed by McCann (1998c) involved simple obsessional following in which a teenager repeatedly followed his former girlfriend after she ended their relationship. He violated a court order of protection, was arrested, and was subsequently hospitalized after he threatened to kill his parents for trying to keep him away from the girlfriend.

These case examples reveal that individual cases of stalking in adolescents tend to involve subtypes that are similar to the empirically derived subtypes of stalking that have been found in adult stalking offenders. In considering the individual case reports of stalking among both children and adolescents, the anecdotal evidence provides an affirmative response to the question raised at the beginning of this chapter. Stalking is a phenomenon found in younger individuals. The next issue that requires exploration is the extent of the problem in younger populations.

The Prevalence of Stalking Among Children and Adolescents

One of the major issues that must be clarified is whether stalking occurs in relatively rare and isolated cases, or whether the problem is more common and pervasive among children and adolescents. A number of factors interfere with establishing precise prevalence rates of stalking in young people. Only in the past few years or so has empirical research been conducted on adult populations of stalking offenders. Because stalking may sometimes be viewed, although mistakenly so, as a crime that occurs only among adults and in specific contexts such as domestic violence cases, it is somewhat understandable that attention has not been paid to this social problem in children and adolescents.

Several sources provide either direct or indirect evidence that stalking is a growing problem in children and adolescents. In this section, research studies on the significance of stalking among college and high school student populations are reviewed. Furthermore, extensive data are available on behavioral disturbances and other obsessional forms of harassment in young offenders that are related to or overlap with stalking. This growing literature shows that various patterns of violence in adult relationships, such as sexual offenses, domestic or relationship violence, sexual harassment, and dating violence, also exist in adolescent populations at levels that are similar to levels in adult populations (Barbaree, Marshall, & Hudson, 1993; National Victim Center, 1995). Therefore, a review of prevalence data on dating violence, sexual harassment, and related forms of violence may provide some insight into the extent to which obsessional following and harassment are significant problems in young people.

Research on College Students

There has been some valuable research done on the phenomenon of stalking among college students. Although this research is preliminary, and only a handful of studies exist, something can be learned about the relative significance of stalking as a problem among younger populations by studying college students. Even though college students are older than adolescents and are in some respects more representative of adult populations, there are many important factors that support the use of this age group as a reference point for beginning a review of the prevalence of stalking in younger people. The college years represent a transitional period of development between late adolescence and early adulthood, typically spanning the period from ages 18 to 22. College students are more independent and mature than adolescents, yet they also have a significant degree of emotional and financial dependence on the family, as do adolescents. Also, the college years represent a more intense period of exploration of and commitment to intimate relationships that occurs within a somewhat structured setting. There are likely to be dating patterns that involve a greater number of broken relationships or unreturned affections that may precipitate more frequent stalking or obsessive relational intrusions. More specifically, college students generally live in close proximity to one another, where there is a greater level of access and intensity of contact with one another that may create an atmosphere where stalking and obsessional following are more likely. Because college students live in dormitories or apartments near college campuses and their movements are often confined to geographical areas defined by campus size and pedestrian pathways, it is often easier for the stalking offender to monitor, follow, and track the object of his or her obsessive pursuit.

In an epidemiological study of the prevalence of stalking and victim coping strategies, Fremouw, Westrup, and Pennypacker (1997) studied two samples of college undergraduates at West Virginia University. Their study represents the most ambitious attempt to document prevalence rates and types of victim coping strategies in college students. In the first sample of 294 undergraduates, Fremouw and colleagues found that 26.6% of young women and 14.7% of young men reported that they had been stalked, with a total self-reported stalking rate of 21.4%. *Stalking* was defined as "knowingly, and repeatedly following, harassing, or threatening someone" (p. 667). In a second sample of 299 undergraduates from the same university, 35.2% of young women and 18.4% of young men reported being stalked, with a total self-reported stalking rate of 27%. When Fremouw and colleagues combined the two samples to yield a group of 593 college undergraduates, the overall rate of self-reported stalking was 24.2%, with 30.7% of young women and 16.7% of young men reporting being the victims of stalking. In 80% of the cases, the victim knew the stalker, and more young women had dated the stalker seriously at some point (43%), whereas fewer young men (24%) had dated the stalker. In about 16%–18% of the cases, the stalker was a stranger. Thus, stalking in college students appears to be common and characterized by victims who know the perpetrator and have had either a casual or serious dating relationship with him or her.

An interesting finding in this study was the very low number of students who reported stalking another person. Although it may not be particularly remarkable that stalking would be underreported by those who engage in the behavior, the very small number of individuals who admitted stalking was much lower than the number of students who reported being stalked. In the first sample of 294 students, Fremouw and colleagues found that no young women and 3 young men (2.3%) admitted stalking another person. Overall, these findings were interpreted by these researchers as indicating that "stalking is not a rare phenomenon" among college students, and there tends to be a "strong under-reporting" of stalking by perpetrators (p. 668). However, the methodology reported in the Fremouw study does not specify a time frame for when the stalking occurred, and thus it must be inferred that the figures are general lifetime prevalence rates. Still it remains unclear the portion of stalking that occurred more recently in the college years, as opposed to that which occurred earlier in adolescence.

Another study that provides some evidence of the extent to which stalking is a problem on college campuses is a survey of 760 college undergraduates at East Carolina University (McCreedy & Dennis, 1996). Results from this study revealed that 25.1% of the students sampled had received a lewd or threatening telephone call, where 81.7% of those receiving such calls were young women, and 31.1% of the calls were defined specifically as threatening. Also, 6.1% of the total sample reported having been stalked at some time in their lives, with 84.9% of stalking victims being female, 84.9% of victims residing off-campus, and 87.0% of victims being White. The report by McCreedy and Dennis provides additional data on how stalking is handled among college students. About two-thirds (66.6%) of the cases were reported to police, and 40.0% of the cases involved an offender who reportedly knew the victim well. Stalking victims also reported a significantly higher concern about attending night classes (43.5%) as compared to the total sample (26.8%).

Although additional prevalence data are needed on the occurrence of stalking among college students, these two studies provide interesting observations about the phenomenon of stalking in this age group. First, the two studies reported rather different prevalence rates, with McCreedy and Dennis (1996) reporting a 6.1% overall prevalence rate for stalking, and Fremouw et al. (1997) reporting a 24.2% prevalence rate. However, if threatening telephone calls are considered in the McCreedy and Dennis study, then the overall rate approaches that found by Fremouw and colleagues. Also, if one considers the overall prevalence rate of 8% of women and 2% of men reporting having been stalked, as cited by Tjaden (1997), then research in university settings suggests that stalking is at least as prevalent among college students as it is in the general population and may even be somewhat higher in this population if, as Fremouw and colleagues pointed out, stalking is not rare among college students and may be an underreported crime.

Another investigation on the prevalence of stalking among college students approached the issue differently than the previous two studies. Gallagher, Harmon, and Lingenfelter (1994) conducted a survey of 590 chief student affairs officers from both two- and four-year colleges that were members of the National Association of Student Personnel Administrators. Rather than obtain a survey of students, these researchers collected data from college administrators on the degree to which they had to intervene in cases of stalking. In this study, *stalking* was defined as "when students become so obsessed with someone they continue to express their affection for, to pursue, or to harass the individual long after being told to desist" (pp. 41–42). Gallagher and his colleagues reported that 34.5% of the chief student affairs officers sampled had to intervene in one or more stalking cases within the previous year.

There were other important findings in this study as well. For instance, Gallagher and colleagues reported that a broad range of responses were taken by student affairs officers in response to stalking. A warning was sufficient in 15% of cases, and 21% of the cases required both a warning and mandated counseling for the offender. Additional remedies included denying stalking offenders access to residence halls (18%), bringing judicial board sanctions (31%), and suspension or dismissal from school (15%). Also, 24% of victims sought a civil order of protection in addition to any school sanctions. Among the 590 student affairs officers responding, there were 57 instances of students being injured by their pursuers, and 5 homicides by obsessional followers were reported within one academic year. Another interesting finding by Gallagher and his colleagues was that the percentage of chief student affairs officers who reported having to intervene in stalking cases increased as the size of the academic institutions increased. For example, in schools with fewer than 5,000 students enrolled, 28.5% of the student affairs officers reported having to intervene in at least one stalking case; schools with more than 15,000 students enrolled had 49.4% of the student affairs officers reporting a need to intervene in one or more stalking cases in the preceding year.

It is difficult to establish precise prevalence rates for stalking, as well as injuries and homicides in stalking cases, from the data provided by Gallagher et al. (1994) because the total number of college students encompassed in the study was unreported. However, these findings are noteworthy in two respects. First, they documented that a very large percentage of college administrators are finding stalking to be a growing and significant problem among college students. Second, unlike the studies by McCreedy and Dennis (1996) and Fremouw and colleagues (1997), which were each conducted at one university, the Gallagher study was conducted on a broad national sample of college student administrators. As such, this latter study lends strong support to the conclusion that stalking is a pervasive and highly disruptive problem among college students.

An interesting aspect of this research on the prevalence of stalking in college students is that no time frame was specified when students were asked if they had been stalked. In fact, the standard question in both the Fremouw and Gallagher studies, where the students were questioned directly, was to ask students if they had *ever* been stalked. Thus, it remains unclear if a large or small portion of stalking begins in the college years or whether students are responding based on events that occurred in adolescence or earlier. It is possible that prevalence rates of stalking among college students reflect both recent and earlier instances of stalking. Research on the prevalence of stalking in younger populations and longitudinal research on stalking victims may ultimately serve to clarify this issue.

Research on High School Students

The research on stalking prevalence rates among high school students is much more limited, although there are more detailed data on related problems such as dating violence and sexual harassment that will be discussed later. However, one relevant study was reported by the National

Victim Center (1995). The study was reportedly conducted in Massachusetts, and it examined the number of restraining orders that were issued for threatening, abusive, and stalking behaviors perpetrated by teenagers. During the 10-month period of study, 757 restraining orders were issued to threatening teenagers. This finding corresponds to 2.5 restraining orders being issued each day during the period of study.

This individual study is difficult to interpret properly because abusive behaviors were apparently collapsed with threatening and stalking behaviors. Therefore, it is unclear as to how many of these restraining orders were specifically for stalking or stalking-related behaviors. However, the fact that so many restraining orders were issued against adolescents for behaviors that are very similar to one another suggests that stalking and other forms of threatening behavior may be quite prevalent in teenage populations.

Clearly this single study does not provide adequate data on national trends or specific prevalence rates of stalking in adolescent populations. However, even if this Massachusetts family court study is remotely indicative of national trends, then it suggests that stalking in teenage populations is a significant social problem.

Related Forms of Obsessional Harassment in Young People

Dating and Courtship Violence

There is a pervasive view that stalking is primarily manifest in cases of domestic violence; indeed, the most common form of stalking in adult populations is done by an obsessional man who stalks a prior intimate female sexual partner (Meloy, 1998b). For this reason, it is often argued that anti-stalking laws are directed primarily at protecting women from domestic violence (Fielkow, 1997). However, there are some problems with viewing stalking merely as a form of domestic violence, because this obsessive form of harassment occurs in many contexts involving strangers or casual acquaintances and for reasons other than control or domination, such as revenge, delusional thinking, and sexual preoccupation. In short, stalking is an obsessive form of harassment that is closely linked, but not unique to domestic violence.

Nevertheless, violence and abuse that occurs in dating and courtship relationships can involve obsessional forms of harassment that are closely tied to stalking and thus deserve careful consideration. In particular, stalking may constitute one type of courtship disorder (Meloy, 1996, 1998b). Freund, Scher, and Hucker (1983) discussed courtship disorders as a disruption in normal human sexual interactions. More specifically, Freund and his colleagues noted that humans engage in a logical sequence of courtship behavior that begins with the location of a potential sexual partner, proceeds to a period of pre-tactile interaction such as looking or talking with the potential partner, progresses to actual physical contact, and leads ultimately to intercourse. Of course, a wide range of behaviors and cultural rituals are part of this process of locating and interacting with potential mating partners, and successful completion of this process may take months or even years. However, Freund and his colleagues found empirical evidence to support their hypothesis that many paraphilias and anomalous sexual behaviors, such as voyeurism, exhibitionism, and so forth, are manifestations of problematic courtship behavior. For example, exhibitionism reflects disturbed pre-tactile interaction, and voyeurism reflects disturbed location of a potential partner. Consequently, at least some forms of stalking can be viewed as a disruption in the seeking of and interacting with a potential sexual partner, because stalking can sometimes involve obsessional following and pursuit that is directed toward a potential partner that is unavailable, unreceptive, or unwilling to reciprocate the obsessional follower's interest.

Because some forms of stalking can be viewed as a courtship disorder, the nature and prevalence of abuse and violence in dating relationships is important because the literature on courtship violence is likely to provide interesting insights into stalking. Moreover, there is a growing body of literature on dating and courtship violence that indeed helps broaden the understanding of stalking in young people.

There are strong data that show the prevalence of dating and sexual violence in adolescent populations is comparable to the rate of such violence in adult populations. In one study of 204 high school juniors and seniors, Roscoe and Callahan (1985) found that 91% of their sample reported having been involved in a dating relationship at some time. More importantly, 35% of the students knew someone who had been in a physically violent dating relationship, and 9% indicated that they had experienced physical violence by a dating partner. Five percent of the students admitted being physically violent at some point in a dating relationship. Girls were more likely to be victims of violence (65%) than were boys (35%). In addition, dating violence was more likely to occur in brief relationships (i.e., less than 6 months) than in longer relationships. Findings that have the greatest implications for understanding stalking are those pertaining to the perceived motivation for violence. That is, some of the more common precipitants for violence were jealousy, sexual denial, and substance abuse. Also, only 58% of the adolescents involved in a violent relationship found it easy to end the relationship.

In another study of dating violence, O'Keefe, Brockopp, and Chew (1986) surveyed 256 high school students and found that 35.5% of the sample experienced some form of violence. Their finding is deceiving because these researchers collapsed several categories of subjects to form larger clusters. Therefore, the 35.5% of students in the O'Keefe study has been cited as an estimate of the prevalence of dating violence among high school students (Bennett & Fineran, 1998). However, this statistic appears impressive because it is based on three groups of students: victim only, perpetrator only, and both victim and perpetrator. Thus, the percentage cited in this study should be more appropriately characterized as the prevalence of students' first-hand experiences with some form of dating violence, rather than a true rate of victimization. Also, O'Keefe et al. (1986) included threatening statements as a form of violence. The importance of this form of harassment is that it is threatening behaviors, and not actual violence, that is the critical feature that defines stalking, although violence is an important concern in stalking cases. However, threats are relevant to stalking because it is the threatening nature of certain behaviors that constitutes one of the prongs of the legal definitions of the crime when they occur more than once and are directed toward a specific individual.

In the results cited by O'Keefe and her colleagues, threatening behaviors were not a primary focus of study. However, results from this investigation provide some estimates of the prevalence of threatening behavior that can be extrapolated from the data. Of 66 dating violence victims in the O'Keefe sample, 4.5% reported being threatened with a weapon, and 45.5% were threatened with physical assault. Of 62 dating violence perpetrators, 1.6% reported threatening a partner with physical assault. It is interesting to note that these rates of threatening behavior are similar for both victims and perpetrators. With such high levels of threatening behavior in the dating relationships of students in this sample, the critical question becomes what portion of the threats experienced by students in this sample were repetitive and might have constituted stalking or obsessional following? Although there are no data to provide an answer to this question, the analysis provided by O'Keefe and colleagues suggests that if intimate relationship violence, including threats, is a hidden social problem that occurs as frequently in teenage dating relationships as in adult populations, then obsessional forms of harassment and stalking may also occur at rates similar to those found in adult populations. However, further research of obsessional harassment among teenagers is needed to test the validity of this hypothesis.

Other research supports the observation that the rates of dating violence among high school students do not differ from the rates of such violence in adult populations. Bennett and Fineran (1998) found that 43% of the 463 high school students they sampled reported being the victim of sexual or severe physical violence in the previous year and that perpetrators of violence were most likely to be current or former dating partners or a peer whom the victim knew. Bergman (1992) found that the prevalence of sexual and dating violence among 631 high school students varied as a function of gender and type of violence. Sexual violence occurred among 15.5% of the girls, and 24.6% reported being victimized by either sexual violence or physical violence, or both. Among the boys, the rate of victimization was 4.4% for sexual violence, with 9.9% reporting sexual violence, physical violence, or both. It is interesting to note that although Bergman found that violence tended to occur, the victims often did not disclose it to parents or school officials. Thus, underreporting may prevent true prevalence rates of recurring violence from being known.

In addition, Bergman examined the prevalence of verbal violence among these students, which was broadly defined as threats of harm toward the victim or others and verbally abusive behavior. This form of violence was reported by 11.3% of the sample, with 7.4% of the girls and 13.2% of the boys reporting being the target of verbal threats. Again, these later findings are particularly relevant to the phenomenon of stalking in high school students because it is the threatening nature of the perpetrator's actions that characterizes many forms of repetitive behavior such as stalking. However, it is also important to note that these findings by Bergman merely provide some estimate of the prevalence of threats among high school students and do not specify what portion of these threats are, in fact, recurrent or might constitute actual stalking. Also, these results do not provide any data on non-verbal threats, such as following and letter writing, which are common forms of indirect or implied threat that occur in stalking cases. Thus, although the research on dating and courtship violence in high school students provides support for the fact that various types of relationship violence among adults occur at similar rates among adolescents, it can be inferred, but not confirmed or substantiated from this data, that stalking is as prevalent among high school students as it is in adult populations. More epidemiological and survey data are needed, however.

Sexual Harassment

Another form of threatening and harassing behavior that overlaps somewhat with stalking is sexual harassment. What makes this particular form of harassment deserving of attention is that it has been studied among fairly large samples of children and adolescents. Although sexual harassment and stalking are different forms of harassing behavior, there is some overlap that warrants their comparison. Whereas sexual harassment is generally defined as unwanted and unwelcome sexual behavior, stalking refers to a pattern of repetitive harassment directed at a specific individual that is meant to create fear in the victim. Therefore, the underlying motive behind stalking may or may not have sexual connotations, whereas sexual harassment specifically involves sexual motives. Moreover, certain behaviors that are sexually harassing (e.g., voyeurism) may not necessarily be stalking if the victim is not aware of or directly threatened by them. Nevertheless, there are parallels between these two forms of behavior such as attempts to control or exert power over the victim and the repetitive nature of the harassment.

One large scale study was conducted in 1993 by the American Association of University Women (AAUW) Educational Foundation on sexual harassment in America's schools. The findings reveal several noteworthy yet surprising trends about sexual harassment in schools. More specifically, four out of five students (81%) have experienced some form of sexual harassment at some point during their school lives. This finding holds for both boys (76%) and girls (85%). One-third of these students who reported being sexually harassed indicated that their first experience of harassment was before the seventh grade. The most common form is peer-to-peer harassment, although adult-to-student harassment was also noted to be prevalent (18%).

A careful analysis of the data from the AAUW study reveals several factors suggesting that stalking may be a significant subset of sexual harassment that occurs in schools. However, it should be noted that there is no indication that stalking occurs at a rate anywhere near that of sexual harassment, although stalking behavior appears to be related to some forms of sexual harassment. For instance, 66% of girls and 49% of boys who reported having been harassed also experienced unwanted sexual advances often or occasionally. Although some sexually harassing behavior such as mooning, making sexual comments or jokes, and intentionally touching the victim in a sexual manner may not constitute stalking behavior per se, other forms of sexual harassment are similar to the behaviors used by stalkers to harass their victims. For example, 32% of students who have been sexually harassed reported receiving unwanted pictures or notes, and 7% reported being spied on while they dressed or showered at school. About 37% of sexually harassed students reported being the target of rumors. These latter behaviors mirror many behaviors used to stalk others.

Another interesting set of findings in the AAUW study had to do with the reasons why students engaged in sexually harassing behaviors. Peers perpetrated most of the sexual harassment. Among girls who were harassed, 81% reported being harassed by a boy acting alone, and 10% reported being harassed by a girl acting alone; of boys who had been harassed, 57% were harassed by a girl acting alone and 25% were harassed by a boy acting alone. Some of the reasons why students engaged in sexually harassing behaviors also mirrored some of the motives behind stalking, such as thinking the person liked the behavior (25%), wanting a date with the person (22%), wanting something from the person (18%), and wanting victims to think the perpetrator had some control over them (6%). Other evidence for the obsessive nature of sexual harassment among students is found in some of the ways in which victims have been affected by the harassment. The behavioral consequences for victims of sexual harassment included staying away from familiar places in school or on school grounds (23%), stopping attendance at a particular activity (10%), and changing the way they come to or go home from school (10%). These findings suggest that a portion of sexual harassment in schools is perpetrated by one person against a specific victim where stalking-like behavior is used as a repetitive and obsessive form of harassment.

In a study of 561 students ages 11 to 16, Roscoe, Strouse, and Goodwin (1994) found results that further support the findings discussed above that sexual harassment is common in schools and that subsets of sexually harassing behavior may involve stalking and obsessional following. Roscoe and his colleagues found that 50% of girls and 37% of boys in their sample experienced some form of sexual harassment, although it is worth noting that these prevalence rates were lower than those reported in the large-scale AAUW study. Nevertheless, six broad categories of sexually harassing behavior were defined in a survey by these researchers: sexual comments, physical contact, telephone calls, letter/note writing, pressure for dates, and sexual advances. At least two of these categories, telephone calls and letter/note writing, are common forms of stalking behavior found in child and adolescent obsessional followers (McCann,

1998c; 2000; Urbach et al., 1992), as well as in adult stalking offenders (Meloy, 1998b). The other forms of sexual harassment defined by Roscoe and colleagues are also behaviors that have been found in some cases of stalking by child and adolescent obsessional followers.

The results reported by Roscoe and colleagues (1994) revealed that 20.7% (18.5% of the girls and 22.9% of the boys) of their sample reported receiving telephone calls that were harassing and 19.1% (18.5% of the girls and 19.6% of the boys) reported receiving letters or notes that were considered sexually harassing. Higher rates of sexual comments (43.3% of total sample) and physical contact (31.9% of total sample) were reported by the students. These results indicate that unwanted advances or approaches are common among junior and senior high school students. It is quite possible that a portion of these cases involve stalking behaviors, but there is no way of knowing how many of these unwanted advances or approaches were repetitive and threatening, based on the way the data are reported. Moreover, it is unclear as to what percentage of these unwanted behaviors are perceived as threatening by the students, even though the students in this study uniformly rated such behaviors as unwanted. This latter distinction is again important, because it is the threatening nature of the behaviors as perceived by the victim that is one of the factors that defines repetitive harassment as stalking. Given the high percentage of students experiencing sexually harassing behaviors—if even a small percentage of this harassment rises to the level of stalking, it suggests that this social problem is prominent in school-age children.

Sexual Aggression in Children

The research on stalking in younger age groups has been limited primarily to college student populations and, to a lesser extent, to high school students. Likewise, related forms of obsessional harassment such as dating violence and sexual harassment provide indirect evidence of potential stalking in school-age children. However, much of the research on these related forms of harassment has focused on adolescents. The anecdotal case evidence reported earlier in this chapter reveals that stalking has been observed in younger children who are in the pre-adolescent years, or younger than 13. For instance, Snow (1998) reported two cases of stalking by children ages 10 and 11, and McCann (2000) found, from a survey of documented reports of stalking by young people, one case involving a 9-year-old boy as a perpetrator. Therefore, it is worth looking at other forms of obsessional harassment in pre-adolescents as a means of learning whether or not stalking-related behaviors occur with any frequency in children.

One form of behavioral disturbance in children that appears to overlap somewhat with stalking is sexual aggression. Araji (1997) provided a comprehensive review of the literature on sexually aggressive behavior in children who are age 12 or younger. In her review of several classification systems that have been used by various clinicians and researchers to differentiate normal from inappropriate or problematic sexual behavior in children, Araji concluded that sexually aggressive behaviors represent an extreme end of the sexual behavior continuum. More specifically, sexually aggressive behaviors that are manifest in children "have an aggressive quality, involving use of force, coercion (social and physical), and secrecy" (p. 35). More importantly, most conceptual models of sexually aggressive behavior in children defined the acts as "*patterned* rather than isolated events" (p. 35; emphasis added). It is this latter portion of the definition of sexually aggressive behavior that parallels aspects of the definition of stalking and obsessional following in that a pattern of threat or harassment is required, not one specific act or instance of harassment.

Araji (1997) also noted several other characteristics of sexually aggressive behavior in children that closely parallel the way in which stalking has been defined and characterized. More specifically, these acts:

> . . . may have a compulsive, obsessive nature; they may be aimed at the self, but by the time behaviors become sexually aggressive they usually involve other victims; behaviors may be opportunistic but many are planned, calculated, and predatory; and the sexual behaviors usually exist in combination with other antisocial behaviors such as conduct disorders (p. 36).

Again, the parallels between stalking and sexually aggressive behaviors in children imply that both may involve obsessive and coercive behaviors that are aimed at exerting power and control over the victim in some cases. In fact, Pithers, Gray, Cunningham, and Lane (1993) noted two major factors that should be used to differentiate normal from problematic sexual behavior in children—whether the sexual activities are coerced through intimidation or force and whether the child displays a compulsive and obsessive preoccupation with the behavior. Again, these factors parallel several themes that exist in the literature on stalking behavior, because it is possible that children can display obsessive sexual preoccupation with a specific object or victim.

There are also data available that reveal sexually aggressive behaviors as prevalent among children younger than 13. For example, Pithers and Gray (1998) noted that almost 40% of all child sexual abuse is perpetrated by individuals younger than 20, and children ages 6–12 account for between 13% and 18% of all substantiated child sexual maltreatment. Pithers and Gray based their conclusions, in part, on their review of 1991 Child Protective Services records from Vermont (Gray & Pithers, 1993). These records indicated that of 135 cases that remained open on children or adolescents who had acted out sexually against another person, 51 (37.8%) were between the ages of 6 and 12, and these 51 cases accounted for 13.2% of all substantiated cases of child sexual abuse in Vermont during the year in which data were reviewed. In addition, Araji (1997) reported data from other studies that show sexual aggression to be quite prevalent among children. For example, she noted that one study of sex crimes in New York revealed that the number of offenses perpetrated by children younger than 12 was greater than the number perpetrated by 13- to 15-year-old individuals. Araji also cited data from Oregon, Washington, and Rhode Island that indicate a rise in sexually aggressive behavior among children ages 12 or younger. As such, the data have led Araji (1997) and Pithers and Gray (1998) to note that sexually aggressive behaviors are an under-recognized and growing problem among pre-adolescent children.

Although the research on sexual aggression in children suggests that some forms of this behavior may rise to the level of stalking, there are limitations with viewing this body of literature as direct evidence of the nature or extent of stalking as a problem among younger children. Although it is interesting to note that some unpublished data reveal about 25% of child perpetrators of sexual aggression use direct threats against their victims (Araji, 1997), with threats being a major defining feature of stalking, it is not at all clear how many cases involving sexual aggression involve repetitive acts of harassment toward a specific victim as opposed to multiple single acts with different victims. Cases of the former type would more closely parallel typical stalking cases, whereas those of the latter type would not. In addition, the motivation of many individuals who stalk may involve purposes other than sexual preoccupation, such as anger, revenge, or unusual psychotic fixations. However, given the lack of research on the specific nature of obsessional harassment among children, it is unclear if forms of harassment other than sexual aggression are significant problems.

Despite these limitations, the literature on sexual aggression in children is useful for providing some insight into the nature of stalking in younger people because many of the etiological features that have been used to explain sexual aggression have also been found in the stalking literature. For instance, Araji (1997) noted that deviant fantasies, dysfunctional and abusive family life, poor attachment patterns, the inability to recognize proper interpersonal boundaries, and severe conduct disturbances have been identified as risk factors associated with sexual acting-out in children. In later discussions on stalking, many of these themes will reemerge, because they have also been identified in one form or another as being associated with heightened risk for stalking behavior.

Conceptualizing the Problem of Stalking in Young People

Before examining the nature of stalking in young people more fully in the next chapter, it is useful to comment in this last section on some of the challenges in defining and conceptualizing the problem of stalking or obsessional following in children and adolescents. Many of these challenges stem from defining appropriate age boundaries for various phases of development, such as differentiating childhood from adolescence and adolescence from adulthood. A useful first step in outlining the problem of stalking in children and adolescents is to define appropriate age ranges for these periods of a person's life. There are a number of ways to classify someone as a child or adolescent. For example, legal definitions often define young people, or juveniles, as anyone younger than age 18, because individuals who are 18 and older are considered for legal purposes to be adults (Suarez, 1994). Legal definitions may be useful for delineating who is and is not a minor for purposes of identifying those individuals who are covered under a particular law, but there are clear limitations to a purely legal approach to defining someone's status as a minor. Within the psychological literature there are a number of factors that can be used to define age status such as cognitive levels of development, social relationships, and psychosocial challenges that may prevail at a particular point in one's life. Biological factors, such as the onset of puberty, are often used to distinguish whether someone is a child or adolescent. However, there are individual differences that exist using biologically based criteria. In short, there are no clear guidelines for distinguishing important developmental transitions such as when a child becomes an adolescent or when an adolescent becomes an adult.

With respect to the issue of stalking, a number of theoretical and clinical concepts, such as attachment, identity, and interpersonal dynamics, are used to conceptualize some of the psychodynamics of stalking. Many of these factors are important across the life span and are not necessarily confined to a specific developmental period. On the other hand, some factors such as sexual attraction and preoccupation or serious mental illness are relevant to some forms of stalking and are more significant at a particular phase of development. Therefore, for the purposes of the topic of stalking in children and adolescents, I define the transition between childhood and adolescence as occurring around the onset of puberty, because this marks a change in the person's sexual interests and identity, as well as a shift in primary attachment from family to peers. In addition, I define the period of adolescence generally as the teenage years from age 13, or the onset of puberty, to age 19. The upper end of this age range is relevant because there is a developing literature on stalking and obsessional harassment in college students that is informative, and the college years are a transitional phase between adolescence and early adulthood. The lower end of this age range (i.e., age 13) is useful because it corresponds to the age below which much of the literature on sexual aggression in children has focused. That is, with sexual aggression being a form of harassment that is related to stalking in some ways and because childhood has been defined as ages 12 or younger in this literature, the age ranges adopted for discussions in this book correspond to those in other bodies of literature.

Although puberty and the college years are useful markers for transitions in development, a number of other factors can be used to further differentiate young people into distinct phases of development. For example, moral and cognitive development differentiates very young children from latency–age children. In addition, social factors such as the primacy of family relationships versus peers or romantic relationships serves as a useful marker to distinguish early and late adolescence. Therefore, although puberty and strict age ranges serve as relatively clear markers for delineating phases of development, a number of other factors that cannot be as easily attributed to a specific developmental phase are considered throughout this book.

A very important challenge in identifying and conceptualizing the problem of stalking in children and adolescents is striking a balance between the pressure that leads to either underinclusion or overinclusion of young people in the class of stalking offenders. In other words, there may be a tendency to minimize the severity or chronic nature of a given child or adolescent's harassing behavior as less intrusive than it really is. On the other hand, there is the equally dangerous risk of overpathologizing or criminalizing relatively harmless child or adolescent behavior as stalking.

An example of this problem was reported in a case of alleged sexual harassment in a public school several years ago. A 6-year-old boy was accused of sexual harassment after he kissed a female classmate on the cheek (Sexual Harassment Guidance, 1997). This example of a clear over-reaction by school officials to student behavior prompted the Office of Civil Rights in the Department of Education to develop written guidelines to help schools formulate appropriate responses to cases of alleged sexual harassment in schools. This form of overreaction is a critical concern when dealing with how to conceptualize and define stalking behavior in young people. A balance needs to be struck between the two extremes of failing to recognize serious obsessional harassment that may constitute stalking in young people and inappropriate criminalizing or overpathologizing of innocuous forms of behavior in younger populations.

Cupach and Spitzberg (1998) have used the term *obsessive relational intrusion* as a general term for repetitive pursuit and personal invasion that encompasses a continuum of relatively innocuous behavior on the one hand, such as love notes or brief periods of infatuation. On the more severe end of the continuum lie more pathological forms of obsessive intrusion such as sexual harassment, threats, and stalking. This concept is useful because it permits flexibility in the way these behaviors are defined in terms of severity, intent, and impact.

CONCLUSION

This chapter reviewed the evidence from individual cases as well as the limited empirical research available on the social problem of stalking in children and adolescents. There is evidence that stalking is a phenomenon that is observed among children and adolescents. However, there are very limited data on the extent of the problem. Research on high school and college student populations reveals that stalking is a significant problem. A review of research on related forms of obsessional harassment in younger populations, such as dating violence, sexual harassment, and sexual aggression in children, also provides indirect, but not conclusive, evidence that stalking is a subtype of these prevalent forms of threatening and harassing behavior in children and adolescents. Although the literature reviewed in this chapter supports the conclusion that stalking occurs in younger people, the types of behavior, dynamics, and offender psychopathology that exist in these cases require expanded coverage. In the next chapter, these issues are explored in greater detail.

3

The Nature of Stalking in Young People

A major question that should be addressed when various forms of psychopathology or abnormal behavior are identified in both children and adults is whether these behavioral patterns can be conceptualized the same regardless of the age of the individual. Difficulties can arise when some psychological principles or concepts used to describe and explain adult behavior are applied to younger populations (McCann, 1998a). In other words, children and adolescents are not "mini-adults" who differ only with respect to physical size and chronological age. Rather, children and adolescents face unique developmental challenges that call for age-appropriate concepts and principles that can be applied to understand young people and their problems. Of course, some constructs such as attachment, identity, self-concept, and the like that are used to describe personality and social behavior are applicable across the life span. However, some of these constructs or issues are more or less relevant at various points during a person's life.

Because of these developmental considerations, there have been efforts to examine the unique issues raised when trying to understand social problems and various forms of psychopathology in children and adolescents that have traditionally been associated with adults. Some examples include juvenile sex offenses (Barbaree, Marshall, & Hudson, 1993), homicides committed by children (Ewing, 1990), malingering and deception in adolescents (McCann, 1998a), and sexual aggression in children (Araji, 1997). The purpose of this book is to perform a similar type of analysis on the social problem of stalking. Several challenges are inherent in such a task, including the fact that the psychological environments and personality development of children and adolescents vary as a function of age and level of maturity.

One of the major characteristics of adolescents, for example, is that they are very much influenced by peers, and the social relationships of adolescents often have a profound effect on shaping behavior. Likewise, teenagers are often highly influenced by popular media, including television, movies, and current cultural trends such as those in music. These social dynamics can complicate the study of stalking in younger populations as illustrated by an unusual stalking game, "Assassins," that has been described by Martello and Balsly (1996). According to the rules of this game, high school students pay $5 to enter the game, and each student is given the name of another student to shoot with a dart. After the first round, half of the participants are eliminated, and the remaining students are then given the name of another remaining student. This process continues until two students are left, and they then split the prize money, which can total anywhere from $400 to $600, depending on the number of original participants. This game was the subject of a 1985 movie *Gotcha*, starring Anthony Edwards, in which college students pursued each other with paint-ball guns.

What is fascinating about this game is not that it tends to trivialize a serious social problem such as stalking; rather, some of the comments made by students participating in the game, as well as the reactions of school officials and members of the law enforcement community, reveal that the game has prompted responses very similar to those of victims in genuine stalking cases, resulting in considerable confusion. For example, the following comment was made by a participant of this game who described how he would pursue other students: "You do all your research on your person. After you'd shoot [them], I usually ended up talking to them for about an hour. It actually introduced me to a lot of people" (Martello & Balsly, 1996, p. A1). This comment reflects the preparation and effort that is often exerted by someone who stalks another person and also how pursuit is often viewed as a means of increasing one's social contacts, as least in the mind of the person doing the stalking. Likewise, one victim's perspective was provided by another participant of the game:

> I could never go to my house unless someone at my house was home, because I didn't want to pull into my garage without someone coming out and checking around before I got out, so I would have to drive around for like an hour and a half before someone came home. (p. A1)

One would expect this type of reaction from an actual victim of stalking.

Another aspect that blurs the boundary between an adolescent game and the real problem of stalking is the reaction of school officials and police officers. School administrators have discouraged students from participating in this stalking game, and on one occasion police officers confiscated a gun from one of the participants because it was believed to be a real weapon, not a dart gun.

This unusual form of entertainment and competition among high school students underscores one of the difficulties with conceptualizing and studying the problem of stalking in younger people. There is often a blurry boundary between forms of pursuit and obsessional following that are less threatening and more socially acceptable or even sanctioned within peer groups. In this chapter, I outline the behavioral characteristics and dynamics that occur when stalking involves children and adolescents. More specifically, the material illustrates how stalking or obsessional following is manifest in cases involving younger perpetrators and victims.

Toward this end, the first section of this chapter discusses a prototypic case of stalking that involved a teenage offender. This case encompassed many salient issues that are often found in stalking cases involving younger perpetrators, although no single case can realistically provide examples of all relevant phenomena. Still, a detailed case example can provide a more accessible framework and context within which to think about age-related issues. Following this single case example, I then review a sample of stalking cases involving children and adolescents to examine some of the behavioral patterns and clinical features of child and adolescent obsessional followers. Also reviewed are some stalking-related behaviors that have been observed in clinical and forensic settings and are interesting facets of some cases, including fixations on public figures and patterns of obsessional following that have been observed between parents and children, a phenomenon that I call "intrafamilial stalking." Finally, the chapter closes with an overview of the various forms of psychopathology that have been observed in stalking offenders. In this discussion, the research on adult populations of stalking offenders is briefly reviewed, and the relevance of this literature to child and adolescent obsessional followers is discussed.

A CASE OF ADOLESCENT STALKING

A psychological evaluation was conducted on George, age 16, who had recently been transferred back to a group home setting after violating the conditions of his probation while living at home. The purpose of the evaluation was to provide an assessment of his psychological treatment needs and to make recommendations for case management given the numerous problems he had encountered when adjusting to a less structured setting. At the time of the evaluation, he had been convicted as a youthful offender on charges of harassment under the formal stalking provision of the criminal code in the state where the offense occurred.

George had a very lengthy history of involvement in the juvenile justice system dating back to age 13 when he was placed on a Person in Need of Supervision (PINS) petition by his mother due to escalating behavioral problems. Throughout his school history, George had difficulties with poor motivation, had a specific learning disability in reading, and was easily distracted. He was behind at least three grade levels in his reading achievement and had always been somewhat of a social outcast who had very few friends or acquaintances. As he approached adolescence, George's motivational problems became more pronounced, and he began to skip many days of school. Also around the start of adolescence, when teenagers typically begin showing signs of puberty and increased sexual awareness, George began to develop a sexual fixation on a single woman who lived alone in his neighborhood. He would follow the woman to her bus stop, ride the same bus that she did, and get off when she got off the bus. Initially this behavior was not considered threatening until George's approach behavior escalated over a period of time. He began to make inappropriate sexual comments to the woman that were perceived as threatening because of their highly charged content. The woman took out a civil order of protection, which George subsequently violated, and he was charged with harassment and placed on probation.

While on probation, George committed another offense of assault when he made a threatening remark to the same woman that she perceived as an intent on George's part to commit a sexual act against her. He was charged with sexual assault and sent to a juvenile correctional facility for 18 months, his first placement outside of the home, when he was age 14. During his incarceration, George was described as easily distracted, poorly motivated, uncooperative with staff, and noncompliant with the requests or demands that were made on him. Following his release, he was placed in a conditional release program whereby he was required to attend school, to abide by an order of protection barring him from having any contact with the woman he was stalking, and to attend regular appointments with his probation officer. Within 3 months, George violated the conditions of his probation. He made contact with the victim by following her once again, and he was returned to residential placement for 6 months. At the time of the evaluation, he had been residing in a group home for about 2 months.

In addition to the stalking behavior, George presented with several significant findings on the examination. His psychosocial history revealed that he had long-standing conflict with his parents. George saw his mother as untrustworthy in that he blamed her for initially placing him on a PINS petition and for reporting behavioral problems to his probation officer. His father was a career military officer who was away for large parts of George's early life, and as George entered adolescence, he began to rebel and withdraw from his father, who attempted to take a heavy-handed approach to his son's acting out. In many ways, George lacked any attachment or connection to either parent, but he was particularly indifferent to his father. There was no history of medical difficulties and yet George had a history of marijuana abuse that was heavy during those periods of time when he was not in residential or group home placement.

Other findings from the evaluation revealed that George had several previous psychological evaluations during the course of his placements. He was consistently observed to be very aloof, with flat affect and poor eye contact. His responses to questions during interviews were brief and his emotions were disengaged from the serious problems he had experienced, although there were periods of irritability that emerged when he was pressed to discuss how he felt about his involvement in the system. Although his thought processes were generally intact and there was no evidence of delusional thinking or hallucinations, there was a poverty in his speech and thought content. He had routinely denied suicidal or homicidal ideation or intent, and there was no history of such behavior. Nevertheless, his negativity and impoverished speech made it difficult to fully explore his ideation, fantasies, or other psychological data related to his stalking behavior.

In general, George was noted to have extremely poor social skills. He had no close friends, related peripherally to other residents in the group home, and manifested prominent schizoid personality characteristics. He also had been diagnosed with conduct disorder due to his legal troubles, but did not appear primarily psychopathic. His prognosis for benefitting from traditional psychotherapy was very poor given his chronic resistance and active rejection of support or assistance.

Several aspects of George's case are useful for illustrating the nature of stalking in a younger offender. One of the more significant factors was that his stalking behavior was so chronic and severe that he was formally charged and convicted of criminal harassment, which was the statutorily defined charge for stalking at the time. In addition, George's stalking behavior persisted over the course of several months and resulted in him violating an order of protection and the requirements of his probation. Therefore, ample evidence existed that his stalking was not merely a case of adolescent infatuation or "puppy love" and instead constituted a criminal pattern of behavior. Another significant aspect of this case was that George manifested symptoms of psychopathology, which undercuts any argument that he was a well-adjusted individual who merely got carried away with his pursuit. Rather, he displayed symptoms of schizoid personality disorder, conduct disorder, and subtle disturbances in his thinking that pointed to a need for mental health treatment. As such, his case illustrates how stalking, even if perpetrated by a youthful offender, often requires responses from both the criminal justice and mental health systems.

There are other interesting attributes of this case that raise questions about the nature of stalking in younger offenders. That George pursued a relative stranger, committed assault, and made repeated sexual advances, raises questions about the demographic and clinical characteristics of younger stalking offenders in general, perpetrator–victim patterns, and risk factors for violence. More specifically, it would be important to know what types of psychological characteristics might describe a stalking offender and factors that define victim preferences, the behaviors used to stalk victims, and the motivations for stalking among younger offenders. These questions cannot be answered by looking at a specific case and require instead research studies on larger samples of stalking offenders. The next section explores these issues in greater detail.

PATTERNS OF STALKING BEHAVIOR IN CHILDREN AND ADOLESCENTS

Research has been undertaken to examine various clinical characteristics and behavioral patterns of adult stalking perpetrators (e.g., Harmon, Rosner, & Owens, 1995; Kienlen, Birmingham, Solberg,

O'Regan, & Meloy, 1997; Meloy & Gothard, 1995) but there is no such research on child and adolescent stalking offenders. Much of the literature on stalking in young people has been confined to isolated case reports. Well-controlled comparative studies on the ways in which child and adolescent obsessional followers differ from other youthful offenders are needed. Likewise, research on the clinical and demographic characteristics of young stalking offenders also needs to be conducted.

One attempt to provide some preliminary descriptive data on child and adolescent obsessional followers was a summary of case reports by McCann (1998c, 2000). For example, McCann (1998c) provided evidence from individual case reports that subtypes of stalking in adolescent obsessional followers matched the often used typology developed by Zona, Sharma, and Lane (1993; see chapter 1 for detailed discussion on typology). In a broader analysis of both child and adolescent stalking cases, McCann (2000) conducted a review of the professional literature and media reports of stalking by a child or adolescent. From this analysis, a sample of 13 cases was identified from the author's clinical and forensic case files, the published professional literature, and detailed media reports. There was no control group against which the sample was compared, and in some cases relevant data such as clinical diagnosis or specific demographic information were missing, thus rendering the study limited as to its generalizability. Instead, what this summary of cases represents is a preliminary report on some of the demographic and clinical characteristics of young stalking offenders. One aspect that is worth noting is that all of the cases had some form of contact with either the mental health or criminal justice system specifically in response to the youth's stalking behavior. As such, all of the cases involved relatively clear instances of obsessional following by a child or adolescent.

The sample of child and adolescent stalking offenders in McCann (2000) had a mean age of 14.1 years, with a range of 9 to 18 years. Most of the obsessional followers were male, and most of the victims were female; this finding is consistent with research on adult populations (Meloy, 1996, 1998b). The relative ages of the victims were evenly split:

about half of the victims of young stalking offenders were adult and about half were same-age peers. Another interesting trend in the sample studied by McCann was that just over half of the stalking offenders made an explicit threat toward the victim, which again parallels the finding in adult populations that at least one-half of those who stalk threaten their victims (Meloy, 1996, 1998b). The types of motivation that guided stalking in the sample of young offenders included a desire for sexual contact as well as anger or revenge, which parallels the two major patterns of stalking identified by Harmon et al. (1995) in a sample of adults referred to a forensic clinic serving a criminal court. In addition, McCann found that 31% of the child and adolescent obsessional followers in his sample were violent toward the victim, which falls within the range of 25% to 35% of violence in adult stalking offenders that has been observed across various research studies (Meloy, 1996). Other trends that were noted included the fact that physical approach, telephoning, and letter writing were the most common behaviors used to stalk victims in McCann's (2000) small sample. These methods of pursuit are also common in adult samples.

Despite the parallels between this small sample of child and adolescent stalking offenders and the research findings from studies on adult offenders, the results from McCann (2000) are limited by a small sample size, unavailable data in some cases, and the lack of a comparison group. However, this study raises some questions that require further study. For instance, the youngest offender identified in this sample was age 9, and the case involved a youth who made more than 200 telephone calls of a sexual nature to a girl in his class. Thus, the question becomes what level of cognitive, social, emotional, moral, and behavioral development is necessary before a child can engage in a pattern of harassment that constitutes actual stalking. The answer to this question requires theoretical input from many components of human development. In the next chapter, various approaches to developmentally conceptualizing psychopathology are used to address issues on the etiology of stalking behavior.

Another trend noted in McCann's (2000) data that raises questions for further study is that the modal form of stalking in this small sample was a young male making repeated unwanted sexual advances toward a female adult or same-age female peer. This pattern is consistent in some ways with the data presented earlier on the wide prevalence of sexual harassment in school settings. In fact, casual acquaintances (64%) were the most common form of perpetrator–victim pattern, followed by strangers (21%) and prior intimate partners (14%). Meloy (1998b) noted that the most common pattern of stalking in adults, but not the only such pattern, involves obsessional men who stalk a woman with whom they have had a prior intimate sexual relationship. As McCann (2000) speculated, the difference in psychosexual development and level of intimacy that differentiates adult and adolescent relationships may account for this difference in prevalence of perpetrator–victim relationships. Because adolescents are experiencing greater uncertainty about their identity and expanding their sexual exploration, their capacity or opportunity for intimacy is less than it is for adults. Therefore, the young obsessional follower may develop fixations that involve sexual feelings that are directed more at casual acquaintances rather than prior intimate partners. Again, this explanation is speculative and requires further study. Some of the issues to be addressed in the following chapter on the etiology of stalking may provide further insight.

The material presented herein may sensitize clinicians and researchers to the problem of stalking in younger populations so that appropriate cases will be accurately identified and larger samples for study can be developed. Until such research exists, it may be useful to draw from the stalking research on adult samples to help conceptualize cases involving children or adolescents. A careful blending of research findings on adults and an appraisal of the developmental psychopathology literature will provide a framework for understanding the way in which various psychological disturbances that are associated with stalking manifest themselves similarly or differently in children and adolescents (more will be said about these issues later in this chapter, as well as in the next). However, it is first necessary to explore some stalking-related behaviors that have been distilled from observations made in specific cases. These related forms of pursuit include fixations on public figures and stalking that occurs within the family.

Other Forms of Stalking-Related Behavior

Fixations on Public Figures

In late 1997, two 13-year-old boys from Tennessee were charged with sending a threatening e-mail message to First Lady, Hillary Rodham Clinton. The message stated that a sniper was outside of the White House and that an explosive device was in a satchel somewhere on the White House grounds. After an investigation by the U.S. Secret Service, juvenile court proceedings were initiated against the youths, and they were charged with threatening and harassing Mrs. Clinton. If perpetrated by adults, this crime would have been punishable under federal law by both fines and several years in prison.

When federal agents appeared shortly after the message was sent, the youths were said to be extremely afraid and apologetic. The message was apparently meant as a prank, and there was no serious threat intended. Because of their ages, the boys were adjudicated in juvenile court, and therefore details about their background are protected from public disclosure. Ultimately, the court took into account the lack of serious threat, the fear and remorse expressed by the boys, and the lack of prior legal difficulties in their background. In the end, the judge took the charges under advisement, which meant that as long as the boys stayed out of trouble for one year, the charges would be dismissed, and the youths would have no criminal record.

This case illustrates how the specific act of threatening a political figure can be perpetrated by adolescents, despite the fact that most people might expect such behavior primarily in adults who have some political or attention-seeking agenda (H. V. Hall, 1998). However, a number of factors make it difficult to know the extent to which threats against public figures are made by children and adolescents. As in the case example described above, legal charges brought against teenagers are likely to be initially filed in family or juvenile court where there are greater confidentiality protections and privacy given to those charged with crimes. Moreover, record keeping is hampered by the fact that the ages of perpetrators for various offenses are either unavailable or not kept, so it is difficult to know how frequently young offenders threaten or harass public figures.

The behavior of the two adolescents who sent a threatening message to the First Lady would not meet the legal definitions of stalking because there had been no course of conduct. In other words, this was a one-time threat with no pattern of repetitive or recurrent harassment. Nevertheless, there are a number of reasons why an adolescent might form an obsessive attachment to a public figure. An obsession may appear on the surface to be pathological, but closer examination might reveal more benign motives. As in the case discussed, many threats made by juveniles toward public figures may be made as a prank or done on a dare from peers. Oftentimes, adolescents have difficulty appreciating the long-term consequences of their actions and the short-term gains of impressing friends, creating mischief, or in other ways committing harmless turmoil can serve as a motive behind immature threats as in the case of the Tennessee teenagers who threatened Mrs. Clinton.

There are other motives that can result in an obsessive attachment to a public figure that can ultimately turn into a primary fixation that could result in the stalking of that public figure. In mental health settings, I have observed some children and adolescents, with severe deficits in self-concept, inadequacy, intellectual limitations, or other factors that contribute to social alienation, forming very strong fixations on same-age celebrities. These fixations often occur with celebrities whose public persona is viewed by the young person as an idealized image that is desired but unattainable. In other words, the obsessive fixation becomes a way of coping that compensates for underlying feelings of inadequacy.

The case of Terry provides an example of this process. Terry, age 14 and White, had been admitted to an acute psychiatric inpatient facility for suicidal ideation and superficial gestures in which he threatened to kill himself. This crisis arose after Terry was discovered in sexual play with a younger child (age 11) who, like Terry, was living in a foster home. Terry had been in special education classes throughout the duration of his formal schooling and was diagnosed with mild mental retardation. He had been severely neglected during the early years of his life, and both of his biological parents were ineffective caretakers who had their parental rights terminated. This early loss of a major attachment figure is a recurrent theme that emerges in the early lives of individuals who stalk (Kienlen, 1998). Terry had lived in various foster homes throughout his life and had been hoping to be adopted, but a family never showed much interest. His personal hygiene was marginal, and his social skills were delayed; he had no same-age friends, and prominent themes of rejection, inadequacy, and neediness dominated his interactions with others.

During the course of his mental health treatment, it became clear that Terry had developed a fixation on a male child actor who had starred in several successful movies. Terry's fixation included repeated statements of his intent to travel to Hollywood to meet this actor and to become friends. Terry would write numerous notes and letters to the actor, although they were rather superficial and vague in content, given his intellectual limitations. When asked about his reasons for wanting to become friends with this celebrity, Terry would provide vague references to the child star being "nice" and likely to be a "good friend." It was apparent that the public persona of this celebrity was an idealized portrayal of all that Terry felt was lacking in his life; the star was attractive, popular, well-liked, intellectual, and competent as portrayed in his movies. Terry's unrealistic expectation of friendship, although non-violent in its intent, was clearly a compensatory fantasy-based union in which the child actor could help Terry overcome his feelings of rejection and inadequacy by joining into an idealized friendship. However, the future implications of Terry's propensity to become obsessively fixated on a celebrity served as a warning sign that he was prone to develop distorted attachments, despite no immediate threat being present.

Not all such obsessional fixations in children and adolescents are as pervasive as Terry's. However, there is psychological compensation that operates in many such fixations. Young people are no different than adults who pursue celebrities in wanting to have a sense of belonging, elevated status, and peer acceptance when they identify closely with a particular celebrity, musical group or artist, or other figure in the popular media. These fixations become obsessive and dysfunctional when they are more pervasive and consume the teenager's existence to the point where other aspects of his or her life suffer. For instance, school performance may decline, the teenager may develop unrealistic expectations about his or her relationship with the public figure, and in some instances the teenager may develop delusions about the celebrity such as erotomanic beliefs that one is loved by the public figure.

One empirical study on expressed motivations for contacting celebrities provides some insight into the reasons why individuals contact public figures and the differences between appropriate and inappropriate motivations and expectations. Leets, de Becker, and Giles (1995) surveyed fan behavior in a sample of 294 university students, as well as a sample of fan letters received by one Hollywood celebrity. This study is particularly useful because it used a college student sample with a median age of 19, representing late adolescence. Several interesting findings emerged from the data, including the fact that most of the letters received by the celebrity and sampled for this study were received from pre-adolescents (42%) and adolescents (16%). Thus, over half of the letters coded for expressed reasons to want contact with a celebrity came from children or adolescents. The college students in this sample provided self-reports of reasons why they might contact a celebrity through a letter; these included a desire for information, the need for association, a request, sexual contact, entertainment, and the need to express oneself. One expressed motivation, a desire for association, was the only variable that could differentiate those who had actually contacted a celebrity from those who had not. When actual letters received by a celebrity were sampled, the major motivations or expectations were curiosity or a need for information (16%); the desire to express adulation (39%); and a request for an autograph, letter, or money to support a fund-raising drive (46%). Overall, Leets and her colleagues concluded that normal motivations or expectations for contacting celebrities that are consistent across age groups include curiosity, a desire for information, expression of adulation, the need for association, and a favor or request.

Leets and her colleagues compared the major reasons for normal fan behavior with the inappropriate motivations and expectations for contacting public figures that were studied by Dietz and his colleagues (Dietz, Matthews, Martell, et al. 1991; Dietz, Matthews, van Duyne, et al. 1991). The major feature that differentiated appropriate from inappropriate contact with celebrities was the reasonableness of the expectations. Therefore, unusual motivations such as a request for marriage, sexual liaison, valuable gift, or having children are unreasonable expectations that characterize abnormal or inappropriate fan behavior. In addition, irrational, hostile, or threatening communications that suggest the person has projected inappropriate or unusual attributes or motives onto the celebrity would also characterize abnormal expectations of individuals who make inappropriate contact with a celebrity. A psychodynamic explanation for this phenomenon is that individuals who make inappropriate contact with celebrities or who have pathological fixations lack a cohesive identity that results in immature attempts to obtain an identity through unrealistic associations with celebrities. More is said about this hypothesis in the next chapter.

When assessing an individual's fixation on a public figure to determine whether it is benign or pathological, Leets and her colleagues suggested paying close attention to the person's capacity for distinguishing between fantasy-based expectations and reality-based ones. Sometimes the person may spontaneously recognize that his or her expectations are merely a form of wish-fulfillment, whereas in other cases the person can make this distinction with subtle confrontation or challenge. However, in other cases the person cannot draw the distinction between fantasy-based and reality-based expectations, and the result is a pathological fixation. In the case of Terry, his expectations of friendship were unrealistic, and even with direct confrontation he did not alter his belief or expectation that he could become friends with the celebrity if given the proper opportunity to meet him.

A noteworthy collateral concern in cases of obsessive fixation in younger populations is suicidal gestures or actual completed suicide in response to the death of a public figure who is the object of adolescent idolizing. One example is the 1994 suicide of rock star Kurt Cobain. One study found no increase in completed suicide in the Seattle community where Mr. Cobain lived that could be tied to his well-publicized suicide (Jobes, Berman, O'Carroll, Eastgard, & Knickmeyer, 1996). However, there was a significant increase in the number of suicide crisis calls following his death. Various aspects of media coverage for this event, the violent method in which Mr. Cobain took his life (i.e., gunshot), and community outreach efforts are all hypothesized to have contributed to the lack of copycat suicides following the rock star's death. Although these findings support community outreach and education as preventive measures, the increase in suicide crisis calls points to the fact that many young fans were affected by Mr. Cobain's death. Thus, prevention of adolescent suicide connected to obsessive fixations on public figures in the popular culture may be more successful when there are efforts to educate and provide outreach support services to youths during the time of such publicized crises.

Differentiating between an age-appropriate infatuation with a celebrity or teen idol by a child or adolescent and an obsessive preoccupation that can give rise to stalking is not always a clear line. Teen magazines and fan clubs are a part of youth culture that reinforce infatuation with idols from movies, television, and music. However, in some instances this preoccupation can rise to disturbing levels and can include actual stalking in some cases. There are some criteria that can be used to determine when harmless youth infatuation with a celebrity may cross the line into a pathological obsession. If the youth's fixation interferes with his or her functioning in school or peer and family relationships, the fixation could be considered extreme. Another indication of difficulty is if the youth engages in some crude form of approach behavior toward the celebrity that is not appropriate, has minimal likelihood of achieving success, is not sanctioned by the celebrity, or has no rational purpose or goal. For instance, attending a concert or autograph session are examples of appropriate or sanctioned approach behavior. One example of a poorly organized effort at approach by an adolescent occurred with Robert Bardo, the man who stalked and later killed actress Rebecca Schaeffer. At the age of 14, he stole money from his mother and traveled to Maine to meet a same-age celebrity (Tharp, 1992). The approach was not sanctioned, was disorganized, and had a very limited likelihood of success. Another sign that a youthful fixation on a celebrity has taken on extreme levels is if the fixation is associated with other signs of psychological disturbance such as psychotic thinking, delusions, depression, suicidal ideation or gestures, severe anxiety, or social withdrawal. It is important to balance the need to identify certain risk factors for stalking in young people against the risk of labeling age-appropriate and benign behaviors as disturbed or pathological. However, obsessive fixations on public figures and celebrities is a critical issue that can serve as a useful early sign of later problems; thus careful attention must be given to a child or adolescent's preoccupation with a public figure to make sure that it is not extreme or interfering with his or her functioning.

Intrafamilial Stalking

The most common form of stalking in adults involves a male obsessional follower and a female victim with whom he has had a prior intimate sexual relationship (Meloy, 1998b, 1999b). In addition, three types of stalking victims have been identified and used to classify various perpetrator–victim patterns: (a) prior intimate sexual partners, (b) acquaintances, and (c) strangers. In clinical and forensic settings, however, a unique pattern has been observed in stalking cases that involve children and adolescents. More specifically, in very few cases a perpetrator–victim relationship involves a parent and child as either obsessional follower or victim. Elsewhere it has been noted that this relationship is somewhat unique to stalking cases involving young people and could be characterized as prior intimate partners where there has been a non-sexual, live-in relationship (McCann, 2000).

One well-publicized example of this phenomenon is the case of 17-year-old Olympic gymnast Dominique Moceanu. In the fall of 1998,

Ms. Moceanu's coach, Luminita Miscenco, and the gymnast's father, Dimitru Moceanu, got into a lengthy and heated verbal argument that ultimately led to Ms. Moceanu and her coach fleeing the gymnasium where she was training (Raboin, 1998). Ms. Moceanu quickly packed some personal belongings and went to stay with her coach. Apparently much of the conflict between the gymnast and her family stemmed from the father's excessive control over his daughter's career and most aspects of her life. Some disputes were reported concerning the manner in which the gymnast's parents managed the fortune she had amassed over her career.

The issue of stalking, however, did not emerge until shortly after Ms. Moceanu filed court papers seeking legal emancipation from her parents. That motion was granted in the fall of 1998. In late November of that same year, Ms. Moceanu filed for a temporary protective order against her father because it was alleged that he had stalked his daughter after her separation from her parents. Police detectives in Houston, Texas, investigated an allegation that Mr. Moceanu was attempting to hire someone to kill one of his daughter's friends and her coach (Longman, 1998). Although there was insufficient evidence to make an arrest, the threats and alleged stalking by her father resulted in the fear in Ms. Moceanu that is common among stalking victims:

> I am terrified that my father will soon be successful in harming me or one of my friends or associates. This threat of danger from my father hangs over me every day and puts a tremendous physical and mental strain on my mind. (Raboin, 1998, p. 1C)

This case of alleged stalking of a daughter by her father represents a well-publicized example of the phenomenon I call *intrafamilial stalking,* in which the perpetrator–victim relationship involves a parent and child. In another case encountered in a forensic context, the roles were reversed, and an adolescent stalked his mother to such an extent that the mother was required to obtain an order of protection against her son.

These unusual cases illustrate many dynamics that are generally found in stalking cases. In the case of Ms. Moceanu, for instance, there was a triangulation between the gymnast, her father, and third parties such as friends and her coach. Such triangulation may increase the risk of violence when third parties are perceived by the obsessional follower as hindering access to the object (Meloy, 1996, 1999a). In the case of Ms. Moceanu, her friend and coach were reportedly perceived by the father as preventing the gymnast from returning to her family and perhaps alienating her further from her parents. Of course, this could be the perception of the pursuer, while other factors such as fear of control might be motivating the object to avoid or extricate himself or herself from the influences of the pursuing parent.

Intrafamilial stalking is somewhat unique to children and adolescents. When a child stalks a parent, or vice versa, the perpetrator–victim relationship is one in which there is more than a casual acquaintance relationship, but the relationship also differs from the situation in which a prior intimate sexual relationship existed between the perpetrator and victim. However, intrafamilial stalking fits more closely with the prior intimate relationship pattern of perpetrator and victim interactions because the person being stalked at one time lived with the person who is pursuing him or her. Therefore, many conflicted emotional ties may still exist, making the nature of the attachment and fixation different from that which exists when stalking occurs among casual acquaintances or strangers.

A very important concern with the concept of intrafamilial stalking is the possibility that patterns of disturbed or conflicted interactions between a parent and child may be mistakenly characterized as stalking. That is, one might argue that intrafamilial stalking is nothing more than the application of the term *stalking* to describe patterns of conflict in families that results in sensationalism. Indeed one might question whether the media misapplied the term in the case of Ms. Moceanu and her father merely to sensationalize the conflict. Although this observation raises an important point, the pattern of obsessional following between parents and their children in a few isolated cases strongly suggests that stalking is a fitting way to conceptualize the behavior in such cases.

It should be recognized, however, that there are many different variations of conflicted behavior that may exist between parent and child. For instance, children can be oppositional and repeatedly defiant and parents may be abusive and controlling toward their children, which may constitute a regular pattern of behavior. Therefore, the question remains: at what point does repetitive acting-out or chronic controlling behavior become a pattern of intrusive and threatening behavior that rises to the level of stalking?

Based on observations that have been made in a very small number of cases of intrafamilial stalking, I have formulated three general guidelines that can be used to define such cases that may protect against inaccurately identifying conflict that occurs between a child and his or her parent as stalking (McCann, 2000). First, there must be a pattern of threatening or harassing behavior directed toward a specific individual that meets the definition of stalking or obsessional following. Second, some legal action must be taken specifically in response to the threatening behavior. Such legal action might involve police investigation of threats, such as occurred in the case of Ms. Moceanu, or the victim might seek an order of protection. In one case on which I consulted, a mother had been stalked by her son while he was on a court petition for delinquency. However, the mother also had to obtain a civil order of protection against her son specifically because of his threatening behavior toward her. Third, the harassing or threatening behavior should occur during a period of time when the parent and child are living apart. This criterion prevents blurring of the definitions of stalking and domestic violence or child abuse that occurs when family members are living together. Again, the pattern of threats observed in the case of Ms. Moceanu occurred after she had left her parents and was living elsewhere with her coach. In another case where a teenager stalked a parent, he had repeatedly followed the parent, made threatening telephone calls, and made harassing comments after he had been removed from the family home and had been placed in a group home for adolescents.

These three criteria are somewhat strict, but they serve as guidelines that can help delineate cases that involve threatening and harassing behavior that is more than just conflicted or abusive behavior between a parent and child. Intrafamilial stalking is likewise a very unusual but interesting phenomenon that has been observed in clinical and forensic settings. However, no data are available on the prevalence of this particular behavior, and more study is needed to determine if it is rare and occurs in isolated cases or if it represents a small subtype of stalking that occurs in disrupted family situations.

Psychopathology and Stalking

Any discussion of the psychiatric diagnoses that are found among child and adolescent obsessional followers must address the relevance of certain psychiatric diagnoses that are first identified in childhood or adolescence, such as conduct disorder and attention deficit-hyperactivity disorder (ADHD). In this section, the types of psychopathology that may be associated with stalking in younger offenders are examined.

It was originally noted by Meloy (1996) that many of the early case studies reported on stalking were devoted to the diagnosis of erotomania. According to the *DSM-IV* (American Psychiatric Association, 1994), *erotomania* is classified as a delusional disorder subtype in which the person maintains a delusional belief "that another person, usually of higher status, is in love with the individual" (p. 301). The *DSM-IV* also states that the delusion often pertains to a belief of idealized romantic love or special union with the object, rather than sexual attraction. Aside from the case reports that have appeared in the literature, most research on adult stalking offenders reveals that erotomania is not a common diagnosis (Harmon et al., 1995, 1998; Kienlen et al., 1997; Meloy & Gothard, 1995), although erotomania is found to some extent in groups of obsessional followers (Zona et al., 1993). Although erotomania has been identified in adolescence (Urbach, Khalily, & Mitchell, 1992), it remains unclear how common or rare this diagnosis is in populations of young stalking offenders. Therefore, even though erotomania appears to be associated with stalking behavior in adolescents, it remains unclear if this diagnosis is extremely rare or is merely a low frequency diagnosis.

The more common clinical syndrome diagnoses among adult stalking offenders on Axis I of the *DSM-IV* appear to be substance abuse, mood disorders, and schizophrenia (Meloy, 1998b). Again, there are no systematic data on young stalking offenders, so broad conclusions cannot be drawn at this time. Individual case reports by McCann (1998c) revealed that schizophrenia has been associated with stalking in adolescents, but again it is unclear how common this occurs in larger populations. The small sample of child and adolescent obsessional followers reported by McCann (2000) had too many cases with missing diagnostic information, which prevents any firm conclusions from being drawn. Therefore, the research does not provide any clear answer as to the prevalence of various mental disorders among young stalking offenders. This area requires further research.

One issue that merits attention is the application of specific psychiatric diagnoses that are often first made in childhood or adolescence. Two diagnoses, conduct disorder and ADHD, are relevant because these conditions are associated with an increased risk for criminal behavior. According to the *DSM-IV, conduct disorder* is defined by "a repetitive and persistent pattern of behavior in which the basic rights of others or major age-appropriate societal norms or rules are violated" (American Psychiatric Association, 1994, p. 85). By definition, conduct disorder is associated with higher levels of antisocial behavior, but much diversity exists among children and adolescents with this disturbance, because their problematic behavior can be differentiated in terms of frequency, intensity, repetitiveness, and chronicity (Kazdin, 1996).

Case studies exist that reveal conduct disorder as a diagnosis in younger stalking offenders (McCann, 1998c, 2000). However, the presence of conduct disorder in a child or adolescent obsessional follower does not necessarily imply an antisocial or psychopathic motive for the stalking behavior. Although the *DSM-IV* noted that "a substantial portion" of children and adolescents with conduct disorder will manifest antisocial personality disorder in adulthood (American Psychiatric Association, 1994, p. 89), the research literature shows that childhood conduct disturbances can take many different courses. Tolan and Gorman-Smith (1998) have provided a comprehensive review of the developmental pathways of criminal behavior in children and adolescents, showing that delinquent behavior can shift in intensity and severity over the life span. This finding is consistent with Moffitt's (1993) delineation of adolescence-limited and life-course-persistent antisocial behavior. The significance of these issues for young stalking offenders is that the presence of conduct disorders does not necessarily imply an antisocial or psychopathic motive. Research on adult stalking offenders, for example, has shown that personality disorders are prevalent, but that antisocial personality disorder is less prominent than it is in other criminal offenders (Meloy, 1998b; Meloy & Gothard, 1995). This finding supports the theoretical hypothesis that stalking is more a disturbance of attachment (Kienlen, 1998), because psychopathic or antisocial individuals are pathologically lacking in the need for attachments. Therefore, conduct disorder in children or adolescents who stalk may reflect a behavioral pattern associated with impulsivity, aggression, and so forth rather than an antisocial or psychopathic personality disturbance (McCann, 1998c).

Another diagnosis among children and adolescence that has been the focus of clinical and research attention in recent years is *ADHD*, which the *DSM-IV* defines as "a persistent pattern of inattention and/or hyperactivity-impulsivity that is more frequent and severe than is typically observed in individuals at a comparable level of development" (American Psychiatric Association, 1994, p. 78). There is strong research evidence that the presence of ADHD creates a heightened risk for criminal behavior, particularly when it occurs with conduct disorder as a co-morbid diagnosis (Barkley, 1997, 1998; Tolan & Gorman-Smith, 1998). Again there is no research on the prevalence of ADHD among young stalking offenders, or in the childhood histories of adult stalking offenders for that matter. However, one published case study of stalking in a sexually sadistic adolescent had ADHD as one of the major diagnoses (Johnson & Becker, 1997). Therefore, the role of ADHD as a risk factor for potential criminal or violent behavior in stalking offenders needs to be studied more systematically.

One final issue that should be noted is the role of psychotic disturbance in stalking behavior. The most common forms of psychotic disturbances among adult stalking offenders include erotomania, which was
discussed earlier, and schizophrenia. Although psychotic disorders are
found in adult stalking offenders, most individuals are not psychotic at
the time they stalk (Harmon et al., 1995, 1998; Kienlen et al., 1997;
Meloy, 1998b; Meloy & Gothard, 1995). Nevertheless, the onset of schizophrenia "typically occurs between the late teens and the mid-30s, with
onset prior to adolescence rare . . ." (American Psychiatric Association,
1994, p. 281). Therefore, although schizophrenia is a common, but not
prominent, diagnosis among adult stalking offenders, it may be even less
prevalent in child and adolescent stalking offenders given the typical
developmental course of the disorder. McCann (1998c) documented at
least one case study of stalking by an adolescent with schizophrenia.
Thus, even if schizophrenia is less common in younger individuals, it
may still be found in some cases.

One additional issue related to this discussion of psychopathology in
stalking offenders that deserves attention is the diagnosis of personality
disorders. Meloy (1998b) noted that personality disorders on Axis II of
the *DSM-IV* are found in a majority of stalking offenders. Again, case
studies have suggested that personality disorders are found in adolescent
stalking offenders as well (McCann, 1998c, 2000), as the case presented at
the beginning of this chapter illustrates. The appropriateness of making
personality disorder diagnoses in children and adolescents is marked with
controversy and some confusion. McCann (1999) briefly reviewed these
issues and noted that the *DSM-IV* permits the diagnosis of a personality
disorder in children and adolescents where maladaptive personality traits
are pervasive and are not limited to the distinct developmental pressures
of the individual's specific chronological age or level of maturity.
Moreover, the *DSM-IV* permits the diagnosis of a personality disorder in
children or adolescents when the features of the specific personality disorder have been present for at least one year (American Psychiatric
Association, 1994). The exception, of course, is antisocial personality

disorder which requires that the individual be at least 18 years of age before the formal diagnosis may be made.

There is evidence that personality disorder diagnoses can be made reliably in adolescents (Johnson, Brent, Connolly, Bridge, Matta, Constantine, Rather, & White, 1995; Marton, Korenblum, Kutchner, Stein, Kennedy, & Pakes, 1989). Also, avoidant and borderline personality disorders show some proclivity to run in families, which supports the validity of these diagnoses in children and adolescents. Nevertheless, the long-term stability of some personality disorders diagnosed in adolescence is tenuous, as some researchers have found rates of various personality disorders diagnosed in adolescents to be lower when the same adolescents were re-examined years later (Mattanah, Becker, Levy, Edell, & McGlashan, 1995; Rey, Morris-Yates, Singh, Andrews, & Stewart, 1995). Personality disorder diagnoses in young stalking offenders need to be considered on a case-by-case basis. That is,

> a personality disorder diagnosis may be warranted in some cases where the adolescent's [or child's] functioning has been impaired by persistent and pervasive maladaptive personality traits, whereas in other cases an adolescent's maladaptive traits may lack the long-term stability required for a personality disorder diagnosis (McCann, 1999, p. 169)

Close adherence to the *DSM-IV* criteria, use of reliable psychological testing, structured interviews, and a broad-based approach to assessment will help clinicians when determining appropriate diagnoses in cases of stalking by a child or adolescent.

CONCLUSION

Literature on the nature and dynamics of stalking in children and adolescents reveals that there are far more questions that need to be answered than there are reliable conclusions that can be drawn at this time. More research is needed, particularly where comparisons can be drawn between samples of young stalking offenders and other youth offenders who do not stalk. The preliminary findings that have been presented in this chapter point to research questions that can be addressed in the future. Much of what is currently known about the phenomenon of stalking in children and adolescents is derived from published case reports. A survey of these case reports suggests that there are some parallels between young stalking offenders and adult offenders, such as the fact that most perpetrators appear to be male; most victims appear to be female; and the types of behaviors used to stalk victims include physical approach, following, telephone calls, and letter writing. There is no one pattern of stalking, victim type, or motivational pattern that characterizes all cases of child or adolescent stalking. That is, specific cases may involve stalking motivated by sexual attraction, revenge, anger, psychotic thinking, or disorganized behavior. Special types of stalking-related behaviors were also reviewed, including fixation on public figures and intrafamilial stalking, which seems to be a unique perpetrator–victim pattern observed in isolated cases. Finally, various issues related to the types of psychopathology that may be encountered in stalking cases were also reviewed. In particular, the case reports suggest that erotomania, personality disorders, schizophrenia, and conduct disorder are found among adolescent stalking offenders, but no conclusions can be drawn about relative prevalence rates. The relevance of special diagnostic issues among children and adolescents were discussed, such as the developmental course of various forms of psychopathology and the assessment of personality disorders in young people. To provide a context for understanding how various forms of psychopathology contribute to stalking behavior, it is necessary to explore how and why stalking develops. Therefore, the proposed causes of stalking behavior are discussed in the next chapter.

4

The Development of Stalking

As the subtitle of this book illustrates, the word *primitive* has been used to describe stalking in young people as a problematic bond or connection that is manifest early in life. In fact, the word generally denotes something that is underdeveloped or occurs early in time. In psychological literature and in psychoanalytic writing in particular, the term has been used to describe defense mechanisms, emotional states, and psychological processes. For example, primitive defense mechanisms such as projection, splitting, and devaluation have been used to characterize less integrated personality states (Kernberg, 1984; Masterson, 1981). Likewise, primitive emotional states such as rage and jealousy have been used to describe the poorly modulated emotions of individuals whose ability to test reality, control affect, and maintain a cohesive sense of self has been compromised.

Several psychological theories have proposed stages of development as a means of characterizing and facilitating the understanding of physical, social, and psychological challenges that a person encounters over the course of his or her life. Numerous examples of stage-oriented theories are present in psychology, including the psychosexual stages proposed in psychoanalytic theory, Piaget's stages of cognitive development, and Erikson's stages of ego development. Difficulties in the separation–individuation stage of development have also been related to a person's vulnerability to primitive modes of psychological functioning (Mahler, Pine, & Bergman, 1975). Although stage-oriented theories have limitations, because individual differences exist in the rate of maturation and chronological age demarcations are difficult to apply with uniformity, the notion that people develop in stages highlights the fact that adaptive development depends on successful resolution of certain challenges or demands before the person can experience further growth and change.

The notion that psychological processes can be primitive has been applied in various contexts to understand psychopathology from a developmental perspective. Dutton (1998) has recently provided a succinct review of how the notion of primitive psychological factors can serve as a useful mechanism for understanding the origins of spousal abuse and battering, a phenomenon related to stalking:

> When psychiatrists refer to a defense as "primitive," they mean it formed very early in life, even before the "Oedipal stage" of development. Whereas Sigmund Freud emphasized the "oedipal" [stage] around age 3, later psychiatry has focused on the "pre-Oedipal" period as having great importance for the formation of personality. During this earlier phase, our basic notions of selfhood develop, as we wander for the first time from the embrace of our mother. During this initial sojourn it gradually dawns on the infant that it is a separate entity from its mother. This dawning has been described . . . as the "psychological birth of the human infant." It is also during this stage that rage is born and temper tantrums appear. (p. 94)

This passage by Dutton captures the essence of the term *primitive* as it is used in psychodynamic theory to identify the developmental stage of growth to which some forms of serious psychopathology can be traced. Primitive psychological states such as psychotic disturbances, borderline personality organization, and severe antisocial and narcissistic personality disorders have all been identified as having etiological foundations at the earliest stages of development. As such, the word, when used as a qualifier for defense mechanisms, affective states, and self-states, does not refer only to psychotic disturbances (Kernberg, 1992); rather, primitive states also encompass severe personality disorders, some types of sexual pathology, and a heightened propensity for extreme anger and rage.

Another significant theme in the passage taken from Dutton's (1998) book *The Abusive Personality* is that the dynamics of primitive, or pre-Oedipal, stages of development involve attachment, formation of one's identity, and intense emotional states involving rage and anger. Successful navigation of the primitive stages of development means that the person develops with more mature and well-integrated ego functions, such as the capacity to test reality, the ability to modulate and tolerate intense emotions, a cohesive and clear sense of self, as well as stable and secure attachments with others.

In this chapter, the major theoretical models for understanding stalking, particularly from the perspective of the perpetrator, are reviewed. Currently, one major model of stalking that has been set forth is a psychodynamic formulation in which stalking is viewed as a disturbance of attachment. However, I expand on this view of stalking and address equally important psychodynamic issues, including the formation of personal identity and the nature of primitive emotions such as rage, jealousy, and anger. A major thesis offered in this chapter is the notion that stalking is a disturbance not only of attachment but also of identity in which the person's capacity to develop healthy relationships and to cope with rejection or abandonment are impaired due to feelings of inadequacy and a diffuse sense of one's own values and ideals. Another secondary theme of this chapter is the notion that the psychological vulnerabilities that predispose someone to develop an obsessional fixation on another person and to engage in stalking behavior have their origins in the earliest phases of development. Consequently, the early development of personal vulnerabilities that predispose someone to stalk implies that stalking can arise in later childhood, particularly the later latency phase of development, or adolescence.

The first major section of this chapter begins with an overview of Meloy's (1996, 1998b) psychodynamic model of stalking. Next, issues involving attachment disturbances; impaired identity formation; and primitive emotions involving anger, rage, jealousy, and envy are discussed in greater detail. Finally, some alternative models for understanding stalking are presented. The chapter then closes with a brief appraisal of the value of each theory, and suggestions are offered for using current theoretical models to guide future research.

A PSYCHODYNAMIC MODEL OF STALKING

One explanatory theory of stalking behavior is Meloy's (1996, 1998b) psychodynamic model. In many ways this model serves as a useful organizing framework for the other issues that are discussed later in this chapter. After briefly presenting Meloy's formulation, specific components of his theory are expanded upon, such as attachment pathology, identity disturbances, and intense rage-based emotions such as envy and jealousy. Although all of these factors play a role in many forms of stalking behavior, the psychodynamic model is the first comprehensive framework that places each of these early developmental challenges into a theory that results in an explanation of the dynamics of stalking, at least from the perspective of the psychology of the perpetrator.

The psychodynamic model of stalking behavior has six major stages (Meloy, 1996, 1998b). In the first, the person develops *a narcissistic linking fantasy* in which he or she fantasizes about a special or idealized relationship with a particular person. Specifically, the person maintains thoughts "of being loved by or loving, admired by or admiring (idealizing), being exactly like (mirroring) or complementing (twinship), or sharing a destiny with a particular object or person (merger)" (Meloy, 1998, p. 18). It is interesting to note that Meloy, in citing the work of Person (1995), stated that such narcissistic linking fantasies are found in normal individuals and can serve adaptive functions in relationships throughout a person's life. Specifically, narcissistic linking fantasies serve to motivate the pursuit of a stable, long-term relationship and can also serve as motivation to form attachments to others. Empirical support for the normative basis of such fantasies was presented in the previous chapter where research on college students showed that narcissistic linking fantasies were a common reason that students often sought out contact with a celebrity or public figure (Leets, de Becker, & Giles, 1995).

The normative nature of narcissistic linking fantasies is important to acknowledge from a developmental perspective, because the fantasies of adolescents and children tend to be more primitive (Person, 1995). That is, fantasies in younger people tend to be more narcissistically focused on special or idealized relationships with public figures such as teen idols, superheroes, and other figures in the media. If the fantasies of children and adolescents are more primitive, in that they are more narcissistically based, then one might expect that these fantasies would lead to a higher prevalence of obsessional harassment in younger people. However, there is no support for higher prevalence rates of stalking or similar forms of harassment in younger people (although bullying is a very common form of obsessional harassment that is related to stalking; see chapter 5). In fact, children and adolescents who stalk represent the lower end of the age distribution of stalking offenders.

Therefore, if children and adolescents have a greater propensity to engage in narcissistic linking fantasies, the question is why younger people are not more prone to stalk. The answer appears to lie in the fact that narcissistic linking fantasies are not the cause of stalking behavior, but rather serve as the starting point. The more critical variables in the psychodynamics of stalking that determine whether someone will ultimately obsessionally follow another person occur when the person experiences rejection or failure in achieving the desired relationship with the object. How the person copes with this rejection is more important in understanding whether the person will engage in stalking. The psychological factors that dictate how the person will cope have their roots in the earliest stages of development.

The second stage of the psychodynamic model involves behavioral approach toward the object of fantasy that may range from an appropriate set of behavioral rituals that result in a relationship, such as a request for a picture or autograph from a celebrity, socially approaching a stranger, or developing a close working relationship. However, with each of these behavioral approaches comes the risk of either acute or chronic rejection, and it is at this critical juncture which, according to Meloy (1996, 1998b), the differentiation between an appropriate reaction to rejection and stalking is made. In normal individuals, rejection may precipitate grieving the loss of the idealized object; the person grieves the loss and moves on to the possibility of a new relationship with a different idealized object. Likewise, rejection by an acquaintance with whom the person desires a more intimate relationship may precipitate hurt, anger, or rejection, but those emotions are channeled adaptively into appropriate outlets. An example of this phenomenon is a terminated employee who sets out to prove that a boss was wrong for firing him or her by being motivated to succeed with another employer.

On the other hand, Meloy (1998b) noted that "in stalking cases . . . a different course of events unfolds. The subject, because of his pathological narcissism . . . is extraordinarily sensitive to rejection and the feelings of shame or humiliation that accompany it" (p. 19). As a result, the next series of stages in Meloy's psychodynamic theory of stalking involve the obsessional follower defending against these feelings of shame and humiliation, which are unacceptable and intolerable, with feelings of rage. Consequently, the idealized object becomes devalued and the person's rage "is a central component in motivating the behavior of the stalker," and there is a desire to hurt, control, or even destroy the object (Meloy, 1998, p. 20). In addition, Meloy suggested that both envy and jealousy are emotions that play a role in the rage that is used to defend against the shame and humiliation.

In the final stage of Meloy's psychodynamic model of stalking, he suggested that the act of stalking results in controlling, hurting, or devaluing the object and thus the original narcissistic linking fantasy is restored, as is the pursuer's psychological equilibrium. This concept is interesting, and Meloy (1998b) made a compelling argument by citing anecdotal evidence of how this process can occur through his discussion of the case of John

Hinkley, Jr., in his pursuit of actress Jodie Foster. As result of Mr. Hinkley's assassination attempt on President Ronald Reagan, Mr. Hinkley ultimately linked himself with Ms. Foster in the minds of the public, and it also assured that the actress would never forget who he is. Therefore, Meloy's psychodynamic theory basically implies that the pursuit and obsessional following serve to restore and maintain the psychological equilibrium of the pursuer.

One of the key stages in this psychodynamic model that is significant from a developmental perspective is the obsessional follower's response to real or imagined rejection because it triggers a primitive response that is based on impaired ego development in the pursuer. In short, one of the key issues appears to be the expectations the pursuer has of the effect his or her stalking behaviors will have on the object and the capacity of the pursuer to adaptively cope with rejection. For example, an individual who has unrealistic expectations or psychotic beliefs of being destined to marry the object is at heightened risk of experiencing harsh rejection because these expectations far exceed realistic possibilities. These situations are likely to occur when individuals pursue celebrities or strangers (Leets et al., 1995). Also, if the individual who pursues the object has weakened ego functions, such that there are weak boundaries between self and other, then rejection is likely to be perceived as a loss of part of the self, aside from loss of the object. Such a severe threat to personal integrity may trigger a strong protective, and potentially aggressive or violent, response to rejection or impeded access to the object. In short, the person who has a weakened ego is unable to test reality when under stress, to make clear demarcations between self and other, and to manage intense and unpleasant emotions in response to rejection. As such, the psychological deficits that predispose an individual to stalk arise at a very early stage of psychological development when the person is learning to develop the capacity for healthy attachment, the ability to test reality, a cohesive sense of self that is differentiated from others, and the capacity to manage intense rage and anger. All of these functions have traditionally been conceptualized as developing in the primitive stages of development.

Because the theory outlined by Meloy implicates attachment, identity, and intense emotions, such as rage, anger, envy, and jealousy, each of these issues is discussed in greater detail in the remainder of this section. It is also important to recognize that situational factors and other developmental issues, such as the onset of formal operations (the ability to think abstractly) and puberty, can also influence the relative level of psychological maturity that may be required before stalking or obsessional following will be manifest in a particular individual. Nevertheless, the purpose of the present discussion is to examine psychodynamic issues in greater detail.

Attachment Disturbances

The concept of attachment has become an accepted and important construct for explaining interpersonal relationships. According to attachment theory, "early experiences of infants with their care givers influence subsequent well-being and behavior through their effect on 'working models' of the self and others" (Greenberger & McLaughlin, 1998, p. 122). Based heavily in the work of Ainsworth (1989) and Bowlby (1973, 1980, 1982), attachment theory has been set forth as a model for explaining externalizing and internalizing behaviors in children (Cowan, Cohn, Cowan, & Pearson, 1996), various forms of psychopathology in adolescents (Allen, Hauser, & Borman-Spurrell, 1996; Rosenstein & Horowitz, 1996), and aggressive behavior in children (Lyons-Ruth, 1996). Stalking has also been conceptualized as a disturbance in attachment (Kienlen, 1998; Meloy, 1992, 1996, 1998b).

Attachment is not merely another word to describe interpersonal relationships. Rather, attachment constitutes an affectional bond with another person, where an *affectional bond* is "a relatively long-enduring tie in which the partner is important as a unique individual and is interchangeable with none other. In an affectional bond, there is a desire to maintain closeness to the partner" (Ainsworth, 1989, p. 711). Attachment also encompasses bonds with individuals who provide protection and comfort in times of danger and stress (Bowlby, 1973, 1980, 1982). A critical tenet of attachment theory is that the affective bond with a specific person is not interchangeable with another person. However, secure attachments in the early stages of life form the basis for personal confidence, assurance, and security that permits the child to explore his or her environment. Through exploration, he or she engages in other attachment behaviors, which are any actions that result in a preference for closeness and a lasting connection to another person (Bowlby, 1980).

In very young children, attachment to primary care givers is crucial and involves such behaviors as clinging in strange or frightening situations, distress when separated from the care giver, checking on the location of the parent when playing, and seeking attention from the care giver. According to Hazan and Shaver (1994), attachment behaviors are biologically programmed to ensure survival; because infants are extremely immature, both psychologically and physically, they must rely on adults to provide care and protection. Attachment increases the likelihood that the infant will survive by facilitating complementary systems of behavior with adults. Furthermore, Hazan and Shaver outlined the three defining features of attachment behavior: proximity maintenance, safe haven, and secure base. *Proximity maintenance* involves behaviors that are directed at keeping the young child near the attachment figure and resisting separation. A *safe haven* implies that a primary attachment figure is someone to whom the infant can turn for comfort, support, and reassurance. Attachment figures provide a *secure base* from which the child can explore the environment and return after brief separations. The goal of attachment is to maintain feelings of security, enhance self-confidence, and enhance feelings of trust and predictability in relationships, because early attachments form the basis for later social relationships (Bartholomew, 1990).

The work of attachment theorists has been directed not only at understanding how attachments form, but also at understanding the effects of disruption or the severing of early attachments on functioning later in life. Bowlby identified a three-stage response in infants who were separated from their care givers (cited in Hazan & Shaver, 1994). In the first stage of *protest,* infants cry, actively search for the care giver, and resist any efforts by others to sooth distress. A second stage of *despair* was noted in which infants became dysphoric, passive, and sad. In the third stage of *emotional detachment,* infants exhibited a lack of emotional investment in others. These stages represent an infant's reaction to disruption in attachment, but they can also represent adaptive coping mechanisms:

> . . . reactions of anxiety and protest, even detachment, are highly adaptive responses to separation from one's primary protector. A child expresses distress because it usually brings the care giver around. . . . The characteristic inactivity of despair keeps the child quiet and still, allowing for recuperation. Detachment makes possible the resumption of normal activity, possibly even the search for a new attachment figure. (Hazan & Shaver, 1994, p. 5)

This normative view of an infant's response to disruptions in attachment is particularly useful for understanding the dynamics of stalking. In adolescent and adult relationships, the formation of lasting attachments is based on the experiencing of severed attachments repeatedly until a stable and secure set of attachments are formed. Karen (1994) described such a process in which people seek out intimate relationships but the romantic relationships in adolescence and early adulthood typically end, which often results in an attempt at reconciliation (i.e., protest), followed by a period of grieving over the loss (i.e., despair), and then acceptance (i.e., emotional detachment). The person can then search for a new attachment figure. As Karen (1994) stated,

> In healthy mourning, the individual gradually reorganizes. He [sic] allows himself to separate from the lost person and begins to reach out to form new attachments. Pathological mourning, in contrast, either never lets up or is disavowed and continues to control the person unconsciously. (p. 100)

Meloy (1998b) described this process as a dynamic that goes awry in obsessional followers in that a perpetrator does not successfully grieve and instead experiences shame and humiliation as opposed to despair in the face of rejection and loss. Consequently, the person defends against this shame and humiliation with rage and engages in stalking behavior in an attempt to control, harm, or destroy the attachment figure and restore a narcissistic linking fantasy. In the terminology of attachment theory, stalking behavior can be conceptualized as a fixation on protest activity and an avoidance of feelings of despair and detachment.

The Importance of Internal Working Models

A very interesting question that is yet to be addressed has to do with the connection between disturbances in early childhood attachments and stalking in later life. More specifically, how exactly do early attachment experiences affect close relationships in adolescence and adulthood? One key concept in attachment theory that helps address this question is the notion of *internal working models*. According to Bowlby (1973), the numerous interactions between an infant and his or her caregiver lead to the development of expectations, mental representations, and cognitive representations of the self and others. More specifically, infant–caretaker interactions result in the child having expectations of whether caregivers consistently respond to needs, whether the child is the type of person to whom others will respond positively, who are the reliable care givers, and where attachment figures can be found. According to Hazan and Shaver (1994), these internal working models involve beliefs, emotions, and expectations about the self and others that result in psychological blue-prints that guide the person through subsequent close relationships.

Because internal working models incorporate views of both the self and others, various attachment styles can be identified on the basis of whether the person has a positive view of self or others. Bartholomew (1990) laid out four styles of adult attachment that are represented by the person's model of self (i.e., positive vs. negative) and others (i.e., positive vs. negative). The first is a *secure attachment pattern* in which the person has a positive view of both self and others. Individuals who are securely attached are at ease in intimate relationships and are able to strike a suitable balance between healthy dependence and autonomy.

The three remaining attachment styles suggest problematic functioning in intimate relationships. A *preoccupied attachment pattern* is found in individuals who have a positive view of others but a negative view of the self. These individuals have feelings of inadequacy and unworthiness and actively seek approval from others. The early attachment patterns of individuals with a preoccupied style are characterized by "inconsistent and insensitive parenting" in which the child attributes a lack of parental love to his or her own inadequacies (Bartholomew, 1990, p. 163). A *dismissing attachment pattern* is characterized by a negative view of others and a positive view of the self. Individuals with this attachment style are emotionally distant; do not find value in close, intimate relationships; and see themselves as adequate, independent, and not needing close relationships. The early infant–caretaker patterns of individuals with a dismissing style include emphasis on achievement, impoverished emotional displays of affection, and defensive avoidance of others who may be abusive. In the *fearful attachment pattern,* the person has a negative view of both self and others. Individuals with the fearful style are avoidant, and they experience conflict due to a lack of trust in others, as well as a fear of rejection or ridicule. The early childhood attachment experiences in the fearful style include rejecting and emotionally unavailable caregivers.

Linking Attachment Disturbances to Stalking Behavior

Attachment theory provides many useful concepts and theoretical principles that help explain some of the dynamics of stalking behavior. Moreover, research on attachment theory provides insight into the developmental issues that may explain early manifestations of stalking in childhood and adolescence. For instance, Hazan and Shaver (1994) noted that attachment behaviors change in terms of the targeted individual. In infancy and early childhood, parents or primary caregivers are the main attachment figures and serve all the purposes of attachment, including proximity maintenance, safe haven, and secure base. Therefore, infants and young children look to parents or caregivers for emotional support, comfort, consistency, and accessibility to meet needs. However, Hazan and Shaver also noted that attachments to peers become more important in later childhood, with increasing emphasis on the peer group into adolescence. By adulthood, peers and intimate partners are primary figures for attachment, with parents providing a secondary secure base of attachment that remains present but less significant. Hazan and Shaver (1994) also found that

> attachments begin with proximity seeking (motivated by security needs when directed toward parents and by exploratory and affiliative needs when directed toward peers). In late childhood and early adolescence, close proximity provides the context that eventually fosters support-seeking (i.e., safe haven) behavior. Repeated interactions in which comfort is sought and provided or distress is expressed and alleviated may lead to reliance on the responder as a base of security. (pp. 8–9)

This developmental change in the target of attachment behaviors from parents to peers, as well as the gradual increase in emotional investment that is placed on attachment figures other than parents, may hold the keys to understanding how and when in the life span stalking first develops. In Hazan and Shaver's analysis, it is not until late childhood and early adolescence that strong emotional and affiliative needs outside the family become a major motivational process in attachment-seeking behavior. Therefore, the strong bond that a stalking offender has with his or her object would not be fully formed until late childhood or adolescence, and thus attachment theory suggests that formal stalking behavior would not be clearly manifest until the later stages of childhood, just prior to adolescence. Harassing or stalking-like behavior in younger children (e.g., teasing, bullying, repetitive coercion, etc.) would more likely represent a form of disturbed proximity-seeking behavior without the deeper emotional investment found in affiliative bonds with peers that arise in later childhood. Furthermore, Hazan and Shaver noted that a secure base of attachment does not fully transfer from parents to peers until adulthood, when more permanent intimate relationships are being sought and developed. Consequently, the stalking behavior of children and adolescents is more likely to occur in situations in which the object has some emotional or support-giving role associated with safe haven attachment behaviors. However, where the object has been a source of secure base and has represented a more lasting attachment figure, stalking in this situation would be more likely to occur in late adolescence and adulthood.

There is some empirical support for these observations that are derived from attachment theory. For instance, data show that the most common stalking pattern in adults is an obsessional male who stalks a female with whom he has had a prior intimate relationship (Meloy, 1998b), whereas in children and adolescents the most common stalking pattern appears to be an obsessional male who stalks a female peer or adult who is an acquaintance and not necessarily a prior intimate partner (McCann, 2000). Furthermore, in a study of peer sexual harassment among teenagers, a social problem that overlaps with stalking, Fineran and Bennett (1999) found in a sample of 342 high school students that sexual harassment by peer acquaintances was more prevalent than either sexual harassment by a stranger or sexual harassment by a dating or former dating partner. This finding was the same for both victims and perpetrators, meaning that if a high school student either perpetrated or was a victim of sexual harassment, the relationship between victim and perpetrator was most likely to be that of a casual acquaintance. More significant was the fact that Fineran and Bennett found the most threatening form of sexual harassment (i.e., harassment most likely to generate fear in the victim) was between acquaintances, rather than between strangers or intimate partners. As such, research tends to support the hypothesis that the dynamics of stalking and obsessional harassment in child and adolescent populations involve attachments that are more likely to be, but not exclusively, those in which the pursuer has begun to seek out closer attachments but has not yet fully reached the longer-term commitments involved in which the person has formed a secure base.

There are additional research findings that support early attachment disturbances as a significant factor in identifying an individual's propensity to stalk another person. The work of Ainsworth, Blehar, Waters, and Wall (1978) showed that there were three basic patterns of attachment that could be reliably identified in caregiver–infant interactions. *Secure interactions* involved those in which the infant would become distressed when the mother left, could be comforted upon her return, and would actively explore the environment while she was present. *Anxious/ambivalent interactions* consisted of the mother showing inconsistent responsiveness and the infant becoming angry, anxious, and preoccupied with the mother to the extent that minimal exploration occurred. *Anxious/avoidant interactions* were characterized by infants who were shamed by parents and who were not distressed by separations; these children avoided contact with the mother and focused on inanimate objects. In addition to these three attachment patterns, Main and Solomon (1990) identified *disorganized/disoriented interactions,* which show inconsistency in parent–child interactions and in which there is an "apparent lack of, or collapse of, a consistent strategy for organizing responses to the need for comfort and security when under stress" (Lyons-Ruth, 1996, p. 67).

The disorganized attachment pattern in infancy, which has attributes of both ambivalent and avoidant patterns, has been identified in about 15% of infant–caregiver interactions (Lyons-Ruth, 1996). Moreover, this attachment pattern may be of particular significance in the development of a person's propensity to stalk in childhood and adolescence, because it appears to be a precursor of coercive childhood behavior. In early interactions with caregivers, infants who are exposed to a disorganized pattern tend to engage in behaviors that attempt to control the parent. In later development, children who display a disorganized attachment pattern have no working model for organizing and predicting the reactions of others, and thus coercive behavior becomes the mechanism through which the child attempts to aggressively control the environment. One form of coercive behavior that constitutes an aggressive attempt to control others and manage chaotic emotions in later life is stalking.

There is also some research that provides more direct support for a link between early attachment disturbances and stalking behavior. Meloy (1992, 1996) first pointed out that stalking behavior represents a form of disturbance in attachment and that a fruitful area of research might be the childhood and adolescent attachment patterns of individuals who stalk or obsessionally follow another person. Following this theoretical line of inquiry, Kienlen, Birmingham, Solberg, O'Regan, and Meloy (1997) examined the childhood attachment experiences of adult stalking offenders. A substantial portion of the sample, 63%, reported a loss or significant disruption in their relationship with a primary caretaker in childhood. Many of these disruptions occurred prior to the age of seven. Fifty-five percent of the stalking offenders studied by Kienlen and her colleagues also reported a history of some form of childhood abuse, including physical, psychological, or sexual abuse. Another important factor observed in the study was that a large majority of the stalking offenders, 80%, experienced serious stressors within 7 months of the beginning of the stalking behavior, with personal losses being the most common stressor. Among the losses reported were breakup of an intimate relationship or marriage, job loss, estrangement from children, and loss of a parent. Kienlen and her colleagues suggested that these findings support the psychodynamic theory of stalking as a disturbance in attachment wherein early childhood losses give rise to a preoccupied attachment pattern and that subsequent losses in life give rise to coercive and controlling behavior, including stalking, as an effort to compensate for such losses.

Further empirical support for these observations is found in a recent study by Fein and Vossekuil (1999) who reported on the Exceptional Case Study Project conducted by the U.S. Secret Service. Fein and Vossekuil studied 83 individuals, ranging in age from 16 to 73, who were known to have attacked or approached with the intent to attack a prominent public official or figure since 1949. In this sample, nearly half of the individuals experienced a significant personal loss in the year prior to their attack or approach toward the target. Again, personal loss or setbacks surrounding an important attachment or personal status was a significant factor in the histories of these individuals. Likewise, Verlinden, Hersen, and Thomas (2000) found that a recent relationship loss, stressor, or loss in status is a common occurrence among assailants in school shooting cases.

Finally, the relationship between disrupted attachment patterns in adults as outlined by Bartholomew (1990), and various subtypes of stalking behavior has been outlined by Kienlen (1998). The three disturbed attachment styles, namely preoccupied, fearful, and dismissing, have been proposed as a means for explaining some patterns of stalking observed in clinical and research samples. For instance, the preoccupied attachment style is manifest in those individuals who view others positively but who have a poor self-image and feelings of inadequacy. Stalking patterns in those with a preoccupied attachment pattern may involve a need to validate one's self-worth by actively seeking attachment to another person (Kienlen, 1998; Meloy, 1996). The fearful attachment style is characterized by negative self-worth and fears of rejection, resulting in ambivalent attachments and angry and jealous instability. Kienlen (1998) noted that fearful attachment may lead to stalking when a supportive intimate relationship ends and thus results in rage and anger. The dismissing attachment pattern involves emotional distancing from others in order to protect a positive self-image. In this pattern, stalking may represent a behavior that is driven by a need for revenge or anger that seeks to avenge a narcissistic injury brought about by rejection and humiliation (Kienlen, 1998; Meloy, 1996). Because each of the adult attachment patterns identified by Bartholomew (1990) has been found in adolescents (Allen et al., 1996; Cowan et al., 1996), these attachment dynamics in stalking offenders outlined by Kienlen (1998) and Meloy (1996, 1998b) can also be used to explain some of the stalking patterns found among adolescents.

Although the theoretical literature on attachment appears to be of some use in understanding the dynamics of stalking and the empirical literature offers preliminary support for viewing stalking as a disturbance of attachment, there are some additional considerations that should be recognized. Most significant is the fact that even attachment theory recognizes that it is not only the view of others that is important in understanding interpersonal relationships but the view one has of the self. Insecure attachment patterns involve a negative self-concept, whereas dismissive attachment patterns involve a positive self-image that is prone to narcissistic injury. Consequently, another psychodynamic construct that deserves analysis is identity. It is posited below that stalking involves not only a disturbance in attachment, but also a disturbance of identity. Primitive emotions of anger, envy, and jealousy can emerge from both attachment disruptions as well as injuries to one's identity.

Identity Disturbances

The concept of *identity* has been an important component of most theories of personality; it refers to the view a person has of himself or herself and the thoughts and emotions that are associated with one's role in society. According to Millon and Davis (1996), the *self* is a major domain of personality that reflects a stable sense of who one is and the manner in which a person appraises the value of himself or herself in relation to other people. The concepts of self and identity are very closely related to one another and one of the most comprehensive discussions of identity and how it develops was outlined by Erikson (1968). According to Erikson, the person develops a way of identifying himself or herself as someone who arouses pleasant or favorable reactions from others or as someone who evokes negative or unpleasant reactions from others. In this way, interpersonal relationships become an important mechanism through which a person develops a sense of who he or she is and a set of emotions that give value to one's self that are primarily positive, negative, or a mixture of both.

Identity is a particularly important concept for understanding the psychodynamics of stalking behavior, because the person's vulnerability to shame and humiliation can precipitate the issues that evoke defenses of rage, anger, and controlling behavior (Meloy, 1996, 1998b). In addition, the various forms of psychopathology in stalking offenders reveal marked disturbances in the person's ability to regulate intense emotions, tolerate rejection, and test reality (Meloy, 1992). As such, there is strong evidence to suggest that many individuals who stalk have severe character pathology at a borderline or psychotic level of personality organization as outlined by Kernberg (1984). Those individuals who are organized at a borderline level of personality use primitive defenses such as splitting, projective identification, and denial; they also experience identity diffusion in which they have a poor sense of who they are and their self-perceptions vacillate dramatically in response to stress. However, borderline personality is distinguished from psychotic personality organization in that the borderline individual maintains intact reality testing, except in times of acute stress. The concept of borderline personality organization has been emphasized in certain forms of stalking and violent attachments (Meloy, 1989, 1992) as well as in male batterers who present with a cyclical pattern of abuse in intimate relationships (Dutton, 1998). From a theoretical perspective, then, identity diffusion in borderline personality organization is a significant deficit in ego functioning that can help explain some of the dynamics of stalking.

Erikson's (1968) conceptualization of the developmental processes through which identity emerges also provides a very useful framework for understanding how some psychodynamic factors contribute to stalking at specific stages of childhood and adolescence. Therefore, it may be useful to first present a brief overview of Erikson's theoretical model of identity formation.

Erikson's Stage-Theory of Personality Development

Erikson is perhaps best known for advancing a stage-theory of personality development that consists of eight phases spanning the entire life span. The period of infancy consists of the *trust vs. mistrust* stage in which the child learns whether or not the world is basically predictable and others are consistent in their responsiveness to the child's needs. If the child finds that his or her basic needs are not consistently met, then he or she comes to view the world as an unpredictable place where others cannot be trusted. In the second stage of Erikson's model, *autonomy vs. shame and doubt,* the child learns to develop self-control without a resulting loss of self-esteem. The major challenges revolve around toilet training, but successful resolution of the demands of this phase result in the ability to express and assert one's self without shame or self-doubt. Conversely, the improper resolution of psychosocial demands in this stage results in obsessiveness, rigidity, self-doubts, and a heightened sensitivity to experience shame. It is during this phase that the shame and humiliation that arise from acute or chronic rejection in the stalking offender have their psychodynamic origins.

The third stage of Erikson's model is *initiation vs. guilt,* in which the child begins to develop an understanding of how he or she interacts with the environment. With the onset of language and greater independence at moving around in the world, the child who successfully navigates through this stage develops a sense of freedom and purpose to develop personal interests and goals. Those who do not successfully meet the demands of this stage become inhibited, apathetic, and restricted in their capacity to manage angry feelings, resulting in cycles of aggression followed by guilt. In the fourth stage of ego development, *industry vs. inferiority,* the latency-age child experiences what Erikson called a "psychosocial moratorium" in which the focus becomes learning about the basic nature of work and production. Successful resolution of this stage results in feelings of satisfaction in being able to make things, complete school projects, and obtain knowledge about one's world. Unsuccessful resolution of this phase results in estrangement from one's self and feelings of inferiority.

In adolescence, the stage of *identity vs. identity confusion* arises where the major task is for teenagers to develop a stable and consistent sense of who they are. This occurs by integrating all of the developmental elements of their identity that arose earlier in life (i.e., trust, autonomy, initiative, and industry issues) with their future goals and aspirations. If this fails or if earlier developmental issues create severe deficits or conflicts (e.g., pervasive mistrust in the world), the adolescent will develop feelings of confusion and uncertainty about who he or she is.

Following adolescence, three additional developmental stages have been proposed in Erikson's theory, namely *intimacy vs. isolation, generativity vs. stagnation,* and *integrity vs. despair.* These stages focus on issues pertaining to the development of lasting intimate relationships, feelings of productivity and having made a contribution to society, and integrity about one's life overall, respectively. A detailed review of these latter three stages will not be provided because the primary focus of this discussion is the utility of Erikson's early stages for explaining the psychodynamic and etiological foundations of identity disturbances as they relate to the phenomenon of stalking in children and adolescents.

A major assertion in Erikson's theory that is often neglected is the fact that each stage of ego development follows a pattern of epigenesis. In other words, a specific challenge or conflict is prevalent at one particular time, but the major psychological implications of these conflicts are present throughout the life span and can have profound effects both before the main conflicts in a stage have arisen and after they have subsided. For example, during adolescence the primary conflict is between developing a clear identity and sense of self versus experiencing identity confusion. However, Erikson (1968) noted that each of the four preceding stages, and the extent to which they are successfully resolved, will have a direct impact on the adolescent's identity later in life. For instance, when the infant learns that the world is essentially predictable and others are trustworthy, the long-term effects are positive, and the development of one's identity is facilitated. Infants who trust others and feel secure will anticipate mutual reciprocation in relationships with others; the person develops a positive self-image and healthy identity by giving others recognition while expecting and receiving the same from others. However, if the infant comes to view others with mistrust and learns that the world is unpredictable, then the long-term effects can be quite negative and will impede the development of a healthy and stable identity in adolescence. Infants who are basically mistrustful will become more estranged and isolated from others, which can carry over into subsequent stages of development, including adolescence. In short, early childhood experiences help shape later identity development by determining if the child is comfortable being assertive, anticipates proper roles of others, and can identify skills and tasks in school that will lead to growth. Otherwise, a child who fails to resolve early conflict will develop autistic withdrawal, self-doubt, inhibition, and apathy, leading to confusion about one's identity.

Another aspect of Erikson's theory is the notion that each of his eight stages of ego development are present in either prominent or less significant degrees throughout the life span. Thus, the development of identity in adolescence depends on the learning of time perspective and pre-dictability in infancy, self-certainty in the toddler years, role experimenta-tion in the initiative/guilt stage, and so on throughout childhood. The key component in Erikson's theory of epigenesis of identity is that adoles-cence is not the only period at which identity develops. Rather, the earliest stages of life both affect and are affected by the person's need to develop a stable and integrated sense of self.

Theories of Identity Formation

The notion that early childhood experiences play a critical role in later personality development is not unique to Erikson's theory. Rather, many theories of identity formation have also proposed that the early mother–child relationship is where the infant learns to distinguish self from other and also learns to manage rage and anger that inevitably arise from frustration in early relationships. The manner in which these frus-trations are resolved results in the splitting of the self and object into good and bad parts. This is the foundation of object relations theory (Klein & Riviere, 1964; Masterson, 1981). In a comprehensive and integrative review of personality development, Millon and Davis (1996) argued that in most theories of personality the earliest periods of development result in the development of trust in others and confidence in adapting to one's environment. Once these early tasks are mastered, the late latency-age child and adolescent begin to assimilate sexual roles and develop a sense of identity.

Because of basic challenges and tasks that must be mastered by the infant and very young child, it is not until the later years of the latency stage and adolescence that the person begins to engage in the behavioral patterns that can result in stalking behavior. The latency stage, originally identified by Freud as the period between resolution of the Oedipus com-plex and adolescence during which children experience inactivity of sex-ual drive and a consolidation of sex roles and broadening social contexts, has traditionally been viewed as occurring from about age 5 or 6 through age 11 to 13 (Meissner, 1985). The latency phase represents a useful demarcation of an important developmental stage that precedes adolescence. It is during latency that the child "becomes the producer of various products and the performer of tasks that are essential for survival within a given society" (Kernberg & Chazan, 1991, p. 68). Also, the latency period has been identified as the period in which both socialized and unsocialized forms of conduct disorder have been noted to arise. Once the person reaches puberty, the development of secondary sex characteristics, induced by hormonal changes, produces a shift in adolescence where the focus becomes consolidation of a clear identity that is based in part on establishing sex role identification. Consequently, the social relationships of latency age children differ from those of adolescents in that there is a gradual shift from same-age, same-gender peer emphasis in latency to greater exploration and experimentation with heterosexual relationships in adolescence.

Implications for Understanding Stalking Behavior

An understanding of how identity develops has significant implications for explaining the onset of stalking at earlier ages. Based on the nature of social development outlined above, it is suggested here that stalking is likely to first occur in the later stages of the latency period. This does not imply that all individuals who engage in stalking will first manifest their stalking in latency because better empirical data are required on when stalking first occurs in samples of offenders; rather, it is suggested that the earliest age at which stalking is developmentally feasible is in the latter part of latency. The earlier stages of development create psychological vulnerabilities in both attachment capacity and identity formation that renders the person prone to engage in stalking behavior. In a review of published and clinical cases of stalking in children and adolescents, McCann (2000) found that the youngest stalking offender in any case report was 9 years old, which represents the middle to later part of the latency stage. Moreover, the earliest stages of development are where propensities to experience shame and self-doubt arise and also where the person learns to modulate rage reactions. In the psychodynamic model of stalking presented earlier, feelings of shame, humiliation, and rage are viewed as primary dynamic forces that drive the need to control and dominate the object in stalking cases (Meloy, 1998b).

101

More recent research on identity formation in adolescence has implications for understanding the phenomenon of stalking in younger populations. Since Erikson's (1968) work on identity, other researchers have studied four basic manifestations of identity in adolescence based on two different dimensions: "the extent to which individuals have (or have not) experienced an identity crisis and the extent to which individuals have committed to an ideological and interpersonal possible self" (Klaczynski, Fauth, & Swanger, 1998, p. 187). More specifically, some adolescents have an *achieved* identity status in that they have had a crisis and made a successful commitment to a stable sense of self in relation to others. Other adolescents have a *foreclosed* identity status in which they have experienced a crisis but have not yet made a commitment. Still other adolescents may be in the *moratorium* identity status in which they are experiencing a crisis but have not yet made a commitment. The *diffused* identity status refers to adolescents who have not experienced a crisis and have no commitments. Adolescents with an achieved or moratorium identity status tend to be more cognitively developed, have an internal locus of control, engage in career planning, and are more analytical in their thinking. In contrast, adolescents with a foreclosed or diffused identity status hold more traditional gender role attitudes, have more social anxiety, and display fewer prosocial behaviors (Klaczynski et al., 1998).

These further refinements to Erikson's original conceptualization of identity suggest that adolescents who have not experienced a crisis in identity are prone to experiment less with various interests and adaptive behavior. There is some evidence to suggest that adolescents who have not experienced an identity crisis are prone to be rigid in their thinking and to hold authoritarian beliefs and attitudes (Adams, Ryan, Hoffman, Dobson, & Nielson, 1985). Consequently, problems in identity formation may result in adolescents who have inflexible coping styles and heightened need for control which, coupled with self-doubts and insecurities, can contribute to the onset of stalking behavior.

Another significant theme that runs through the literature is the notion that identity both develops from and affects the interpersonal relationships of latency age children and adolescents. Therefore, it can be hypothesized that the challenges of forming an identity, which naturally occur during these periods of development, may be both affected by and have an impact on how the young person interacts with others. As a result, the nature of stalking perpetrated by individuals in late latency and early adolescence may be qualitatively different from stalking perpetrated by older adolescents and adults.

Some case reports indicate that multiple object fixations have been identified in cases of adolescent stalking whereby the perpetrator fixates on different objects at various times (McCann, 1998c). Although there is scant empirical data on the presence of multiple object fixations in adults, Menzies, Fedoroff, Green, and Isaacson (1995) found in a small sample of adult erotomanic patients that multiple concurrent object fixations, along with general antisocial propensities, was a significant predictor of violence. Moreover, McCann (1998c) and Urbach, Khalily, and Mitchell (1992) reported cases of adolescents who were psychotic and stalked other people in which there were multiple object fixations. One hypothesis that emerges from this limited literature is that severely disturbed obsessional followers, particularly those adults or adolescents who are psychotically disturbed, may have a much more diffuse and undifferentiated personality structure that results in poor management of intense rage and anger, coupled with very diffuse and weak identity formation, that results in changeable identification with multiple objects. Of course, this hypothesis warrants more intensive empirical study.

One other hypothesis on the relationship between stalking behavior in younger people and identity formation has been gleaned from a small sample of young stalking offenders. McCann (2000) found that the most common form of stalking in a sample of 13 child and adolescent stalking offenders was unwanted sexual advances being directed at an acquaintance. In adult populations, the most common form of stalking is an obsessional man who stalks a prior sexually intimate partner (Meloy, 1998b). This difference between young stalking offenders and adult offenders, although based on a very limited sample size, suggests that the differences in psychosexual and psychosocial development between adults and children may result in slightly different patterns of stalking. As noted earlier, adults are typically challenged to seek intimate relationships, particularly in early adulthood. On the other hand, late latency and adolescence are periods of an expanding rehearsal of behavioral repertoires, identification with sex roles, and sexual exploration that are part of the process of identity formation. Therefore, the disruption in both attachment and identity formation that contribute to stalking behavior may result in a greater risk for stalking in relationships with casual acquaintances, rather than intimate partners, among children and adolescents. In fact, stalking of prior intimate partners is generally precluded among preadolescent children because of limited sexual development during early and middle latency. This hypothesis of diffuse identity resulting in diffuse (and multiple) object fixations in stalking requires further study not only in samples of child and adolescent obsessional followers, but also in samples of adult stalking offenders.

Jealousy and Envy

It may be recalled that a major psychodynamic factor believed to motivate stalking behavior is rage that is used to defend against shame and humiliation produced by rejection (Meloy, 1998b). In addition, the emotions of envy and jealousy are also believed to play a role in motivating stalking. Both of these emotional states have negative and potentially violent consequences for those individuals who experience them to a significant degree (Guerrero & Andersen, 1998). Because envious and jealous people experience uncertainty, interpersonal relationships can suffer if these emotions go unchecked or cannot be assuaged through reassurance by the partner or the availability of evidence that the person's jealousy is unfounded.

There is strong evidence to support the conclusion that envy and jealousy are key emotional factors in spurring relationship violence among young people. For example, Gagne and Lavoie (1993) conducted a survey of 151 adolescents ranging in age from 14 to 17 as to their perceptions on the reasons why males and females act violently or abusively in dating or romantic relationships. The results from this study revealed that adolescents view jealousy as the most significant factor that causes both young men and young women to be physically or psychologically abusive in romantic relationships. This finding has been found in other studies which have shown that in dating relationships of high school and college students, jealousy is always cited as the most frequent cause of violence (Laner, 1990; Stets & Pirog-Good, 1987).

To better understand how envy and jealousy can serve as emotional factors in stalking, it may be helpful to recognize that

> envy might also play a role, because if the object is sufficiently devalued, she was not worth having in the first place. Jealousy . . . infers competition for the "love" object . . . with the goal to possess her so that no one else can have her. (Meloy, 1998b, p. 20)

This observation by Meloy is significant because it implies that envy and jealousy are related but different emotional states that can have slightly different effects on the thinking of the stalking offender. Thus, it would be useful to explicitly define and differentiate envy and jealousy in greater detail.

Differences Between Envy and Jealousy as Emotional States

An excellent analysis of the differences between envy and jealousy is provided by Guerrero and Andersen (1998). These researchers noted that although jealousy and envy are often considered to be related, they are different emotional states. For instance, Guerrero and Andersen noted that jealousy generally involves emotional experiences such as fear, sadness, or anger, whereas envy is a less passionate emotion that involves more cognitive processing whereby the person typically appraises himself or herself as being less adequate and desires a quality or object that another person possesses. More specifically, jealousy and envy both involve some form of desire for a quality, object, or attribute, but they differ with respect to who possesses the attribute, quality, or object; the emotions that accompany each; and the manner in which society views envy and jealousy.

Guerrero and Andersen noted that the concept of relationship possession distinguishes envy and jealousy in that the feeling of jealousy arises when the person experiences a threat of losing a valued relationship that he or she already has. On the other hand, envy arises when the person does not possess a valued relationship with someone, or a particular trait or quality, and wants to possess it. This difference between envy and jealousy is significant because it implies that envy and jealousy are emotional states that are based on different psychodynamic processes. More specifically, the fact that jealousy involves a triad and is based on feelings of threat or danger over losing a valued relationship that one already has implies a problem with feelings of attachment with another person and the danger of losing the relationship to a third person. On the other hand, envy involves a dyad and requires a comparison between one's self and another person in which negative self-appraisals result in the observation that one does not measure up or does not have a valued object, quality, or trait. As such, an insecure identity or inadequate self-concept is relevant to understanding the basis of envy.

A second major factor that distinguishes envy and jealousy, according to Guerrero and Andersen, is the nature and intensity of related emotions and perceptions that accompany each of these primitive affects. More specifically, feelings of jealousy are associated with greater feelings of mistrust of one's love object, fear or anxiety, uncertainty about the state of the relationship, and loneliness from feeling left out or abandoned either physically or psychologically by the love object. On the other hand, envy is different in that it is associated with higher levels of disapproval of one's feelings, longing for what someone else has, motivation to improve one's self, and degradation and feelings of humiliation and inferiority. Again, one can see how jealousy is closely connected to the notion of insecure attachment, whereas envy implicates a weak or diffuse identity due to the self-devaluation, inferiority, and need for some object or personal quality in order to feel complete. Therefore, jealousy and envy are related, but distinct emotions that imply different psychological disturbances.

A third factor that Guerrero and Andersen identified as a way of distinguishing jealousy and envy is the manner in which each of these affective states have been viewed in historical and social contexts. These researchers noted that jealousy has traditionally been viewed as a stronger and potentially more violent emotion than envy, whereas envy tends to be viewed as socially inappropriate but unavoidable because our society tends to foster comparisons between people. At one time, jealousy was viewed as a socially appropriate and acceptable response to infidelity in relationships. Today, however, jealousy is viewed as a negative emotion that can be damaging to one's interpersonal relationships (Mullen, 1991). In fact, one study on college students who were actively dating found that feelings of jealousy have an adverse impact (Peretti & Pudowski, 1997). More specifically, the jealous individual tends to experience loss of affection, insecurity, anxiety, inadequacy, low self-esteem, rejection, and feelings of rivalry that all impact negatively on the person's psychological well-being. Whether the way society has changed its view of jealousy is due to a change in social norms or an increase in our understanding of the negative consequences of extreme jealousy, there appears to be a general consensus that strong feelings of jealousy are damaging to the stability and satisfaction derived from interpersonal relationships.

Linking Envy and Jealousy to Stalking Behavior

As a result of these observed differences between jealousy and envy, attempts have been made to outline the manner in which these concepts, which have sometimes been used interchangeably, are actually related but different emotions that have distinct implications for understanding clinical phenomena. Spielman (1971) noted that both jealousy and envy arise from a narcissistic injury in which the person experiences a threat to self-esteem, security, and adequacy. However, jealousy is distinguished from envy in that extreme jealousy is accompanied by suspicion, mistrust, and paranoid ideation.

Because of the differences between envy and jealousy, the affective states associated with these emotions, such as fear, sadness, and anger, must be interpreted differently depending on whether the primary emotion is envy or jealousy. Anger in jealous states is generally related to feelings of rivalry, betrayal, and a need to seek revenge. In envious states, anger is often "rooted in resentment, hatred, and frustration" (Guerrero & Andersen, 1998, p. 49). Another emotional reaction associated with envy and jealousy is fear. However, the fear in jealous states is generally associated with fear of abandonment or loss, whereas in envious states fear is based on feelings of failure, rejection, and uncertainty about one's self and future. Likewise, the depression and sadness of jealous and envious states differs in that jealous sadness stems from loss or abandonment, whereas envious sadness stems from feeling excluded, a lack of personal wish fulfillment, and feelings of having fallen short of one's expectations. Again, the implications of the meaning of these associated emotional states is that jealousy is based in feelings of insecure or faulty attachment, whereas envy is based in feelings of uncertainty about one's self or identity diffusion.

Jealousy and envy, along with the associated affects of anger, sadness, and fear, are connected to a large extent with stalking behavior. Recall from the discussion of Meloy's (1996, 1998b; 1999b) psychodynamic model that the narcissistic linking fantasy that results in feeling admired, superior to, idealized, and destined to be with the love object creates a tenuous state of psychological equilibrium that can result in narcissistic injury, a common precipitant of both envy and jealousy (Spielman, 1971). Consequently, if the person experiences acute or chronic rejection, this evokes attachment issues that can spur feelings of sadness, rejection, and loss that, in turn, provoke jealousy. Additionally, the feelings of shame and humiliation that result can also spur feelings of inadequacy, insecurity, and inferiority, which produces envy. As such, the prevailing emotions associated with stalking behavior, whether they are anger, sadness, fear, or a combination of several of these emotions, should be interpreted differently based on whether the prevailing emotion is envy or jealousy.

Another line of research on the nature of jealousy that may have implications for understanding the motivations of stalking, particularly stalking driven by jealousy, is the work of Buss (1994). More specifically, Buss has shown that certain relationship events activate a physiological response that is associated with jealousy and that these responses differ in males and females based on different adaptation needs that have been observed over the course of human evolution. In a series of studies on college undergraduates, Buss, Larsen, Westen, and Semmelroth (1992) found that while both young men and young women showed jealous reactions to threats of a mate's sexual and emotional infidelity, the women showed stronger jealous arousal to cues involving a mate's emotional infidelity (i.e., feelings of emotional attachment without a sexual relationship), whereas the men showed a stronger jealous reaction to threats of a mate's sexual infidelity. Buss and his colleagues therefore hypothesized that jealousy in men may diminish with an increase in the woman's age because her reproductive value decreases. Of course, the relevance of this research is that it suggests jealousy becomes a motivation for stalking behavior for younger people when romantic and sexual exploration begins, usually around the onset of puberty. Thus, one hypothesis that can be set forth is that the onset of interest in sexual or romantic interpersonal relationships may mark a developmental phase during which stalking may first begin to appear as a pathological form of social behavior. This hypothesis requires more systematized study.

ALTERNATIVE THEORETICAL MODELS

In the previous sections, extensive coverage was given to psychodynamic principles such as attachment, identity, and primitive emotional states as a means of understanding stalking behavior. Although other approaches to conceptualizing human behavior can be applied to this social problem, the psychodynamic approach has been a major focus of the inchoate body of literature on stalking. Nevertheless, there are some notable exceptions to this trend. The focus of this section is to provide an overview of two other theoretical approaches that have been used to help understand stalking. In addition, the utility of these approaches for understanding this social problem among children and adolescents is reviewed.

One major alternative approach has been the behavioral psychological technique of functional analysis of behavior set forth by Westrup and

Fremouw (1998). In their review of the stalking literature, Westrup and Fremouw noted various problems with the definitions of stalking that have been used, the manner in which this behavior has been studied, and the limitations of existing models for explaining stalking. For instance, these researchers questioned the use of the terms *obsessional harassment* (Harmon, Rosner, & Owens, 1995) and *obsessional following* (Meloy, 1996; Meloy & Gothard, 1995) to describe stalking offenses because the modifier *obsessional* implies thoughts, impulses, or images that are unwanted or intrusive, whereas many of the thoughts experienced by those who stalk may be wanted and experienced as pleasurable. Moreover, terms such as *harassment* and *following* that are sometimes used synonymously with stalking do not, according to Westrup and Fremouw, adequately capture the full range of stalking behavior. Of course, there are equally persuasive counter-arguments for retaining these alternative terms (see Meloy, 1998b), such as the fact that these terms emphasize the pursuer's preoccupation and common patterns of pursuit found in stalking cases. Moreover, terms such as *obsessional harassment* or *obsessional following* are less sensationalistic than the terms *stalking* or *stalker*.

Additionally, Westrup and Fremouw noted that the empirical literature is limited by the fact that descriptive studies have not provided any consistent clue as to the causes of stalking; many studies have been correlational in nature, and no study has examined effective methods for predicting or controlling stalking behavior. Consequently, a functional analytic approach was offered as a behavioral method for assessing stalking behavior.

Another approach to conceptualizing stalking has been the work of Cupach and Spitzberg (1998; Spitzberg, Nicastro, & Cousins, 1998; Spitzberg & Rhea, 1999), who approached the problem using communications theory to explore the interpersonal dynamics of stalking. As noted in chapter 1, Cupach and Spitzberg have used the concept of obsessive relational intrusions to study various forms of harassment and stalking in intimate relationships. *Obsessive relational intrusions* are defined as "repeated and unwanted pursuit and invasions of one's sense of physical or symbolic privacy by another person, either stranger or acquaintance, who desires and/or presumes an intimate relationship" (Cupach & Spitzberg, 1998, pp. 234–235). Therefore, obsessive relational intrusion is a concept that overlaps considerably with stalking but that also differs in some important ways. Although stalking and obsessive relational intrusions both involve repetitive behaviors that in extreme forms represent threatening behaviors and unwanted pursuit, obsessive relational intrusions differ from stalking in that they can involve relatively benign forms of intrusiveness that do not necessarily constitute stalking (e.g., sending notes or gifts). Moreover, obsessive relational intrusions are applicable only to relationships in which there has been or is presumed to be an intimate relationship with the victim. Another important facet of how obsessive relational intrusions are defined is the fact that they are based on the notion of physical and/or symbolic privacy, which means that they can involve invasions of privacy and personal space that may not necessarily be threatening.

The functional analytic and communications theory-based approaches represent two alternatives to the psychodynamic model outlined above. In the interests of balance and fairness, these other theoretical models are outlined separately. The implications of each theory for understanding stalking in children and adolescents is briefly discussed.

Functional Analytic Assessment

Functional analysis of behavior is an approach to assessing psychological phenomena that uses principles of classical behaviorism. According to Nelson and Hayes (1996), functional analysis of behavior relies on the assumption that the function or purposes served by a behavior should be the primary focus of assessment; once the functions of a behavior are discovered, the factors that maintain the behavior are known and treatment interventions can then be targeted at these functional purposes. According to Westrup and Fremouw (1998), most of the stalking literature has focused on the characteristics of stalking offenders and the types of harassing behaviors they use to stalk their victims. However, the purposes served by stalking have often not been adequately addressed in the research. Westrup and Fremouw suggested that more useful information on stalking will come from research on stalking victims, perpetrators, and third-party witnesses (e.g., police officers, coworkers) that involves direct interviewing that seeks to determine the purposes of the stalking.

A functional analytic approach to stalking might begin with a comprehensive description of the stalking behavior, including "its topography (i.e., how the action is performed, what it looks like), frequency, duration, and intensity. It is also important to learn the history of the behavior (e.g., when it first occurred, whether it has increased or decreased)" (Westrup & Fremouw, 1998, p. 270). However, a comprehensive functional analysis involves not only an assessment of the behavior, but also the behavioral antecedents and consequences. Therefore, Westrup and Fremouw suggested that much more attention must be given, both clinically and empirically, to the environmental conditions that give rise to stalking behavior as well as the consequences of stalking that either reinforce or lessen the likelihood of pursuit and harassment. Such factors as what the person was doing, thinking, and feeling just prior to the onset of an act of stalking should be studied in greater detail. Likewise, attention must be given to such factors as the outcome of stalking and its effect on the victim, whether or not the pursuer obtained the intended effect, and the psychological impact on both victim and perpetrator.

In a functional analytic approach, an understanding of the controlling factors dictates intervention strategies. Westrup and Fremouw (1998) noted that interventions may involve direct treatment of the stalking offender, but they may also involve modifying behavior of the victim of stalking, including treatment of psychological symptoms resulting from being stalked and modifications in behavior to help curb the stalking behavior. In fact, some cases involve a pursuer who is intractable to change or not actively involved in treatment and modification of the victim's behavior may be the only viable option, such that "effective interventions would best be directed toward the target's responses that are rewarding the stalking behavior" (p. 271).

Although the functional analytic approach outlined by Westrup and Fremouw pointed out many issues that have yet to be explored through research, their model serves more as a guideline for conducting this research rather than a comprehensive explanatory model of stalking. A major limitation at present is the lack of empirical research on stalking that takes a functional analytic approach. Nevertheless, this model highlights critical issues that need to be addressed in research such as what variables precede the onset of stalking behavior and whether specific consequences (e.g. restraining orders) increase or decrease the likelihood of further stalking. Moreover, a functional analytic model would be useful if it incorporated psychological variables that are less directly observable but must be inferred, such as fantasy, object relations, and motivational factors; however, it does not incorporate these useful concepts. The applicability of the functional analytic model to understanding stalking in children and adolescents has potential, but much more clinical and empirical work needs to be done, and its scope must be broadened to include more behavioral and psychodynamic principles.

Communications Theory: Obsessive Relational Intrusions

The work of Cupach and Spitzberg (1994; Spitzberg & Cupach, 1998) examined the "dark side" of human interactions across a variety of contexts and with respect to a variety of social and relationship problems. According to this perspective, "to fully understand how people function effectively requires us to consider how individuals cope with social interaction that is difficult, problematic, challenging, distressing, and disruptive" (Cupach & Spitzberg, 1994, p. vii). A major focus of this research has been the phenomenon of obsessive relational intrusions that represent a pattern of unwanted pursuit and invasion of privacy by someone who wants or presumes to have an intimate relationship with another person.

Rather than a comprehensive model of stalking, obsessive relational intrusion is a construct that represents a form of interpersonal communication and conduct that is applicable to those stalking cases in which the pursuer wants, has had, or has a delusional belief that there is an intimate relationship with the victim. Cupach and Spitzberg (1998) outlined three important features of obsessive relational intrusions that characterize the nature of such behavior. First, obsessive relational intrusions lie along a continuum of behavior, with milder forms of intrusive behavior such as pestering, leaving notes, or engaging in excessive self-disclosure at one end of the continuum and more threatening forms of behavior such as stalking, making threatening telephone calls, and menacing at the other end. In short, obsessive relational intrusions constitute behaviors that range from those that are merely annoying to those that are threatening to the victim. Second, this continuum of intrusiveness suggests that the boundary between what is reasonable and what is obsessive is often unclear. For example, the demarcation between sending notes to communicate an interest in dating and sending threatening letters in response to persistent refusals by the object is quite clear. Often, however, there are behaviors that must be judged with respect to the context of the individual case. Third, obsessive relational intrusions occur within the context of an interpersonal relationship.

There is an emerging body of empirical literature on obsessive relational intrusions that has implications for conceptualizing stalking in children and adolescents. For one thing, Spitzberg and colleagues (1998) developed objective measures of obsessive relational intrusions, including self-report measures of victim experiences and coping strategies. One noteworthy feature of this work is that college undergraduates have been the subject population on which this research has been conducted. Given that these subjects are in a transitional period of development between adolescence and adulthood findings from this research are applicable at least to older adolescents. Spitzberg et al. (1998) tested three hypotheses about the relationship between stalking and obsessive relational intrusions. Their first hypothesis, that being victimized by obsessive relational intrusions (e.g., unwanted messages, exaggerated expressions of affection) in intimate relationships would differentiate students who reported having been stalked from those who had not, was supported by the data. Therefore, obsessive relational intrusions appear to create a heightened risk of stalking in intimate relationships.

A second hypothesis was that young men and young women would show different rates of victimization by obsessive relational intrusions. This hypothesis was not confirmed in that no significant gender differences were found in the frequency of victimization. What is unusual about this finding is that it does not comport with a rather robust finding in the stalking literature that women are more commonly the victims of stalking than are men (Meloy, 1996, 1998b). It may be that gender differences do not exist with respect to less-threatening intrusive behaviors in relationships, but that gender differences emerge as the intrusions become more threatening due to increased male aggression.

The third hypothesis tested by Spitzberg and his colleagues was that obsessive relational intrusion victimization and coping responses would predict the severity of psychological symptomatology in victims. This hypothesis received empirical support and revealed that both a higher rate of relational intrusions and more coping strategies used by the victim predicted more severe symptoms, including anxiety, fear, and hopelessness. As such, the findings suggest that more threatening forms of obsessive relational intrusion in college undergraduates are associated with stalking behavior and have an adverse impact on victims.

In a related study, Spitzberg and Rhea (1999) examined the association between obsessive relational intrusions and coercive sexual behavior among college undergraduates. Again, empirical support was found for the construct validity of obsessive relational intrusion as a form of coercive behavior in intimate relationships. The degree to which students reported being the victim of intrusions was positively correlated with various forms of sexually coercive behavior, including deception, physical force, and psychological coercion. Moreover, obsessive relational intrusions were associated with psychological distress among victims.

The utility of the concept of obsessive relational intrusions for explaining the phenomenon of stalking in younger individuals was briefly discussed in chapter 1. However, it is worth expanding on this discussion to explore some additional ways in which this concept may be applicable. One of the more positive aspects of Cupach and Spitzberg's (1998) description of obsessive relational intrusions is the notion that intrusive and harassing behaviors lie along a continuum. There is always a risk that when various problematic behaviors or psychological disturbances are identified in children and adolescents that certain developmentally appropriate or common age-related deviations from normality may be inaccurately identified as abnormal or disturbed. Some forms of intrusive behavior such as teasing, bullying, or mild harassment are a part of many social interactions in childhood and adolescence. However, it may not always be clear at what point such behavior becomes sufficiently repetitive and threatening as to constitute stalking. The fact that obsessive relational intrusions are conceptualized along a continuum, with annoyances at one end and threatening actions at the other end, offers a flexible approach to defining stalking and obsessional harassment in the intimate relationships of younger individuals.

A limitation of the obsessive relational intrusion construct as applied to stalking cases is that it focuses on an actual or presumed intimate relationship between pursuer and victim. Some stalking cases involve those in which the obsessional follower is motivated by anger, revenge, or some other hostile motive that arises from a relationship that is not sexually or romantically intimate. As the work of Harmon and colleagues (1995, 1998) shows, many stalking cases involve themes of revenge over feeling slighted or unfairly treated in employment settings or non-intimate relationships. Furthermore, some cases of stalking by a child or adolescent are also based on hostile motives (McCann, 2000), such as a student who stalks a teacher out of revenge over a perception of being mistreated or unfairly evaluated in a school setting. Therefore, the concept of obsessive relational intrusion is useful for conceptualizing some but not all cases of stalking or obsessional harassment.

CONCLUSION

There is a developing body of literature suggesting that stalking is a disturbance in attachment that has developmental origins in infancy and very early childhood. The term *primitive* has been used to describe psychological states, defense mechanisms, emotions, and a level of maturity that arises very early in life. During these early periods, the infant is prone to experience fluctuating concepts of self and others, intense rage reactions, and frustrating interactions with others. Therefore, early disruptions in attachment have been posited as a significant etiological factor in the onset of stalking. In this chapter, early attachment experiences, identity disturbances, and primitive emotional states such as envy and jealousy have been explored against the background of Meloy's (1996, 1998b, 1999b) psychodynamic model of stalking. Although preliminary empirical data suggest that stalking represents a form of attachment disturbance, there is also theoretical and some empirical evidence suggesting that stalking also involves disturbances in identity. More specifically, attachment pathology may serve to explain why a stalking offender maintains his or her fixation on the object and why certain personal losses (e.g., divorce, break-up of an intimate relationship) precipitate stalking behavior. However, identity disturbances and deficits in self-concept and ego functioning may help to explain other facets of stalking, such as why a specific target is chosen, the selection of multiple or fluctuating object fixations, and why losses of personal status (e.g., job loss, physical illness) may precipitate stalking behavior. Much more research is needed on the causal factors involved in stalking. However, psychodynamic principles, particularly those involving early life experiences, such as the formation of attachments, the development of identity, and the capacity to manage intense emotions, are particularly useful in understanding the social problem of stalking among children and adolescents. Likewise, the concept of obsessive relational intrusions in intimate relationships offers a flexible construct for conceptualizing some forms of obsessional harassment in close relationships among younger individuals. Because stalking behavior has been observed in late childhood and adolescence, experiences very early in life are important areas of study in the search for how and why stalking develops.

5

The Early Signs

T he first step in studying a phenomenon such as stalking is to conduct descriptive and correlational studies that provide information
on how and why stalking occurs. Another important area of study is the
analysis of antecedents, or early signs of stalking, that might be used to predict the behavior in specific situations or in certain individuals. In this context, early signs of stalking constitute either of the following: (a) problem
behaviors in the social relationships of children or adolescents that could be
viewed as early manifestations of obsessional following in a specific
instance, or (b) childhood risk factors that suggest someone might stalk
another person later in life. One reason for exploring the potential early
signs of stalking in young people is that it broadens the application of material presented thus far by raising awareness of those risk factors that can be
targeted for treatment. In this way, preventive programs can be implemented early on so that the risk of stalking might be reduced. A final reason for
examining potential risk factors for stalking is that some problem behaviors
in childhood that overlap with stalking, such as bullying and sexual harassment, have been more extensively studied and can provide direction for the
design of preventive programs for stalking and obsessional following.

Before discussing these early risk factors, I offer a note of caution on the practical use of the material presented in this chapter. When information is offered for one purpose, such as providing clinical and empirical hypotheses or outlining specific issues that can be addressed in treatment, there is a risk that such factors may be applied for less legitimate purposes, such as identifying specific individuals for restrictive detention or confirming some preconceived notion about a person's guilt or innocence in a criminal case. The present chapter is offered as an overview of clinical observations, anecdotal evidence, and research findings on topics related to stalking that outline hypotheses for understanding how stalking may develop and what preventive strategies might be effective.

The potential for misuse of the material presented herein arises if broad generalizations are drawn about a particular child or adolescent without confirming or disconfirming these hypotheses through the collection of other data in a comprehensive psychological assessment. It is important to note that the process of clinical judgment and prediction may produce errors if clinicians fail to recognize sources of bias in judgment or misapply heuristics, or simple rules for making clinical decisions. Garb (1998) provided a detailed discussion of biases that can occur in clinical judgment. *Confirmatory bias* occurs when clinicians look only for data that confirms their hypotheses but overlook the evidence that refutes their hypotheses. In the present context, the clinician must avoid focusing only on those specific behavioral signs observed in a particular youth that suggest a proclivity to become an obsessional follower without also considering evidence to the contrary. *Hindsight bias* is an error in judgment that suggests once a given event has occurred, the clinician believes that the event could have been predicted. This bias is often framed in the adage "hindsight is 20/20." Hindsight bias is more relevant to the issue of behavioral prediction of violence and is addressed in the next chapter.

Misestimation of covariance is an error in clinical judgment that occurs when clinicians fail to properly describe the relationship between two variables; that is, the clinician may recall times when one variable was present and another variable was also observed but does not recall times when the two variables were unrelated. In the present context, misestimation of covariance is an important issue to recognize. For example, if a particular risk factor for stalking is identified, such as a history of childhood bullying, this observation is based on anecdotal case evidence and an analysis of the conceptual similarities between stalking and bullying. However, there may well be numerous instances in which the presence of bullying in childhood does not lead to stalking in adulthood or, in the reverse, that a person who stalks was not necessarily a childhood bully.

It is also important to recognize that judgments about behavior can sometimes be characterized by specific heuristics, or simple rules, that outline how judgments are made (Garb, 1998). For example, the *past-behavior heuristic* involves clinicians making predictions of future behavior based on the person's past behavior. This approach is not necessarily inaccurate; the past-behavior heuristic is merely a means of describing the decision-making process. With respect to the material presented in this chapter, this heuristic is relevant because some anecdotal evidence suggests that a history of harassing behavior such as obsessive relational intrusions, obsessive preoccupation, and stalking early in one's life are risk factors for stalking in adulthood. Empirical research on the childhood histories of adult stalking offenders, as well as longitudinal study of children who manifest harassing and bullying behavior, is needed to evaluate the validity of this anecdotal evidence.

In light of these difficulties in making judgments about risk factors for stalking, two general themes are explored in this chapter. One topic to be addressed is the relevance of a common and familiar form of repetitive harassment among children that overlaps considerably with stalking, namely bullying. In fact, formal legal recognition of bullying as a type of stalking behavior is found in cases where anti-stalking legislation has been used to legally address chronic bullying among children and teenagers. These interesting cases raise the notion that some forms of bullying may constitute a subtype of stalking in youngsters, whereas in other cases bullying may represent a coercive behavior that is a childhood precursor of a life pattern of controlling and harassing behavior that extends into adulthood. Because early prevention programs have been designed to address bullying, extension and modification of these programs to address obsessional following may also be useful in efforts to prevent stalking.

A second general topic to be addressed in this chapter deals with the various behaviors that serve as early signs of tendencies in a particular child or adolescent to obsessionally harass or follow another person. By examining the psychosocial histories of adult stalking offenders for childhood antecedents of stalking (a process of postdiction rather than prediction), some interesting issues emerge. Also, research on related topics such as obsessive relational intrusions and relationship violence show that key risk factors for stalking in intimate relationships among adolescents can be identified by looking closely at those related problems.

BULLYING AND STALKING

The problem of bullying among children and adolescents is not a new phenomenon. For centuries the systematic harassment and attacking that occurs among young people, mostly among boys, has been widely recognized and even experienced first-hand by many people while growing up. In Norway, for example, 15% of students encounter problems with bullying (Olweus, 1993). Oliver, Hoover, and Hazler (1994) reported data from research in the United Kingdom revealing that 23% of students experience bullying in school. In the United States, the rates of bullying might be higher, with 75% of students reporting being the victims of bullying and 14% experiencing severe trauma from bullying (Hoover, Oliver, & Hazler, 1992, as cited in Oliver et al., 1994). However, Duncan (1999) found a lower rate of bullying among 375 children in the United States; 25% reported being the victim of bullying, and 28% acknowledged being bullies. It has only been in the past few decades, however, that the social problem of bullying has been systematically studied (Olweus, 1993). What makes the topic of childhood bullying particularly relevant to the subject of stalking is the behavioral similarity between stalking and bullying and the application of anti-stalking laws to address the problem of bullying in schools.

Conceptual Comparisons

There are significant parallels between the definitions for bullying and stalking that point to a possible connection between these forms of obsessional harassment. According to one definition, *bullying* is

> repeatedly (not just once or twice) harassing others. This can be done by physical attack or by hurting others' feelings through words, actions, or social exclusion. Bullying may be done by one person or a group. It is an unfair match since the bully is either physically, verbally, and/or socially stronger than the victim. (Hazler, 1996, p. 6)

Olweus (1993), a prominent researcher on bullying, provided a more succinct definition as when someone "is exposed, repeatedly and over time, to negative actions on the part of one or more other students" (p. 9).

Each of these definitions shares common themes that parallel many of the components of legal and behavioral science definitions of stalking. Recall from chapter 1 that the California statute defines *stalking* as follows:

> any person who willfully, maliciously, and repeatedly follows or harasses another person and who makes a credible threat with the intent to place that person in reasonable fear of death or great bodily injury or to place that person in reasonable fear of death or great bodily injury of his or her immediate family is guilty of the crime of stalking . . . . (Cal. Penal Code <sect>646.9(a), 1993)

Also recall that a behavioral construct used to define stalking, *obsessional following,* was defined by Meloy (1996) as when "a person who engages in an abnormal or long-term pattern of threat or harassment directed toward a specific individual" where pattern of threat is defined as "more than one overt act of unwanted pursuit of the victim that is perceived by the victim as being harassing" (p. 148).

A comparison of the definitions of bullying, stalking, and obsessional following reveals several parallels. Bullying requires more than one act of harassment or negative action before the behavior can constitute bullying. This part of the definition parallels the "course of conduct" requirement of stalking statutes (Guy, 1993; McAnaney, Curliss, & Abeyta-Price, 1993) and the pattern of threat component of Meloy's definition of obsessional following. Thus, both stalking and bullying are characterized by more than one incident of threat, harassment, or intimidation. Another component of the definition of bullying is that one or more persons harass, intimidate, or in other ways respond negatively to a specific person. Again, this parallels the component in stalking definitions that require similar actions toward the victim. Many of the behaviors that bullies use to intimidate the victim are similar to those used in stalking cases in which the perpetrator seeks to threaten or evoke fear in the victim. Staring, following, making verbal threats, destroying the victim's property, and other similar actions are used by those individuals who bully or stalk. Yet another similarity that exists between the definition of bullying and stalking is that for threatening or harassing behavior to constitute either of these patterns of threat, the victim must have some awareness of the perpetrator's actions or know that he or she is being bullied or stalked. Therefore, behaviors such as lying in wait, secretly planning to harm the victim, or following the victim without his or her awareness do not constitute bullying or stalking, unless the victim discovers the actions and experiences them as threatening.

Of course, there are some differences between bullying and stalking that should be noted. One major difference is that bullying may be perpetrated by either one person or a group of people, whereas stalking generally refers to a single individual obsessionally following a specific victim. Stalking is generally not considered to be a crime that involves a group of perpetrators working toward the common goal of harassing or threatening a victim. However, some researchers have drawn a distinction between bullying, which is one person harassing or picking on another person, and *mobbing*, a term used to describe a group of individuals attacking another person (Oliver et al., 1994). If one adopts this distinction between bullying and mobbing, then there is greater similarity between the definitions of bullying and stalking.

Another critical difference is the underlying motivation of bullying and stalking. It is generally recognized that bullying involves a need to exert control and dominance over the victim, typically to achieve some position or status in a peer group. Although some professionals have argued that control is the major motivation for stalking (Snow, 1998), it has been argued more convincingly that stalking is a disturbance of attachment motivated by a need to regain some sense of psychological equilibrium by satisfying the fantasy of unification with the victim (Meloy, 1996). In short, the motivation in bullying is primarily aggressive control and dominance, usually over a weaker victim, whereas in stalking the motivation may be control, romantic obsession, psychotic fixation, hostility, or some other emotional bond related to disturbed attachment.

Finally, whereas bullying and stalking may involve similar behaviors that are directed toward the victim, there are some behaviors that are unique to either bullying or stalking. For instance, repetitive and unwanted sexual advances can sometimes be used as a form of stalking, but this behavior is not typically associated with bullying. Likewise, exclusion from a peer group is a common form of bullying behavior that has the usual goal of diminishing the victim's social status. Stalking offenders may attempt to alienate the victim's peer group through such actions as spreading rumors, gossip, or distributing embarrassing materials. However, the goals in stalking cases are likely to include intimidating or arousing fear in the victim.

One other difference between bullying and stalking appears to be societal attitudes about each form of harassment. A study on adolescent attitudes toward bullying suggests that teenagers view bullying somewhat favorably. Social attitudes toward stalking, however, are much more negative, given that criminal statutes create strong sanctions against this form of harassment. Oliver and his colleagues (1994) found that some students believe bullying toughens weaker peer group members and that bullies have a higher social status in the peer group. A majority of students viewed bullying as playful teasing even though the victims may find it to be more harassing. One interpretation of these findings is that adolescents view bullying along a continuum, with milder forms of the behavior having some favorable attributes and more severe forms of bullying having negative consequences. Another interpretation of these findings, however, is that the smaller portion of students who view aspects of bullying as positive (e.g., toughens the victim) may themselves be bullies or have close friendships with bullies.

Because Oliver and his colleagues did not examine differences between bullies and non-bullies in attitudes about bullying, this issue remains unclear. However, research on students' attitudes about bullying and the motives that sustain bullying behavior could be readily applied to the issue of stalking and obsessional following. The work of Cupach and Spitzberg (1998) on obsessive relational intrusions in college students is a more sophisticated attempt at addressing this issue, but their work needs to be extended to include middle and senior high school students.

Legal Connections

The similarities between bullying and stalking are interesting not only for academic reasons; they are legally relevant because the parallels between these two forms of obsessional harassment have been recognized by courts. In two legal cases, one in the United States and the other in England, anti-stalking legislation has been used to address instances in which children have been chronically bullied by other children.

In *Svedberg v. Stamness* (1994), one youth in his mid-teens, Anthony, began a 2-year course of threatening, harassing, teasing, and assaultive behavior toward another youth who was in his early teens, Christian. Anthony would often call Christian names such as "Dumbo" in reference to the victim's large ears. On at least one occasion, Anthony had made a threat that he would kill Christian, although the actual intent behind this threat was never made clear in the case analysis. Over time, Anthony's bullying became more incessant, and over a period of 2 years, Christian's fears became so pronounced that he could not attend school; he became depressed and made suicidal comments during periods of heightened stress. His parents' attempts to have school officials intervene were unsuccessful, as no action was ever taken. Therefore, the victim's parents sought a remedy in the courts. Christian's parents were able to obtain a disorderly conduct restraining order after a judge determined that Anthony's threats, taunts, and harassment were motivated by an intent to negatively affect Christian's safety, security, and privacy. Consequently, Anthony was barred by court order from making uninvited visits to the victim's home or making harassing telephone calls. He was further barred from calling Christian names or engaging in any other behaviors that could be construed as physically or psychologically harmful.

The legal basis for the court issuing the disorderly conduct restraining order was North Dakota's anti-stalking law that had recently been amended to include a restraining order section. When the judge's initial ruling was appealed, the case was ultimately heard by the North Dakota Supreme Court, which upheld the issuance of the two-year restraining order. By upholding the validity of a restraining order that barred bullying behavior using legislation originally drafted to combat stalking, a top state appellate court had essentially endorsed the use of anti-stalking laws as a legal tool for addressing severe bullying among children and adolescents. Moreover, this case raises the question of whether stalking and bullying are overlapping forms of obsessional harassment, or whether bullying might constitute a childhood subtype or precursor to stalking related behavior in later life.

In another legal case involving circumstances that are nearly identical to those in *Svedberg*, anti-stalking legislation enacted in England was used to prosecute three youngsters for chronic bullying behavior. In Leicestershire, England, three youths, ages 12, 13, and 15, had repeatedly threatened and harassed two neighborhood children over a period of several years (Bowcott, 1998). The bullying was of such severity that one of the victims was treated for depression. Although the bullying had been reported to the police, there apparently was little that could be done until England passed its first anti-stalking law, the Protection From Harassment Act (cited in Bowcott, 1998). Originally drafted to protect victims against malicious stalking, the act was used in this case as a test prosecution to determine if chronic bullying could be curbed legally using anti-stalking legislation. It is interesting to note that this case from England and the *Svedberg* case from the United States involved the use of anti-stalking legislation to address severe and chronic bullying in two different legal jurisdictions and countries. This suggests that the parallels between bullying and stalking are not merely of academic interest, but of some practical relevance, and that these parallels generalize across jurisdictional and national boundaries.

There has been some criticism of the use of anti-stalking laws to deal with chronic bullying. Fielkow (1997) argued that the courts are not an appropriate forum in which to seek a legal remedy for bullying through the use of anti-stalking laws; she argued that the school and home settings are where remedies should be sought. In addition, Fielkow noted that anti-stalking laws are intended to protect women from being followed, watched, harassed, or abused by estranged intimate partners, spouses, or strangers. As such, she argued that the use of anti-stalking laws to address bullying is an inappropriate extension and application of these laws.

These criticisms are, in my opinion, unwarranted. The courts are a suitable forum for resolving cases of excessive bullying when, as in the case of *Svedberg v. Stamness* (1994), the victim and his or her family have failed to obtain a suitable and effective response from school officials. Often, bullying behaviors are not confined only to the school grounds; they can extend to the walk or bus ride home, parks, neighborhoods, and the victim's home. As a result, school officials may have either very limited or no authority to enforce a solution to bullying when it extends beyond the boundaries of school property or does not directly affect an educational program. Moreover, the parents of children who bully may be resistant or openly hostile toward any attempts to have limits placed on their child's behavior or to seek mental health treatment for their child. In a later chapter, the issue of what school systems can do to address stalking in children and adolescents is addressed. However, it is worth reinforcing the point that schools have limited sanctions available (e.g., detention, suspension), and often these sanctions are limited in the extent to which they can force a bully into mental health treatment or to control a bully's actions off school grounds. It may be overly optimistic to assume that all instances of bullying can be resolved in the home environment or by cooperation between the parents of the bully and victim. Often, legal action in the form of a restraining order or other protective remedy is needed.

In addition, even though some anti-stalking laws may have been drafted for a specific intended purpose, such as protecting women from domestic abuse and stalking, there is no barrier to using these laws to address other forms of obsessional harassment, so long as the applications are legally permissible. In fact, it is debatable as to whether the protection of women from domestic violence was the sole purpose behind anti-stalking laws. Anti-stalking laws have many other purposes that are equally legitimate, including the protection of celebrities and politicians from obsessive harassment, the protection of individuals from repetitive domestic violence, and maintaining security in the workplace by criminalizing disgruntled employees' harassment and stalking behavior. In fact, the application of anti-stalking laws to combat workplace violence is an appropriate extension of these laws that parallels their application in school settings to prevent bullying. Therefore, anti-stalking legislation can serve as one method by which parents and students can seek legal relief to stop excessive bullying when other approaches have failed.

Theoretical and Practical Implications

The parallels between bullying and stalking give rise to some interesting hypotheses that can be set forth about the ways in which bullying might constitute a risk factor or early manifestation of stalking. Specifically, there are two ways in which bullying may serve as a risk factor for stalking that deserve further study. One hypothesis suggests that children who bully other children are at risk for a form of aggressive stalking later in life that is defined by excessive control and domination of the object. The second hypothesis suggests that a child or adolescent who has been either a victim or both perpetrator and victim of chronic bullying is at risk for a different form of compensatory stalking that is characterized by fixations on unavailable or estranged love objects to compensate for poor social skills and feelings of inadequacy. Some research on bullying offers support for these hypotheses.

The characteristics of children who bully other students are similar to the characteristics of certain aggressive stalking offenders. According to Olweus (1993), bullies are generally physically stronger than their peers and have strong needs to dominate and assert power over other students. In addition, bullies often portray narcissistic personality features in which they feel compelled to act in ways that reinforce their feelings of superiority over others. Bullies also are prone to display eruptive anger and impulsivity, and in most settings they are defiant and oppositional. They favor aggressive behavior as a solution to problems and have little empathy for others. Olweus also noted that bullies typically do not experience anxiety or insecurity, and they have inflated views of their self-worth. They tend to get involved in other antisocial activities at an earlier age. Overall, the typical bully displays "an aggressive reaction pattern combined . . . with physical strength" (Olweus, 1993, p. 35).

Those who bully other students have been shown to maintain their aggressive and controlling behavior over several years. Although bullying tends to reach a peak during adolescence, bullies are at greater risk for having a criminal record as an adult, and they tend to be more aggressive toward others as adults (Hazler, 1996; Olweus, 1993). These trends suggest that bullies are more prone to aggressively control and dominate others as adults in such ways as abusing or battering intimate partners and intimidating co-workers. Batterers frequently engage in behaviors such as following and threatening that sometimes rise to the level of criminal stalking (Walker & Meloy, 1998). Therefore, on a conceptual basis, bullying appears to have a connection to some forms of stalking in adulthood. Specifically, those who bully others during childhood and adolescence may be at greater risk of engaging in more aggressive forms of stalking in adulthood that are motivated by a need to dominate and control the victim.

Another parallel between stalking and bullying that exists at a conceptual level supports the notion that some bullies may be at heightened risk for aggressive stalking in adulthood. In Meloy's (1996, 1998b) psychodynamic theory of stalking, obsessive pursuit is motivated by a narcissistic linking fantasy in which the stalking perpetrator is viewed as having a special, admired, or idealized relationship with the victim. Through acute or chronic rejection by the victim, the stalker experiences feelings of shame and humiliation that are defended against with rage that provides the motivation to hurt, control, destroy, or damage the victim. Stalking results in the narcissistic fantasy of superiority and self-idealization being restored. These dynamics have been identified as underlying some forms of bullying. Olweus (1993) noted that bullies capitalize on relationships with peers in which a power imbalance exists whereby the bully can dominate and control the victim. The assertion of power over others serves to inflate the bully's self-esteem and provides a basis for enhancing feelings of superiority over others. Therefore, the need for self-aggrandizement and satisfaction of narcissistic needs has been identified as a major component of both aggressive stalking and bullying. Although some differences exist in the dynamic formulations of stalking and bullying, such as the nature of the perpetrator's fantasy relationship with the victim, the threats to narcissistic equilibrium in some bullies and stalking offenders suggest that these two forms of controlling behavior share common developmental antecedents involving narcissistic personality disturbances.

A second hypothesis, suggesting bullying may constitute a risk factor for stalking in later life, posits that being either a victim or both perpetrator and victim of bullying in childhood or adolescence produces psychological deficits that create a heightened risk for compensatory forms of stalking. According to research summarized by Hazler (1996), victims of bullying are generally passive and feel vulnerable and helpless. Socially, they tend to communicate poorly with others and become isolated and dysphoric. Bullying victims have low self-esteem and are often shy and self-punitive. There are various types of victims of bullying, including some who are more shy and withdrawn and others who are more provocative and create resentment and frustration in others. A subset of bullying victims who are bullies themselves, often take resentments and anger they feel about being victimized out on others who are weaker (Kumpulainen et al., 1998). In addition, victims of bullying experience intense feelings of anger and revenge fantasies but often mask them behind obsessive and rigid psychological defenses.

Like the research on children who bully others, there is empirical evidence that being the victim of bullying has long-term consequences. Former victims of bullying in childhood can function fairly well socially in adulthood; however, persisting problems with depression and poor self-esteem were found in adults who were victims of persistent bullying in childhood (Olweus, 1993). Another study found that victimization in early childhood predicted later behavior maladjustment, including problems with acting-out, poor attention, and increased sensitivity and dependency (Duncan, 1999; Schwartz, McFadyen-Ketchum, Dodge, Pettit, & Bates, 1998). The findings by Schwartz and colleagues illustrate how victimization can lead not only to depression and low self-esteem but also acting-out. As such, the combination of excessive dependency, sensitivity to rejection, and the propensity to act out in the bullying victim who also bullies weaker peers may create a heightened risk in later life for developing an obsessive preoccupation with an unattainable or idealized love object such as a stranger, celebrity, or other public figure. In these types of cases, the obsessional following would serve a variety of compensatory functions, such as overcoming feelings of inadequacy or loneliness and avoiding the risk of abandonment or rejection that arises in more realistic and attainable intimate relationships.

Not all victims of bullying experience severe maladjustment in adulthood. Therefore, the risk of stalking later in life may instead be found in a subset of bullying victims in childhood. For instance, Duncan (1999) and Kumpulainen and her colleagues (1998) found that the highest levels of disturbance were among victims of bullying who themselves had bullied others. These findings suggest that a certain subgroup of bullying victims experience chronic and intense maltreatment from peers, causing reduced opportunities for adaptive friendship or other appropriate outlets such as the development of specific competencies (e.g., sports, musical performance). However, some of these victims are unable to develop normalized outlets to cope with dependency conflicts or narcissistic injuries, such as support from family or school staff, and they thus develop highly conflicted and ambivalent emotions that lead to provocative behaviors and bullying of younger children. Where social supports may be lacking, feelings of resentment, anger, insecurity, and abandonment fears may intensify over time and under certain circumstances may evolve into obsessional following or stalking.

EARLY IDENTIFICATION OF STALKING PATTERNS

There are two types of behavior that may be useful for identifying those children and young adolescents who are at risk for engaging in stalking in late adolescence and adulthood. The first is based on the general notion that past behavior is a strong predictor of future behavior. Individual cases are analyzed to outline how a pattern of stalking in late childhood and adolescence can be a useful indicator of the potential for more serious and sometimes violent acting out in later life. Because no longitudinal or retrospective research has been conducted on this issue, the present discussion is based primarily on an examination of the histories of adult stalking offenders and correlational research that has been conducted on coercive and intrusive behaviors that overlap with stalking. The second type of behavior that will be examined is early manifestations of coercive and intrusive behaviors in the social and intimate relationships of a particular young person that foreshadow more serious problems. The purpose of the discussions in the following sections is to outline hypotheses for further study and to provide clinicians with hypotheses when assessing and treating a young person that is either closely involved with someone who exhibits these patterns or who is beginning to show signs of coercive and obsessive behavior in intimate relationships.

Prior History of Stalking

When attempting to predict behavior, a past history of the behavior being examined has frequently been identified as one of the best predictors of that behavior in the future. This approach to prediction has been described as the past-behavior heuristic. Using a past-behavior heuristic does not necessarily result in errors in judgment; the heuristic merely describes the process of making judgments about behavior. Nevertheless, because past behavior has been particularly useful as a predictor of future behavior, such as in the area of violence prediction (Monahan, 1995; Quinsey, Harris, Rice, & Cormier, 1998), it is worth raising the question of whether or not stalking behaviors in childhood and adolescence can be used to predict stalking in adulthood. Although no controlled research has been conducted on this issue, there is anecdotal evidence that stalking in adolescence can escalate into more severe forms of stalking-related aggression and violence over time.

The life history of Robert Bardo stands as a testament to what can, and often does, go wrong in the early years of a violent stalking offender's life. Mr. Bardo stalked and later killed actress Rebecca Schaeffer after he was able to locate her home with the assistance of a private investigator (Tharp, 1992). A careful review of Mr. Bardo's background, with particular emphasis on his teenage years, reveals that there were several early manifestations of stalking behavior in his adolescence that were the beginning stages of an escalating pattern of obsessive preoccupation with public figures.

According to a detailed account of Mr. Bardo's history, he had an extremely abusive and chaotic home life in which an older brother made him drink urine and forced him to steal; his father was alcoholic and his mother was paranoid (Tharp, 1992). One psychiatrist who evaluated him prior to his trial for the murder of Ms. Schaeffer believed that the Bardo family contributed substantially to the problems in his life. The first indication of his propensity to form disturbed attachments occurred when he was age 13. After his family moved to Arizona, Mr. Bardo went to visit his sister in Florida, where she worked as a waitress and exotic dancer. Within a year of the family's move, he stole money from his mother, took a bus to Maine, and began to search for Samantha Smith, an adolescent who had gained fame by writing to President Mikhail Gorbachev of the former

Soviet Union. Apparently Mr. Bardo had written to Ms. Smith and received a response. This obsessive pursuit of a famous same-aged peer is significant because it represents one of the first clues to Mr. Bardo's propensity to form disturbed attachments with famous individuals. Although writing a letter to a public figure is not indicative of an abnormal fixation, given that Mr. Bardo approached Ms. Smith in a manner that was uninvited and planned in a manner that had a low likelihood of success, there was clear evidence of his propensity to develop pathological fixations on other people.

This case suggests that disturbed interpersonal fixations in childhood or adolescence may be a predictor of stalking in later life. An empirical study that provides some support for this hypothesis is reported by Burgess and colleagues (1997). In this study, 120 individuals who had been charged with domestic violence felony offenses were divided into those offenders who had stalked their victims (30%) and those who had not stalked their victims (70%). Several variables were correlated with whether an offender had engaged in stalking. Among the variables measured, prior surveillance stalking of the victim was significantly correlated with current stalking behavior. In a step-wise multiple regression analysis, five variables accounted for nearly 40% of the variance in self-reported stalking behavior: (1) prior surveillance of the victim, (2) the offense occurring in an open public place, (3) less provocation by the victim, (4) strangling or choking the victim, and (5) prior stalking by the offender. The multiple regression analysis supports the observation that prior stalking behavior is a significant predictor of current stalking behavior.

Some additional features of Robert Bardo's history point to other early signs of problems in his life. In middle school he was considered to be a loner and a social misfit, even though he was a straight-A student. Mr. Bardo would not talk to other students, would isolate himself, and displayed a preoccupation with aggressive and violent themes. Despite his high grades, he dropped out of school at age 15. It has been noted in research studies that obsessional followers are more intelligent than other criminals, thus accounting for their adept manipulative skills and resourcefulness (Meloy, 1998b; Meloy & Gothard, 1995; Meloy et al., 2000). However, obsessional followers are also underachievers who are often unemployed and who have a series of failed relationships. Mr. Bardo's high academic achievement but abysmal social adjustment in adolescence is an illustration of these patterns in the teenage years.

Another facet of Mr. Bardo's early life confirms a hypothesis presented earlier concerning the potential role of bullying experiences of obsessional followers. An older brother of Mr. Bardo physically abused him, forced him to drink urine, and made him shoplift. As such, Mr. Bardo was a victim of severe bullying by his older brother, and he developed idealized fantasies and fixations on celebrities, presumably to compensate for his ineptness in intimate and social relationships. Empirical evidence reveals that victims of bullying are prone to experience dysphoria, anhedonia, and social isolation; as adults, bullying victims are more likely to have low self-esteem, poor sexual relationships, and depression (Kumpulainen et al., 1998). Moreover, victims are at higher risk for being referred for psychiatric treatment later in life. As an adult, Mr. Bardo had poor sexual relationships and he experienced chronic depression, low self-esteem, and serious psychiatric problems. Although the bullying he experienced as a child cannot be viewed as a direct cause of his stalking behavior, his case supports the hypothesis that a childhood history of bullying victimization is a potential risk factor for stalking in adulthood.

Robert Bardo's fixation with Rebecca Schaeffer began at the age of 16 (Tharp, 1992). However, he developed earlier fixations on other celebrities, including singers Debbie Gibson and Tiffany, but he became fixated on Ms. Schaeffer after seeing her in a movie. This case reveals how the propensity for stalking may develop early in a person's life. An adolescent's inappropriate obsessive fixation on a public figure offers an early-warning sign for more dangerous forms of stalking later in life. More important, that the average stalking offender is a male in his late 30s should not divert a clinician's attention away from considering the possibility that stalking can occur in younger individuals. By remaining aware of this possibility, there is a greater likelihood that stalking behavior can be identified at an earlier age, and appropriate treatment and remedial interventions can be implemented.

There are other case examples found in legal opinions that suggest stalking offenders have engaged in prior stalking behavior. In some of these cases there appears to be an escalation in the seriousness of stalking from less severe to more aggressive and violent episodes. Some courts have used the term *stalking* to refer to behavior that constitutes lying in wait or predatory pre-offense behavior that does not actually meet the legal definition of stalking. For example, in *State v. Laird* (1996), a 17-year-old young man was convicted of first-degree murder, kidnapping, burglary, and several other related charges after he broke into a woman's home, waited for her to return, brutally attacked her when she arrived, and then strangled her. He took her vehicle, dumped her body in the desert, and was arrested the following day while driving her truck. The court opinion notes in its analysis of the youth's level of maturity and planning of the crime that he had been "stalking" the victim the day prior to the murder. Furthermore, it was noted that the youth was familiar with the woman's home and vehicle because he had performed some work on her property about a month before the crime. However, the description of the youth's pre-offense behavior as stalking was not accurate from a legal perspective, because there is no evidence that the victim had been aware of the youth's surveillance. In fact, his actions were such that he kept his presence secret and surprised the victim in her home. Such behavior constitutes a predatory approach toward the victim by lying in wait, whereas there is no evidence that he intended to threaten her or to place her in fear of serious injury as is required in statutory definitions of stalking. Rather, he sought to increase the likelihood that he could gain access to her home without being observed, and he maximized the element of surprise in his attack.

Other court cases provide evidence that some stalking offenders have a history of stalking in childhood or adolescence. In one case report from the Court of Appeals of Minnesota (*In the Matter of Robert D. Hall,* 1997), a 47-year-old man with a lengthy history of sex offenses appealed his involuntary commitment under Minnesota law as a sexually psychopathic personality and sexually dangerous person. In the facts reported by the court, it was noted that Mr. Hall began exhibiting a pattern of serious acting out and aggression at age 6 or 7 when he was "reprimanded" at school for choking girls. At age 14, he began stalking other individuals and also began engaging in exhibitionism and voyeurism. His behavior escalated into more serious and dangerous attacks against women when he was 16. Over much of his adult life he had repeated sexual offenses and numerous placements for treatment; however, the case record does not report any formal treatment until he was about age 25. This case, like the case of Robert Bardo, indicates that stalking behavior beginning in adolescence was part of an escalating pattern of offending that led to more serious and violent attacks.

In other cases involving youthful offenders, one can find evidence of stalking as a precursor to more serious criminal acts. For example, in *State v. Jensen* (1998), a 14-year-old boy was convicted of murdering a taxi cab driver in South Dakota. Even prior to his conviction for murder at such a young age, there was a lengthy history of criminal offenses and school misconduct that included intimidation of students, verbal abuse of teachers and students, and stalking. Another legal case, *In re Paul G.* (1992), also provides evidence of stalking as a precursor to more aggressive and violent acting out in a young sex offender. This case involved the placement of a 15-year-old boy in a juvenile detention facility. His stalking behaviors were cited as evidence of his efforts to coerce and control others during sexual assaults. The ultimate purpose of this evidence, as cited by the court, was to demonstrate the severity of his conduct problems.

The implications of these cases are that if stalking and related offenses are identified early and taken seriously, then appropriate treatment and corrective interventions might serve to prevent or lessen the likelihood of more serious acting-out in later adolescence and adulthood, at least in some cases. Of course, persistent forms of conduct disturbances, such as life-course persistent conduct disorder (Moffitt, 1993), may not respond to early intervention or treatment. In other cases, however, there may be a more favorable response. Further research is needed to establish variables that can help identify which children and adolescents who stalk will respond to treatment and which ones will not. Research on variables such as psychopathy in youthful offenders (Rygaard, 1998), neurobiological dysfunction, and severe personality disorders may be particularly fruitful variables for study.

Coercive and Intrusive Behaviors in Relationships

The early phases of an intimate relationship are often characterized by infatuation, idealized fantasies of a happy future, and intense feelings of sexual attraction. This is particularly true when both individuals in a relationship have mutual feelings of attraction to one another. When idealized fantasies are particularly strong, there is a tendency to overlook personal faults in the other person and to focus instead on the favorable qualities that initially created the attraction. Consequently, it is only after the initial period of infatuation has lessened in intensity, and normal conflicts arise, that the intimacy may have progressed to such a point that it is difficult or impossible to end if one of the partners has developed an obsessive preoccupation that emerges into a pattern of stalking. At that time it may be too late to easily or safely end the relationship.

This pattern of initial infatuation is also present in the dating and intimate relationships of teenagers. In fact, many parents who have teenagers will respond with a strong sense of familiarity when hearing about the parent who finds his or her teenager dating a person who is seen as an undesirable or unacceptable partner. Many battles have been waged between parents and teenagers over the choice of dating partners or steady boyfriend or girlfriend. Therefore, it may be an extremely challenging task to get an adolescent to heed warnings of potential problems that emerge in the initial stages of a relationship. Nevertheless, it is worth reviewing early manifestations of coercive and intrusive behavior that serve as risk factors for stalking or obsessional following in intimate relationships.

The research on obsessive relational intrusions is particularly useful in this regard. Cupach and Spitzberg (1998) noted that many intrusive behaviors are fairly common in relationships. Given the frequency with which some intrusions occur, they may not be particularly useful in predicting more serious problems. The more common forms of intrusion include the following:

- calling on the telephone and arguing
- asking if the person is dating someone else
- watching from a distance
- making hang-up telephone calls
- asking for another chance after a break-up
- making exaggerated statements about one's affections
- failing to take hints that one is unwelcome
- bragging or gossiping about the relationship to others.

Each of these intrusions were reported by over 60% of a sample of 876 college students. Although they may appear to suggest potential problems, the data suggest that they are relatively common in relationships and break-ups.

On the other hand, Cupach and Spitzberg (1998) reported on several rare intrusions in relationships. Given the infrequency with which they occur, these behaviors represent more severe intrusions and may suggest a greater likelihood of stalking and obsessional following:

- sending offensive pictures
- breaking into someone's home
- tape recording conversations without permission
- taking photographs without consent
- sending excessive e-mails
- forcing sexual contact
- making threatening communications.

These behaviors were reported in less than 20% of the sample of college undergraduates studied by Cupach and Spitzberg. The relative infrequency with which these behaviors occurred suggests that they are more severe relational intrusions, and if they occur early in a relationship, they may foreshadow more serious problems such as stalking.

Spitzberg, Nicastro, and Cousins (1998) reported data that may suggest that the number of relational intrusions predict stalking behavior rather than any specific intrusion or behavior. These researchers found that the number of self-reported obsessive relational intrusions differentiated those college students who labeled themselves as victims of stalking and those who did not. One important variable that was not studied, and needs to be, is the timing of obsessive relational intrusions. That is, when jealousy, possessiveness, coercion, obsessiveness, and feelings of betrayal occur in a relationship, the more likely it may be that stalking behavior will occur in the relationship. However, this hypothesis warrants further study.

One example of this reasoning comes from the personal security literature. A well-known personal security expert noted that an excessive degree of possessiveness of the love object or premature investment that includes talk of commitment or marriage in the first few dates is cause for alarm (de Becker, 1997). In addition, de Becker noted that excessive jealousy, possessiveness, inflexibility, and a demand for the person to account for his or her time is also a sign of possible stalking or obsessional following. If a recent relationship has formed and the person begins to make intrusions into their partner's life by questioning peers or family members, there may be a heightened propensity to obsessionally follow the object. Other warning signs in a relationship include a preoccupation with themes of obsessional love, weapons, death, suicide, religion, and a feeling of common destiny with the victim. All of these factors, according to de Becker, should serve as early warning signs that someone may begin stalking if faced with separation or estrangement in a relationship.

Another source of information on the potential early predictors of stalking in children and adolescents comes from literature on developmental antecedents of partner abuse in younger adults. In their discussion of the relationship between partner abuse and stalking, Walker and Meloy

(1998) found that stalking constitutes a very serious form of control and abuse in intimate relationships. Research on the developmental antecedents of abuse in intimate relationships can serve as a useful basis from which to draw inferences about the antecedents of stalking.

One empirical study in this area was reported by Magdol, Moffitt, Caspi, and Silva (1998). This study had a strong prospective methodology and design in which data were collected in a large birth cohort of 1,037 individuals over 20 years. Four major domains of data were collected: socioeconomic factors; family relations; educational achievement; and problem behavior at ages 3, 5, 7, 9, 11, 13, 15, 18, and 21. As such, this study represents an impressive effort to identify risk factors for physical and psychological abuse in intimate relationships that occur in early adulthood.

Results from this study by Magdol and colleagues supported a number of hypotheses. For instance, a close parent–child attachment at age 15 was consistently shown to be associated with a low risk for partner abuse. This finding is particularly relevant to the issue of stalking and obsessional following, which are conceptualized by many other researchers as a disturbance in attachment. Therefore, strong parent–child attachment during adolescence appears to be a protective factor against partner abuse, and possibly stalking, in later life. Other findings in the study revealed that certain socioeconomic factors in the family were related to a lowered risk for partner abuse in adulthood. Specifically, boys in middle childhood who had parents with high-status occupations had a lower risk for partner abuse in adulthood. Also, children who grew up in a household where both parents were present had a lower risk for abuse, particularly if boys lived with both parents in middle childhood and if girls lived with both parents in adolescence. These findings suggest there may be critical developmental periods in which specific aspects of familial stability are important at different times to prevent relationship problems later in adulthood. McCann (1998c) presented a case example of one adolescent stalking perpetrator who was adopted late in childhood and had serious issues surrounding abandonment and acceptance that contributed to his stalking of a former girlfriend.

In addition, Magdol and her colleagues also found that children who dropped out of school were more likely to engage in subsequent partner abuse. Also, early behavior problems before age 15 were associated with later partner abuse, including parent reports of conduct problems in their children, self-reports of aggressive acting-out, and substance abuse. Interestingly, variables from childhood were less consistent predictors of partner abuse in early adulthood than were variables from adolescence. The implication of this finding is that prevention programs directed at reducing the incidence of partner abuse may be most effective when they are implemented in early adolescence.

It is worth noting at this point that some concerns or doubts may exist as to whether these developmental antecedents of partner abuse have any relevance to the prediction of stalking and obsessional following in adulthood. Aside from the significant overlap that exists between violence among intimate partners and stalking, Magdol et al. (1998) noted that the developmental antecedents of partner abuse that they identified are also implicated as predictors of many other adult antisocial behaviors (Loeber & Dishion, 1983). Therefore, the antecedents of abuse identified in their study may serve as general predictive factors for adult antisocial behavior and acting-out, which includes stalking and obsessional following.

CONCLUSION

This chapter reviewed early risk factors in childhood and adolescence that may heighten the risk for stalking later in life. In addition, various behaviors and developmental factors were reviewed that constitute early coercive and intrusive behaviors that may foreshadow more serious problems in intimate relationships. Throughout the chapter emphasis was placed on the fact that there is very little research on variables that can predict stalking behavior. The discussions are offered as a set of hypotheses derived from clinical observations and anecdotal evidence from individual cases. Research on phenomena that overlap with stalking, such as obsessive relational intrusion and partner abuse, offers support for some of the observations presented; however, more work needs to be done in this regard.

One issue that received attention in this chapter was the similarities and differences between bullying and stalking as types of obsessional harassment in children and adolescents. Bullying and stalking are social problems that have existed for quite some time; however, only recently have they been studied in any systematic way. Both bullying and stalking are defined as repetitive patterns of harassing, threatening, or intimidating behavior that are directed at another person. Moreover, similar psychodynamic factors that motivate bullying and stalking behavior have been identified, including threats to narcissistic equilibrium and the need to control others. Moreover, bullying and stalking involve common threatening behaviors such as direct statements of threat, intimidation, and coercion. Nevertheless, there are differences between bullying and stalking such as the type of relationship that sometimes exists between perpetrator and victim (e.g., bullying is generally not used to describe intimidation that occurs in intimate relationships) and the ends achieved by the behavior (e.g., elevation of peer status vs. fear of abandonment). Still, the parallels between bullying and stalking raise interesting questions for further research.

6

The Risk of Violence

S talking behavior is, by definition, threatening and harassing. Furthermore, legal definitions of stalking are based on the notion that victims of stalking develop a reasonable fear of serious injury, independent of whether or not the perpetrator actually intends to harm the victim. As Farnham, James, and Cantrell (2000) have observed, anti-stalking legislation has been enacted "against a background of public apprehension about violence from mentally ill people in general . . ." (p. 199). Although the public perception that all stalking offenders have a psychotic mental disorder is not supported by research (Farnham et al., 2000; Meloy, 1996, 1998b, 1999b; Meloy & Gothard, 1995; Meloy et al., 2000), the question of whether or not a stalking offender will engage in violence toward the victim, a third party, or property remains a focus of research and an important issue to address when assessing and managing stalking cases.

The rate of violence among stalking offenders has been examined in a number of studies (Farnham et al., 2000; Meloy, 1999b). Because violence is generally conceptualized as a situational phenomenon resulting from a complex interaction of variables related to the perpetrator, victim, and situation in which they interact, relevant factors to consider when evaluating violence potential include characteristics of the perpetrator, specific characteristics and behavioral reactions by the victim, and situational variables that may raise or reduce the likelihood of violence. Moreover, variables associated with the likelihood of violence can be further classified according to *static variables,* which are relatively enduring and change little over time, and *dynamic variables,* which are changeable over time and are more amenable to interventions (Monahan, 1992; Monahan & Steadman, 1994). Therefore, the interaction between characteristics of the stalking perpetrator and victim, as well as situational factors that define the context in which the stalking occurs, needs to be examined when assessing the risk for violence in these cases.

Subtle variations exist in the way that violence can be defined. Whereas one approach may be to define violence as actions directed at a person, another approach may include actions directed at either people or property. For example, research on the assessment of violence risk conducted as part of the MacArthur Foundation Research Network considered the throwing of an object as a violent act, as well as more common forms of interpersonal aggression such as pushing, grabbing, kicking, biting, and using a weapon (Silver, Mulvey, & Monahan, 1999). In general, *violence* may be more broadly defined as an aggressive act that is intentional, directed at either a person or object, and results or will likely result in the physical injury of another person. In addition, *persons* may be defined broadly to include animate objects, such as animals as well as people. With respect to children and adolescents where cruelty to animals may occur, acts of aggression directed at animals should also be classified as acts of violence.

Aside from the definition of violence that one adopts, other considerations must be addressed when evaluating a particular individual's propensity for violence. The conceptual framework one adopts to guide decisions about violence potential is important; the two general methods of violence prediction are clinical and actuarial approaches. *Clinical approaches* have traditionally been viewed as involving a professional collecting information, evaluating the individual, and arriving at a general impression that a person will or will not be violent. *Actuarial approaches* to violence prediction are based on empirical and statistical procedures in which variables that correlate highly with violence, based on research studies, are combined with other variables in a statistically derived equation, including discriminant function analysis and multiple regression, to produce a prediction of a person's likelihood for violence.

Because violence prediction is likely to produce some errors, including identifying someone as potentially violent who does not subsequently display violence or identifying someone as not potentially violent who subsequently commits a violent act, there need to be other considerations made when assessing violence potential. For instance, the process of violence prediction has been reconceptualized as violence risk assessment, whereby various risk enhancing and risk reducing factors are identified and result in global estimates of violence risk rather than definitive predictions (Borum, 1996; Heilbrun, 1997). Also, the context in which violence potential is considered is extremely important. Variables such as the base rate, or underlying prevalence, of a violent act in the population from which the person being evaluated is selected also effects the accuracy of decisions about violence (Garb, 1998). Therefore, the base rate of violence in stalking cases is a significant variable that must be considered when evaluating the potential for violence. In addition, the variables associated with violent behavior in children and adolescents differ in some ways from the variables associated with violence in adults. Therefore, consideration must be given to the risk factors that exist for younger individuals.

The purpose of this chapter is to outline general principles for violence risk assessment of children and adolescents and to apply these principles to the assessment of violence potential in stalking cases involving young victims and perpetrators. The first major section of the chapter reviews general principles of violence risk assessment, including clinical versus actuarial prediction and the differing roles and concerns of personal security consultants versus mental health professionals. In addition, the first section reviews principles of evaluating risk for harm to others among children and adolescents. The second section reviews research on the relationship between stalking and violence. Although nearly all of the literature on violence in stalking cases has focused on adults, some of this material can be applied to stalking cases involving younger obsessional followers. Finally, the topic of stalking and homicide is addressed. Although the rate of homicide appears to be rather low in stalking cases generally (Meloy, 1996, 1998b), there are some factors that may reduce the accuracy of estimates of homicide rates in stalking cases. Given the severity and magnitude of the violence in cases of homicide, a brief discussion of these issues is warranted.

GENERAL ISSUES IN VIOLENCE RISK ASSESSMENT

The clinical prediction of violent behavior has been surrounded by controversy, particularly since the publication of Monahan's (1981/1995) book, *The Clinical Prediction of Violent Behavior.* Based on a review of empirical research concerning the accuracy of mental health professionals' ability to predict violence that was available at the time, Monahan concluded that "psychiatrists and psychologists are accurate in no more than one out of three predictions of violent behavior" (p. 47). Consequently, the conclusions offered by Monahan were used in a variety of ways, including the advancement of arguments that professional judgments about dangerousness should be eliminated from legal proceedings (Faust & Ziskin, 1988) or the advancement of better research on risk factors associated with the propensity for violence (Monahan, 1984; Otto, 1992).

Since the publication of Monahan's review in 1981, there have been considerable changes and improvements in the clinical assessment and prediction of violent behavior. These changes are the result of research that has been conducted over almost two decades. For example, there is evidence that mental health professionals' predictions of violence, although not perfect, are better than chance when informed by empirical research and qualified as to context and time frame (Mossman, 1994). Moreover, major improvements have been made in the use of specialized protocols for evaluating specific types of violence, including general criminal violence (Quinsey, Harris, Rice, & Cormier, 1998; Webster, Douglas,

Eaves, & Hart, 1997a, 1997b), sexual violence (Boer, Hart, Kropp, & Webster, 1997; Boer, Wilson, Gauthier, & Hart, 1997; Quinsey et al., 1998; Rice, 1997), and domestic violence (Kropp & Hart, 1997).

Although advances have been primarily in identifying various risk factors and variables associated with violence, there has also been a shift away from the practice of making definitive predictions of violence and toward a practice of evaluating risk propensity or likelihood (Borum, 1996; Grisso, 1998; Heilbrun, 1997; Monahan & Steadman, 1996). Likewise, there has been an emphasis placed on the offering of general classifications of violence risk, such as low, moderate, and high, which more accurately convey the problems with precision when predicting violence (Heilbrun, O'Neill, Strohman, Bowman, & Philipson, 2000). The use of these general classifications conveys useful clinical information when they are based on empirically established correlates of violence and contextual/situational factors.

When mental health professionals undertake assessments of violence potential or dangerousness, there are essentially three types of conclusions or opinions that might be offered in any one case. The first type of opinion involves a statement of specific clinical, social, and historical characteristics that describe the individual. Because no opinion is offered about the implications of these characteristics for violence potential, no errors in prediction result; but such opinions are likely to be of limited use when making legal, treatment, or case management decisions about the person. A second type of opinion is an assertion that an individual has certain characteristics that either increase or decrease the likelihood of violence. By combining a variety of clinical, social, situational, and historical variables that have an empirically established relationship with violent behavior, the clinician can offer general estimates (e.g., low, moderate, or high) or specific estimates of probability where warranted (e.g., 35% likelihood of violence given the presence of certain conditions or variables). Opinions of this type fall under the general practice of risk assessment. They are more informative and useful than opinions of the first type, but are less precise, yet less error prone, than definitive predictions. The third type of opinion is when the clinician offers a definitive prediction: "Yes, this person will be violent" or "No, this person will not be violent." Such statements are prone to error and should be avoided given the many factors that cause violence risk to fluctuate and change over time and conditions.

Risk assessment of violent behavior requires that clinicians not only identify variables that have some empirically demonstrable relationship to violence, but also remain cognizant of how these variables can be grouped, combined, and weighted. For instance, risk factors for violence have been grouped into those that are static and those that are dynamic (Borum, 1996; Monahan & Steadman, 1994). *Static variables* are relatively constant and change little over time; examples of static risk factors include gender (Monahan, 1981/1995), psychopathy (Harris, Rice, & Quinsey, 1993), early childhood maladjustment (Klassen & O'Connor, 1994), and personality disorders (Quinsey et al., 1998; Widiger & Trull, 1994). *Dynamic variables* can fluctuate more readily over time; examples include poor social supports (Klassen & O'Connor, 1989), substance abuse (Monahan, 1981/1995), and threat control override symptoms such as delusions of thought insertion (Borum, Swartz, & Swanson, 1996).

There is extensive literature on the various risk factors that have been established for violent behavior, and a full discussion of these factors is beyond the scope of this chapter, which is limited to giving an overview of violence risk assessment for children and adolescents. Before addressing this topic, two other major factors must be discussed. The first is the difference between clinical and actuarial approaches to predicting violence. The second deals with the role one adopts when evaluating violence potential and the types of errors one seeks to minimize in those roles. In this regard, a comparison of personal security or threat assessment and management consultants and mental health professionals in clinical and forensic settings is outlined with respect to their perspectives and goals when evaluating violence potential. After discussing these issues, the focus then turns to violence risk assessment of children and adolescents.

Clinical vs. Actuarial Prediction

A clinical approach to violence prediction has traditionally been characterized as being based on subjective impressions in which clinicians make their judgments using decision rules and subjective procedures that are not necessarily uniform across professionals and are not always clearly described (Grove & Meehl, 1996). Actuarial, or statistical prediction, on the other hand, is based on mathematical and statistical equations that are mechanical and based on empirically derived algorithms (Garb, 1998; Grove & Meehl, 1996). The relative advantages and disadvantages of clinical and actuarial approaches have been debated extensively in the literature (Dawes, 1989; Dawes, Faust, & Meehl, 1989; Holt, 1986; Meehl, 1954). Overall, the research has clearly shown that actuarial prediction is sometimes as good as, but usually superior to, clinical prediction (Garb, 1998). However, as Litwack and Schlesinger (1999) astutely noted, the distinction between actuarial and clinical assessment "is blurring to the point where there is often no meaningful distinction between the two" (p. 188). They supported this statement by noting that most major actuarial instruments used to evaluate violence potential are comprised of many clinical variables that are based on subjective clinical ratings and diagnostic formulations. For example, the Violence Risk Assessment Guide (VRAG; Quinsey et al., 1998) and HCR-20 (Webster et al., 1997b) include psychopathy, as measured by the Psychopathy Checklist–Revised (PCL–R; Hare, 1991), the presence of a personality disorder, and the absence of schizophrenia as individual variables. Clinical judgment is often required to evaluate these and other variables that enter into actuarial prediction equations and scales.

Consequently, risk assessment of violent behavior is most appropriate when it considers the individual's past history and current clinical status, contextual and situational features that mediate violence potential, potential biases or errors in judgment that may occur, and variables that have research to support their relationship to violence potential.

Private Security or Threat Assessment vs. Mental Health Professional Roles

Private and public security personnel are charged with protecting individuals such as politicians or celebrities, and much of this work depends on making predictions about who poses a serious threat to a specific protectee. For example, the U.S. Secret Service is charged with protecting the family of the President and Vice-President (Coggins, Pynchon, & Dvoskin, 1998). The appraisal of risk in this type of setting requires agents to prioritize resource investment based on an appraisal of what cases involve the highest level of risk for violence.

The private security consultant Gavin de Becker (1997) recently outlined a number of danger signs that should alert individuals to early problems in relationships and other factors that would allow someone to predict violence. In his book *The Gift of Fear,* de Becker stated his belief that violence can be predicted and that there are signs that people can look for to protect themselves from being victimized. He provided several convincing examples in which events leading up to a violent event could have served as clues.

Some behavioral scientists point out the fallibility of predicting violence and might argue that the approach offered by de Becker is prone to error due to what is called *hindsight bias,* or the tendency to erroneously believe that a violent episode could have been predicted by examining the events leading up to the event (Quincy et al., 1998). In addition, some might argue that studying the antecedents of an event that has already occurred runs the risk of erroneously attributing causal significance to factors that may have little, if any, relationship to the violent episode. For example, if the victim was walking down a specific street when a violent attack occurred, it is tempting to conclude that walking down that particular street was a causal factor in the attack. This attribution of causality does not take into account the fact that the attack may have occurred as a result of being stalked and followed and that the attack would have taken place regardless of the path taken by the victim.

This tension between the tenet of behavioral science literature on the fallibility of prediction and the private and public security personnel position that violence can be predicted appears at first glance to be irreconcilable. Is violence preceded by identifiable factors that allow one to predict when it will occur, or are predictions of future violence inherently flawed to the extent that they should never be made? Should predictions of violence be made to avoid being personally victimized, or should all evaluations of future dangerousness be set aside due to errors that can occur in human judgment? A very workable resolution is that both of these arguments have merit and that each can coexist with the other.

The key to understanding the validity of each argument is to recognize that predictions of violence made for personal protective reasons and those made by mental health or legal professionals in a position of authority to police society are two different settings with very different goals, benefits, and costs associated with the accuracy or inaccuracy of a prediction of violence. When a professional makes an assessment of someone's potential for violence, the cost–benefit analysis of this judgment has rather high stakes if an error is made in predicting violence. If the professional says a person will be violent and that person turns out not to be, then the error may result in a nonviolent person having his or her freedom restricted unnecessarily (e.g., remaining civilly committed in a psychiatric hospital, being denied parole). If, on the other hand, the professional predicts that someone will not be violent and that person later commits an act of violence, then the cost of this error is that a person who is a risk to society will be released and cause further harm to others. Therefore, the costs of being wrong about a person's violence potential are very great when professionals offer predictions of violence.

The stakes are somewhat different when violence prediction is carried out on a personal or private level that seeks to maintain someone's safety. Suppose that someone takes a personal security consultant's advice to attend to the fear or uneasiness that is produced when a new relationship starts. The cost associated with ignoring these feelings of fear and continuing the relationship with someone who later becomes violent is that the person's life will be in danger and physical injury may result. On the other hand, the cost associated with the error of taking personal fears seriously and quickly terminating or altogether avoiding a relationship with someone who would not be violent is merely a lost opportunity for a relationship. Predictions of violence made in the course of personal security and safety frequently do not result in serious consequences for the individual about whom the prediction is made; private and public security personnel rarely have the power to have someone arrested and detained, unless there is evidence of potential violence involving threats or other criminal behaviors that may lead to arrest.

In the language of professional judgment, predicting that someone will be violent when that individual never goes on to become violent is a false-positive error in prediction. Predicting that someone will not be violent when that person turns out to be violent constitutes a false-negative error in prediction. The cost of errors when professionals such as judges, mental health professionals, or parole board members make predictions of violence are very high for both false-positive and false-negative errors. On the other hand, the cost of a false-negative error is much higher than the cost of a false-positive error when violence predictions are made with respect to personal safety or private security. A hypothetical example highlights this difference.

Suppose a mental health professional regularly makes decisions about which juvenile offenders should be released from a maximum-security facility and that one of the major criteria for determining which offenders will be released is the potential for future violence. The mental health professional is in a position to have great influence over the decisions made about a number of juvenile offenders and must balance the interests of society to keep dangerous youthful offenders incarcerated against the individual interests of juvenile offenders to be released if there is minimal potential for danger. Given these high stakes, the mental health professional should adhere to standard professional practice, rely on assessment methods that have proven empirical validity, and provide a realistic appraisal of the foundations and limitations of his or her opinion. Moreover, the opinion would in all likelihood be framed generally in terms of an offender posing low, moderate, or high risk for violence.

Now suppose the same mental health professional goes home one day and finds that her teenage daughter is concerned about a boy in her class who has been sending her notes and keeps wanting to go out on a date with her. Suppose further that although the daughter cannot put her finger on it, the boy gave her "the creeps" because he is very persistent and will not take "no" for an answer. In this case, the mental health professional might make a determination as a parent, not as a professional, that the boy poses a serious risk of violence and seeks to prevent any contact between the boy and her daughter. This personal "prediction" of dangerousness involves a consideration of the daughter's safety against a lost opportunity the daughter might have for a relationship with someone who in actuality might not pose a serious risk to her daughter. This personal prediction increases the likelihood that the daughter will be safe, while merely taking away an opportunity for a relationship and resulting in no serious consequence for the boy about whom the prediction is made.

The difference between threat assessment and mental health professionals' predictions of violence is important to make because these two contexts involve different goals, and the relative costs of making an error in judgment is higher in professional settings, whereas personal prediction involves potentially greater threats to personal safety with marginal costs to the person about whom the prediction is made. Consequently, the differences dictate that professionals making judgments about the risk for violence posed by an obsessional follower should be based on empirically established methods and procedures and must be framed in relative terms. Individuals who make judgments about risk for violence in settings where personal safety or the safety of their family is at stake must rely on strategies and actions that maximize the likelihood that they do not become victims of violence. In this way, the goals, methods, and guiding philosophy of threat assessment and mental health professionals' risk assessments are different from one another. Each has its particular place, and the approaches taken in threat assessment should not be applied to or be confused with the risk assessment approach of mental health professionals assessing violence potential. Both approaches have their own unique place in the management of violence in stalking cases.

Assessing Violence Potential in Children and Adolescents

According to Grisso (1998), the evaluation of a particular child or adolescent's potential for harm to others can involve a number of considerations. Among the pertinent issues in such evaluations are concerns about whether the youth requires secure detention before trial, will harm others while in detention, poses a threat to the community, is amenable to treatment, or should be tried as a juvenile or transferred to adult court. Although the scope of the assessment may vary, Grisso recommended that mental health professionals who are presented with a request to evaluate a young person's potential for violence frame the assessment question so that errors of prediction, such as those outlined earlier, will be minimized. Accordingly, Grisso recommended the use of specific guidelines when conducting violence risk assessments:

- Apply risk factors that theory, research, and clinical experience suggest have some relationship to violence.
- Consider the social context in which some violent act might occur.
- Offer estimates of risk rather than definitive predictions.
- Recognize that delinquent youths are heterogeneous, and avoid applying broad predictions of violence across all youths.
- Recognize that delinquent and violent behavior often desists after adolescence.

A survey of these guidelines reveals that they provide a clinically useful set of standards that increase the likelihood that clinicians will not make critical errors in prediction and will not offer broad conclusions about a particular youth that are difficult to substantiate with empirical data. Moreover, they recognize the situational and contextual nature of violence by urging clinicians to consider specific conditions and variables that are likely to raise or lower the relative risk for violence. These guidelines also permit the clinician to make prudent decisions based on risk factors that may have a strong theoretical or clinical basis for increasing concerns about risk. For example, if a particular youth who is stalking a former girlfriend makes a statement that communicates an intent to kill the girlfriend at a specific time and date (e.g., "When prom night comes, you and your new friend are dead.") or under specific conditions (e.g., "Slap another protective order violation on me, and you're dead."), then it would be both reasonable and appropriate to conclude that the potential for violence is raised at that time or under those conditions.

Consequently, more diligent protective measures would be warranted, such as increased police surveillance, involuntary hospitalization, or arrest of the threatener if there has been a violation of the law.

There is an emerging body of literature on general risk factors associated with an increased risk for violence among young offenders. Although a history of previous violence is one of the strongest predictors of future violence, it is important to remember that this relationship is not perfect and that often it is the chronicity, recency, frequency, and severity of the violence that is important to assess (Grisso, 1998). Wiebush, Baird, Krisberg, and Onek (1995) and Hawkins, Herrenkohl, et al. (1998) have provided a comprehensive review of general risk factors for violence in children and adolescents. These reviews group individual risk factors into broad categories, including individual medical/physical conditions, psychological factors, family variables, school factors, peer relationships, and community factors. A brief overview of these general categories is provided; however, the reader is referred to Wiebush and colleagues (1995) and Hawkins, Herrenkohl, and colleagues (1998) for more detailed discussions of these general factors.

Among the medical/physical variables studied, a weak but noticeable relationship exists between pregnancy and birth complications in the perpetrator's mother and later violence (Hawkins, Herrenkohl, et al., 1998; Raine, 1993). However, this relationship is often considered to be of marginal use in individual assessments of violence potential. These variables may be of some utility in making other diagnostic determinations, such as the presence of neurological injury or attention deficit-hyperactivity disorder (ADHD). Moreover, Lewis (1992) noted that stressors during maternal pregnancy and delivery contribute to heightened levels of aggression, which may lead to more interpersonal violence. Likewise, there is research supporting a relationship between low resting heart rate and higher levels of psychopathy and antisocial behavior (Raine, 1993). However, Hawkins, Herrenkohl, and colleagues (1998) stated that these physical/medical variables may be of limited use in individual assessments at the present time.

With respect to psychological variables, much research has focused on the relationship between ADHD and violence. There has been shown to be a positive correlation between ADHD and violence, with the highest rates of future aggression and violence observed among children with ADHD and other co-morbid disruptive behavior disorders such as oppositional defiant disorder and conduct disorder (Barkley, 1997, 1998). Another set of psychological variables that has been studied in relation to future violence are those that have been associated with general antisocial behavior. One of the better predictors of future violence is an early age of onset for violent and delinquent behavior (Hawkins, Herrenkohl, et al., 1998; Weibush et al., 1995). In addition, aggression at a very young age, involvement with any form of antisocial behavior, and endorsement of attitudes and beliefs that are consistent with norm-violating behavior (e.g., dishonesty; violence as acceptable to resolve conflict; bullying; hostility toward authority) are all associated with higher levels of violent behavior. However, it is important to interpret these factors in light of Moffitt's (1993) work, which states that juvenile conduct disturbance may be either limited to adolescence or part of a life-course pattern of antisocial behavior. Some research suggests that of youths who have committed a violent crime before age 18, only about 20%–30% are arrested for a violent act in adulthood (Elliott, Huizinga, & Morse, 1986) and that a small percentage of persistent offenders commit a majority of violent crime (Tolan & Gorman-Smith, 1998).

With respect to familial factors that may serve as risk factors for violence in children and adolescents, the issue of parental criminality has been examined. There is less support for a genetic basis to violent behavior, whereas the genetic loading for criminality is somewhat stronger for property offenses (Raine, 1993). However, violent behavior may be learned, and the transmission of violent norms in families through the witnessing of violence has been supported (Hawkins, Herrenkohl, et al., 1998). Other familial factors that have been associated with, but are not necessarily causally related to, violence include a history of childhood maltreatment (Lewis, 1992), a history of maladjustment in childhood (Quinsey et al., 1998), disruptive and chaotic family relationships, and early separation from parents or leaving the family home before age 16 (Hawkins, Herrenkohl, et al., 1998; Quinsey et al., 1998).

School and educational factors have also been examined with respect to their relationship to violence potential. A history of academic failure, truancy, and dropping out of school all have been associated with higher rates of delinquency and self-reported violence in adolescence (Farrington, 1989; Hawkins, Herrenkohl, et al., 1998; Quinsey et al., 1998). Moreover, intellectual and academic impairment are related to acting-out. Loeber (1990) noted that intellectual limitations are associated with an increased likelihood that a youth will become involved in a delinquent peer group and that learning disabilities and language disorders are more frequent among young people who engage in criminal behavior (Raine, 1993) or commit homicide (Myers & Mutch, 1992).

Other social and environmental factors are associated with violence potential in younger individuals. Hawkins, Herrenkohl, and colleagues (1998) noted that youths who have a peer group that endorses violence, are members of gangs, abuse drugs and alcohol, and are exposed to violence at a young age, particularly in the home, are more likely to engage in violence.

Some research suggests that a relationship exists between risk for violence and video game violence and aggression. Dill and Dill (1998) noted that exposure to violent media such as television, movies, and video games increase aggression and violent behavior in children and adolescents. One of the primary mechanisms is weakened inhibition and greater justification for aggression that occurs as a result of exposure to violence in the media. That is, young people increase their acceptance of violence as an appropriate means of expression by altering their perception as to what is normal and acceptable behavior through exposure to violent media. Similarly, children and adolescents who have violent fantasies and interests may modify their own sense of what is normal aggression when they are able to share their fantasies with peers who hold similar beliefs about violence. Although media violence is not always a direct cause of violence, it may serve as a catalyst in some cases.

The PCL–R (Hare, 1991) has demonstrated very good predictive validity for violent recidivism among adult criminal offenders. Forth, Hart, and Hare (1990) adopted, with good results, a modified version of the PCL–R for use with juvenile offenders. Moreover, Frick, O'Brian, Wootton, and McBurnett (1994) showed that the PCL–R differentiates juvenile offenders who are psychopathic from those who do not have attachment and empathy deficiencies. Therefore, psychopathy is an important variable that should be considered when evaluating violence potential in younger individuals.

Grisso (1998) also offered a number of factors that are important to consider when assessing general risk for harm to others among youthful offenders:

- substance abuse and its effect on the person's behavior
- peer contacts and supports
- family conflict, aggression, and attitudes toward violence
- social stressors and supports
- personality traits such as psychopathy, impulsivity, and anger
- the presence of mental disorders such as depression, ADHD, or psychosis
- prior history of abuse or trauma
- neurological disturbances
- responses to psychiatric treatment
- situational factors such as planning and opportunity for violence, the youth's residence, and resiliency factors.

With respect to resiliency factors, an important but often overlooked concept in risk assessment, Witt and Dyer (1997) reviewed some factors that may serve as protective or risk reducing variables:

- stable and adequate self-esteem
- resilient temperament
- positive social attitudes and disposition
- the capacity for healthy attachment and bonding
- stable and accessible social supports such as parents, positive peer influences, and teachers
- good academic achievement
- the child's attachment to parents.

The research on risk for violence among children and adolescents has not focused on the development of actuarial equations that dictate how these various risk enhancing and risk reducing factors can be weighed or combined. As such, Grisso (1998) summarized the assessment of violence risk in younger individuals as follows:

> Until actuarial base rates are available, however, risk estimates will have to be based on systematic clinical logic that uses . . . risk factors. . . . Reports and testimony about these estimates *must provide a complete description of the data and logic on which they are based.* (pp. 156–157, emphasis in the original)

This approach appears to be the most prudent and reasonable at this time.

Research on Stalking and Violence

When analyzing the rate of violence in stalking cases, it is important to draw a distinction between threats of violence and actual violent behavior. *Threats* are "written or oral communication[s] that implicitly or explicitly state a wish or intent to damage, injure, or kill the target" (Meloy, 1999b, p. 90). Threats may also include indications of potential for harm or violence, without necessarily a direct communication being made. *Violence,* on the other hand, is intentional behavior that results, or is highly likely to result, in injury to the victim. Therefore, someone can make a threat without any true intention of engaging in the threatened action, whereas someone can commit violence against another person without having made a threat. As such, it is important to distinguish between the making of a threat and the posing of a threat (Borum, Fein, Vossekuil, & Berglund, 1999; Fein & Vossekuil, 1999).

The rate of threatening communications in adult stalking cases ranges from about 50% to 75% (Meloy, 1999b). These threats may involve *instrumental threats,* in which the person wants to intimidate or control the victim, or *expressive threats,* in which the person regulates or expresses emotion through the threat (Meloy, in press). In a small sample of child and adolescent obsessional followers, McCann (2000) found that the frequency of threats was just over 50% and similar to the rate of threats observed in adult samples. Likewise, both instrumental and expressive threats have been observed in adolescents. In one case reported by McCann (1998c), a teenager threatened to kill his parents because he saw them as preventing him from gaining access to his girlfriend, who had recently broken up with him and had taken out an order of protection because of his stalking behavior. This youth was attempting to intimidate his parents into backing down in their efforts to control him, despite the fact that they were actually trying to keep their son from violating a court order and facing possible incarceration. Another case involving an adolescent evaluated in a juvenile detention facility involved an expressive threat. The youth had developed an intense and volatile fixation on a staff member who the youth viewed as controlling. During a verbal exchange in which the staff member confronted the youth's behavior and made a verbal request, the teenager verbally exploded, saying "I'm gonna mess you up." There was never any violence following this exchange, and the youth later admitted that he became extremely angry and was merely expressing his rage at that moment. It is important to note, however, that expressive threats do not necessarily imply a lower risk for violence, because there is no research on the rate of violence for instrumental and expressive threateners.

There is also no research on the relationship between threats and subsequent violence among children and adolescents. However, research on adult samples suggests that there may be little association between threatening statements and violence. A negative correlation was found between threats and approach behavior among individuals who threatened a member of the U.S. Congress (Dietz, Matthews, Martell et. al, 1991), and no correlation was found between threats and approach behavior among individuals who contacted Hollywood celebrities (Dietz, Matthews, van Duyne et al., 1991). Likewise, in their study of assassins and near-lethal approachers, Fein and Vossekuil (1999) found that very few assassins made direct threats to the target or communicated threats to law enforcement. Together these research findings suggest that to avoid apprehension or interference, individuals who are intent on committing an act of violence against their target may not communicate their intentions to the victim.

Despite the ambiguity of an association between threatening communications and violence, there may be indirect evidence of violence potential or threats with an intent to harm that are veiled and not clearly evident to the victim. In fact, Fein and Vossekuil (1999) noted that some violent attackers communicate their plans for violence to third parties. One recent case that received considerable media attention was the 1999 mass killing at Columbine High School in Littleton, Colorado. The two teenage perpetrators in that case had reportedly spent a considerable amount of time before the shooting constructing pipe bombs, and speculation was rampant that they must have had assistance with planning and perpetrating the offense. In addition, there were other indirect communications of plans for the assault such as an alleged videotape that was made one year prior to the offense in which a mock shooting was made for a class project. In the aftermath of such acts of violence, law enforcement officials search for other evidence that may reveal pre-offense planning such as journals and diaries, e-mail messages; and access to web sites involving themes of violence, murder, bomb-making, and terrorism.

The importance of these issues for the assessment of violence potential in stalking cases involving young offenders should not be minimized. Although the retrospective reconstruction of risk factors for violence does not produce reliable predictors of violence given the potential for hindsight bias, it can provide valuable clues that direct the assessment process in future cases. When evaluating a child or adolescent who manifests an unusual fixation or who engages in obsessional following, indirect clues to the potential for violence should be explored. These indirect clues can be assessed in several ways. One source of information includes other individuals who know the person being assessed, including parents, siblings, and peers. Collateral interviews with these sources can be useful for gaining an understanding of the youth's interests, peer culture, exposure to violence in the media and community, and expressed attitudes about violence. Another important source of information includes the youth's exposure to weapons, including whether he or she owns any guns or if they are available in the home. If the young person has received training in weapons or reads certain books or magazines, this should also be noted. The presence of a weapon, particularly a handgun, in the home creates a heightened risk among young individuals, even if there is no history or concurrent evidence of psychiatric disturbances or emotional upset (Miller & Hemenway, 1999). This risk factor may be mediated by relatively higher levels of impulsivity among children and adolescents; however, evaluating risk for violence in stalking cases should include issues involving access to guns. If present in the home, a gun's storage should be assessed, including where the gun is kept, whether the gun is stored loaded, whether the ammunition is kept with or separate from the gun, and whether the gun and ammunition are kept locked or unlocked.

Another possible data source for evidence of the potential for violence is the young person's computer use. It is often enlightening to explore the extent to which the youth communicates with others via e-mail, subscribes to specific mailing lists, and visits web sites that have violent or nihilistic themes. If the youth is computer literate and has developed his or her own web site, then asking for the address and reviewing its content may provide important information. In one case, a teenager who was being evaluated for sentencing after a conviction for assault openly discussed his notoriety among peers as a capable "computer pirate" who was able to obtain software and other material that others could not access. Although there was no evidence that the content of this material was of a violent nature, his delight over being able to dupe others was instructive in providing confirmatory evidence of his extreme narcissism, which was a relevant treatment issue. The assault for which he was convicted was precipitated by another youth making a relatively innocuous comment that was construed as an insult. Another case involving a teenage girl revealed that she had a "hit list" published on a personal web page that was intended to evoke humor among her peers. There was minimal evidence of violence potential, and she did not subsequently become violent. In short, assessing issues surrounding computer use and how young individuals access information via computer is a useful area to explore in psychological examinations for indirect evidence of potential threat.

Another issue that is as important as the prevalence of threatening behavior among stalking offenders is the rate of violence. In a review of stalking research, Meloy (1996) found across 10 studies with sufficiently large samples that the frequency of personal violence ranged from 3% to 36% and that most stalkers are not violent. Specifically, 75% of those who threatened did not become violent. The true-positive rate for violence (i.e., those who threatened and subsequently committed violence) ranged from 17% to 32%, with a mean of 25%. The false-positive rate of violence (i.e., those who threatened but did not subsequently become violent) ranged from 68% to 83%, with a mean of 75%. These findings led Meloy (1996) to conclude that "threats may inhibit, disinhibit, or have no relationship to actual violence in any one subject" (p. 158). Therefore, clinicians must assess both the stalking offender's history of threats and their relationship to subsequent violence. In a small sample of child and adolescent obsessional followers, McCann (2000) found a violence base rate of 31%, which falls within the range of reported violence in adult stalking samples.

Despite the fact that most stalking offenders are not subsequently violent, the rate of personal violence is still very high, compared to the base rate of violence in the general population. Therefore, careful attention and assessment of violence potential is required in any particular stalking case. Meloy (1996) also found in his review of stalking research that violence in stalking cases is generally physical assault and battery without the use of a weapon; common violent acts include grabbing, punching, and fondling the victim. The sample studied by McCann (2000) was too small to draw any firm conclusions about the type of violence in stalking cases involving children and adolescents; only four cases were found in which violence occurred, with three involving physical assault of the victim and one involving an attack with a knife. More research is needed on the prevalence of violence in juvenile stalking cases, as well as on the types of violent acts perpetrated in these cases.

Another variable to consider when evaluating the potential for violence in stalking cases involves the object of the violence. Although 80% of the time the violence is directed at the stalking victim, 20% of the time or less the violence is directed at a third party (Meloy, 1996). Triangulation can occur in stalking cases whereby the perpetrator comes to perceive that other individuals are preventing or hindering access to the victim (Meloy, 1999a). This factor may raise the risk for violence, particularly if the belief of hindered access by third parties becomes delusional and the third party is believed to be part of a conspiracy to keep the object unavailable (Meloy, 1999b). As such, third parties such as attorneys, co-workers, law enforcement officials, or new intimate partners may be at heightened risk for being victims of violence if triangulation exists. Violence directed at third parties that stems from triangulation among perpetrator, victim, and a third party believed to be hindering access to the victim should be considered and evaluated when relevant in juvenile stalking cases.

Violence involving destruction or damage to property has also been identified as significant in stalking cases, particularly emotionally spurred aggression toward a symbolic or important object of the victim that is intended to evoke fear, fright, or feelings of invasion in the victim (Meloy, 1999b). The issue of property damage in stalking cases involving children and adolescents has not been studied. However, it appears to be a common experience of students to have property damaged or stolen for various reasons, not necessarily as part of a pattern of stalking. Kingery, Coggeshall, and Alford (1998) reported that about 40%–45% of the young men and about 20%–30% of the young women in high schools reported having had property damaged or stolen at school within a 12-month period. It remains unclear the percentage of these cases that may have involved a pattern of obsessional harassment or following.

There have been other empirical findings on the effect of specific variables on the relationship between violence and stalking. Zona, Sharma, and Lane (1993) found that simple obsessional followers, those who had a prior intimate relationship with the victim, were more likely to be violent. Violence in these cases usually stemmed from the perpetrators' feelings of having been mistreated by the victim. Meloy, Davis, and Lovette (in press) found that the existence of a prior sexually intimate relationship between perpetrator and victim was the factor most strongly predictive of violence in stalking cases. However, Harmon, Rosner, and Owens (1998) found that obsessional harassers who were non-romantically motivated were as likely to be violent as were romantically motivated harassers, including those who felt persecuted. In addition, Harmon and colleagues identified clinical variables that were correlated with violent behavior in stalking cases. The co-morbid presence of a personality disorder and substance abuse, an Axis I clinical syndrome and substance abuse, and substance abuse alone were all associated with high levels of violence.

In another study on risk factors for violence in erotomania, Menzies, Fedoroff, Green, and Isaacson (1995) found that two variables predicted dangerous behavior: multiple object fixations and a history of serious antisocial or criminal behavior. These findings, along with those reported by Harmon and colleagues (1998), suggest that many risk factors for violence in stalking cases are similar to those that are related to violence in general (Meloy, 1998b). However, the findings by Menzies and colleagues that multiple object fixations is predictive of violence in erotomania is interesting. Urbach, Khalily, and Mitchell (1992) reported on a case of erotomania in an adolescent that involved multiple object fixations; this teenager also engaged in at least one act of violence. Also, McCann (1998c, 2000) noted that greater identity diffusion and uncertainty about one's self in adolescence may result in a relatively greater propensity for young stalking offenders to develop multiple or changeable object fixations. Whether or not this is supported empirically remains to be determined, but the relationship between multiple object fixations and violence in juvenile stalking offenders needs to be studied more closely.

Because many risk factors for violence in stalking cases appear to be similar to those associated with violence in general, risk assessment of the child and adolescent stalking offender should include factors commonly associated with violence risk in this age group (these factors were discussed previously). In addition, careful analysis of the case dynamics, including perpetrator–victim relationships, the content of threats that have been made, any use of weapons, substance abuse, prior history of violence, and general clinical risk factors for violence, should be carried out. The approaches to risk assessment outlined by Witt and Dyer (1997) and Grisso (1998) discussed earlier are useful models to follow in stalking cases involving young perpetrators.

Stalking and Juvenile Homicide

A major concern when evaluating the potential for violence is the severity of a violent act, including the extent of harm that is done to the victim. Among the most severe acts of violence are those involving physical injury, torture, and murder. Because stalking and obsessional following involve the perception of threat or harm by the victim, the actual risk of homicide is an important assessment issue in those stalking cases that involve particularly chronic and aggressive forms of stalking. In a comprehensive review of the empirical literature on stalking in adults, Meloy (1996) found that the rate of completed homicides in stalking cases is relatively low at less than 2%. Although Farnham et al. (2000) reported that 5 out of 50 stalking offenders (10%) committed murder, their sample had a bias toward more serious stalking offenders and may therefore overestimate the rate of homicide in stalking cases. As Fein and Vossekuil (1999) noted, however, the research on stalking and homicide is somewhat hampered in that most research on stalking provides demographic and clinical characteristics of those persons who have been charged with stalking; however, this sample is not necessarily revealing of the characteristics of those who stalk and later attack and kill their victim. In stalking cases involving lethal violence, the perpetrator is likely to be charged with murder rather than with stalking. Fein and Vossekuil recommended that stalking researchers take a behavior-based approach to studying homicide and stalking by looking at the behaviors, cognitions, and situational factors that led to an attack on the victim.

The apparent infrequency of homicide in adult stalking cases must be considered within the context of recent data on the prevalence of homicide among juvenile offenders. From 1987 to 1991, the arrest rate for murder among juvenile offenders increased by 90% and has remained constant since 1991 (Farrington & Loeber, 1998). Moreover, juvenile homicide rates vary as a function of several variables such as gender and race of the offender (Hawkins, Laub, & Lauritsen, 1998), as well as whether or not the offender is considered a chronic offender. In fact, Loeber, Farrington, and Waschbush (1998) reviewed several studies and found that chronic juvenile offenders, although they comprise a smaller portion of juvenile offenders, account for anywhere from 50% to 73% of all homicides and that most juvenile homicides are concentrated in inner cities and metropolitan areas. Cornell (1993) noted that from 1984 to 1991, homicide among children and adolescents increased 200% for those homicides that were committed during the course of another crime and increased 83% for homicides committed in the course of some interpersonal conflict. Likewise, young homicide offenders were more likely than adult offenders to use a handgun and to act with an accomplice. Although homicide among children and adolescents has leveled off in the past several years, it appears that isolated homicides that might take place in the context of stalking in an adolescent relationship are relatively rare occurrences, as they are in adult cases. This conclusion is based on the fact that most juvenile homicides are perpetrated by chronic juvenile offenders who have long-standing conduct problems and an antisocial lifestyle. Despite the apparent infrequency of homicides in juvenile stalking cases, homicide can result in some cases of stalking involving children and adolescents. In fact, Heide (1999) noted that homicide could occur within the context of dating relationships that become violent. Although it is unclear how often stalking leads to homicide in cases of dating violence, research in this area may be limited for reasons similar to those raised by Fein and Vossekuil (1999) whereby pre-offense behavior such as stalking is overlooked in lethal crimes.

One typology of homicide among young offenders includes three major groups of homicides (Cornell, Benedek, & Benedek, 1987a, 1987b). The first and rarest type is the psychotic homicide offender, which is characterized by adolescents who were psychotic at the time of the murder. The second type is the conflict perpetrator, which is found in cases where an adolescent had a personal argument or dispute with the victim. A third type is the crime subtype in which the adolescent commits the homicide during the course of another offense such as burglary or rape. Cornell and his colleagues have found empirical support for this typology. The subtype most relevant to stalking cases would be conflict perpetrators in which the juvenile homicide offender has some dispute with the victim. Cornell and colleagues (1987b) found that conflict adolescent homicide offenders most often murder family members or acquaintances, act alone, almost always use a weapon (usually a gun), and are less likely to be intoxicated than other types of young homicide offenders. Interestingly, Heide (1993) found that young homicide offenders who kill parents use a weapon in a manner consistent with a physical-strength hypothesis. That is, where there is a greater discrepancy in perceived physical strength between the young homicide offender and his or her victim, there is a greater likelihood of the use of weapons that are more lethal, such as rifles and handguns. If one extrapolates from these findings, a useful variable to consider when evaluating the potential for lethal violence in young stalking offenders would be the perpetrator's perception of relative strength or weakness of the victim.

It is also important to draw a distinction between many of the school-based shootings that have occurred over the past several years and homicides in stalking cases. As noted earlier, the term *stalking* has sometimes been used to describe the pre-offense behavior of the perpetrator in school shootings cases. However, this use of the term generally refers to lying in wait or a similar act of predation and thus reflects the colloquial meaning rather than the legal meaning of *stalking*. School shooting perpetrators are generally motivated by revenge, and they typically fantasize about the offense in advance of the attack (McGee & DeBernardo, 1999). In addition, nearly all of the school-based shootings have been perpetrated by adolescents who obtained a weapon, typically a rifle or handgun, from the home, and the attacks were premeditated, very lethal, and often maximized the element of surprise (McGee & DeBernardo, 1999). Stalking cases typically involve a variety of motives, and the perpetrator generally seeks to evoke fear in the victim. Nevertheless, the difference between colloquial uses of the term *stalking,* as in school-based shooting cases, and formal legal or behavioral science definitions is important to keep in mind.

In an analysis of various types of juvenile homicide offenses using the typology developed at the Federal Bureau of Investigation's National Center for the Analysis of a Violent Crime and outlined in the *Crime Classification Manual* (Douglas, Burgess, Burgess, & Ressler, 1992), Myers, Scott, Burgess, and Burgess (1995) classified 25 juvenile homicide offenders. Most of the cases (64%) were characterized as personal cause murders, as opposed to criminal enterprise (36%) murders. The most common form of personal cause juvenile homicide was sexual homicide; this finding suggests some bias in case selection given the fact that sexual homicide is relatively rare among juveniles who commit murder (Myers, Burgess, & Nelson, 1998). Because the risk of violence is greater in adult stalking cases in which there has been a prior intimate relationship between the victim and perpetrator, the role of sexual motives must be considered as a potential factor when attempting to identify risk for homicide in cases in which adolescents are involved. There is evidence from published case reports that stalking behavior is present in some cases of juvenile sexual homicide. However, it should be noted that the presence of a relationship between stalking and sexual homicide in adolescents does not necessarily imply that young stalking offenders are at higher risk for homicide. Rather, the data suggest that in at least some cases of juvenile sexual homicide (Myers, 1994), stalking behavior is one form of pre-offense behavior for some perpetrators.

According to Ressler, Burgess, and Douglas (1988), *sexual homicides* are "murders with evidence or observations that indicate that the murder was sexual in nature" (p. xiii). This evidence can be any aspect of the offense, including "victim attire or lack of attire; exposure of the sexual parts of the victim's body; sexual positioning of the victim's body; insertion of foreign objects into the victim's body cavities; evidence of sexual intercourse (oral, anal, vaginal); and evidence of substitute sexual activity, interest or sadistic fantasy" (p. xiii). Moreover, Ressler and his colleagues outlined a motivational model of sexual homicide that involves five major components that interact with one another. The first of these factors is the offender's social environment, in which early family relationships are characterized by parental failure whereby the child is ignored or unprotected and fails to develop healthy attachments. This factor is particularly significant because, as noted earlier, early failure in developing healthy attachments has been identified as a risk factor for stalking. The second factor is the occurrence of specific formative events in childhood and adolescence, namely early trauma such as physical or sexual abuse, developmental failures such as poor social attachments or poor emotional response, and exposure to deviant or poor role models. A third factor is the development of patterned behavioral responses that include specific personality traits such as aggressiveness, narcissism, or social isolation and specific cognitive-processing mechanisms such as excessive reliance on fantasy as a means of managing conflict and tension in one's life. Another maladaptive cognitive-processing mechanism is fixed beliefs and generalizations about life that are dominated by themes of violence, power, or sadism. The fourth factor is the presence of fixed patterns of acting toward others and one's self that are characterized by cruelty, severe conduct disturbances, and gradual progression to more severe sexual acting out. Finally, the fifth factor is a feedback filter in which the sexual murderer justifies his or her behavior and filters out errors or mistakes to protect disturbed fantasies, which results in an increase in knowledge about how to avoid punishment and detection; this information then feeds back into the offender's fantasy life and fuels aggressive and violent sexual fantasy.

According to Ewing (1990), it is difficult to determine the percentage of juvenile homicides that are sexual in nature because crime statistics often do not distinguish between sexual and nonsexual homicides. Also, sexual aspects of some homicides may go unreported or the sexual dynamics of some homicides may not be recognized during the investigation. In fact, Myers and colleagues (1998) studied a group of juveniles who committed sexual murders from the correctional system in one state over a 72-month period and identified 14 offenders out of 1,500 juvenile murderers who entered the system during the period of study. These researchers concluded that slightly less than 1% of all juvenile murders are sexual in nature. Myers and his colleagues noted that their figure was comparable to the national figure of about 0.5% of all adult homicides that are considered to be sexual in nature. However, these researchers echoed the observations made by Ewing (1990) that some sexual homicides go undetected or are misidentified as nonsexual because investigators may fail to recognize or even consider sexual attributes of a crime scene.

With respect to stalking and obsessional following, there is evidence in the literature that in some cases juvenile sexual homicide may occur after a course of stalking by the perpetrator. It is important to note, however, that juvenile sexual homicide appears to be rare. In one study of developmental antecedents of serial sexual homicide, Johnson and Becker (1997) identified nine adolescents who had clinically significant fantasies of becoming a serial killer. One of the nine adolescents studied (11% of the sample) was a 14-year-old White male who began stalking a female peer by following her home, stole her undergarments by befriending the girl's mother to gain entrance to the home, and referred to the girl as his girlfriend despite her requests that he not follow her. Although this boy had not actually killed anyone, he entertained fantasies of killing several people by strangulation or intentionally breaking bones in his victims until they died. Myers and his colleagues (1998) provided data on 14 adolescent perpetrators of sexual homicide in which one case (7% of the sample) involved two boys who had persistently followed and pursued a female peer with whom they were acquainted. The two boys repeatedly tried to convince the girl to go out with them until she acquiesced and agreed to go with them to a fictitious party. Instead, the boys took her to a remote area, savagely attacked her, and left her to die, as they were too anxious to follow through with the sexual attack. Moreover, these two boys had discussed raping and killing another person for years and planned the homicide together.

These two studies by Johnson and Becker (1997) and Myers and colleagues (1998) illustrate that stalking or obsessional following is relatively infrequent in juvenile sexual homicide cases. Moreover, given that sexual homicides among juveniles are rather rare, there is limited data on the degree of risk for homicide that exists in stalking cases involving children and adolescents. Nevertheless, the research appears to suggest some interesting dynamics that may be considered when appraising the level of risk for homicide in cases of stalking involving young obsessional followers. Specifically, it must be noted that the one case of stalking reported by Johnson and Becker (1997) involved a youth who had fantasies of a violent and sexual nature; however, he had not yet engaged in any violence toward humans, although he had been violent toward animals. In the case discussed by Myers and colleagues (1998), it is interesting to note that obsessional following of the victim was carried out by two followers, not one. Traditionally, stalking and obsessional following have been conceptualized as involving a pattern of threat or harassment toward a specific individual that is carried out by one person. However, some cases of obsessional following or stalking perpetrated by young people may possibly involve one or more individuals operating together. It remains unclear if this phenomenon is confined to younger obsessional followers. However, the case example reported by Myers and colleagues (1998) revealed that two boys who obsessionally followed a female peer ultimately acted out their sexual fantasies after a period of intense pursuit, in contrast to the case reported by Johnson and Becker (1997) in which one youth engaged in stalking and had sexually violent fantasies on which he had not yet acted.

The implication of these findings for the evaluation of homicide risk in cases of stalking among children and adolescents are as follows. Because stalking is driven in part by fantasies of having an idealized, special, or destined relationship with the victim (Meloy, 1996, 1998b) and because the risk for violence in stalking cases is greater in cases in which there has been a prior intimate or sexual relationship between victim and perpetrator (Meloy, 1998b), a key factor in determining risk is whether the obsessional follower will act on his or her fantasies when there are dominant themes of revenge, sexual sadism, or aggressive control that are associated with sexual attraction. When obsessional following occurs in cases in which there are two or more pursuers who each share a similar fantasy or motivation for following the victim, there is a greater likelihood that the youth will openly share and discuss his or her fantasies with another person. Moreover, the acceptance of these unusual or bizarre fantasies as an appropriate means of expression will increase, regardless of how inappropriate they are, because they receive validation from a peer. Thus, when there are two or more youths who are concurrently involved in pursuing and following a particular victim, there may be a heightened risk for violence if the youths share similar violent fantasies that provide some of the motivation for their pursuit. When a juvenile obsessional follower is acting alone, he or she may have no outlet to discuss and explore violent fantasies, which may create psychological tension and conflict, but there may be some anxiety about acting on these fantasies if they have not received external validation.

Of course, having no outlet for one's fantasies does not preclude their expression. However, when a child or adolescent has unusual sexual fantasies or bizarre concepts about interpersonal relationships and attachments, he or she may be at increased risk for acting on those fantasies if they receive external validation from a peer who has similar propensities for violence.

CONCLUSION

Despite the fact that little empirical or clinical data are available on the prevalence and characteristics of violent behavior that occurs in stalking cases involving children and adolescents, the seriousness of violence necessitates a discussion of these issues. This chapter reviewed general issues involved in the clinical assessment of violence risk and various risk factors that have been identified among youthful offenders. In addition, research on stalking and violence in adult samples was discussed in terms of its relevance to stalking cases involving children and adolescents. Moreover, general issues related to juvenile homicide were also discussed. Although some anecdotal evidence suggests that stalking occurs in some of the rare cases of sexual homicide committed by adolescents, empirical evidence is lacking.

Several issues may have hampered efforts to study the relationship between stalking and violence among children and adolescents. These issues include the lack of attention to the social problem of stalking by younger people, the tendency to focus on violent acts (e.g. assault, murder) to the exclusion of pre-offense behaviors such as stalking, the tendency to misidentify predatory lying in wait as stalking, or the tendency to misclassify genuine stalking as a different form of behavior. Clearer behavioral definitions and improvements in the methods for identifying stalking in younger people may lead to better research efforts at examining the relationship between stalking and violence, particularly in younger age groups. Until such research becomes available and provides specialized information, general approaches to risk assessment in young offenders and extrapolation from research on violence in adult stalking offenders will assist in the clinical and forensic assessment of young stalking offenders.

7

The Impact on Victims

T he popular literature on stalking is scattered with examples of cases in which victims have sought assistance from various agencies, only to be met with frustration (Snow, 1998). For instance, some stalking victims have encountered skepticism from law enforcement officials and have often been told that little could be done until the perpetrator "does something violent," at which point an arrest could be made. Such an approach offers little solace to the victim of stalking, because it communicates the view that he or she must be assaulted or physically injured before any legal action can be taken. Moreover, although many stalking victims seek the services of an attorney to file a civil order of protection to prohibit further contact with the stalker, disillusionment can result if violations of these orders do not result in strict sanctions by the courts. In addition, stalking victims may seek the services of a mental health professional to cope with the emotional distress that can result from chronic harassment and stalking. However, therapeutic interventions, although supportive, may leave the victim feeling isolated in having to face threats and harassment alone.

The frustration that stalking victims encounter when seeking assistance from legal and mental health professionals stems from a number of sources. One reason professionals may appear to be unresponsive is that myths and misinformation about stalking often exist. For example, my own experiences in forensic settings have revealed that individuals who are charged with harassment or stalking are often referred for evaluations of competency to stand trial because the nature of the offense raises immediate suspicions that the defendant has a mental illness or is incapacitated. Although this may be true for some stalking offenders, most are not actively psychotic (Meloy, 1998b). Another reason professionals may be perceived as unresponsive by stalking victims is that some professionals may be uninformed of the level of seriousness or severity that threatening and harassing behaviors can take in many stalking cases. Because legislation on stalking is relatively new, some attorneys and mental health professionals may be unfamiliar with the legal issues involved in these cases. For instance, I have consulted in cases in which one spouse has persistently harassed the other spouse. An attorney will occasionally conceptualize violations of an order of protection in these cases as instances in which both perpetrator and victim provoke one another. Although this may be occasionally true, stalking often involves chronic, severe, and aggressive threatening behavior, and violations of civil orders of protections typically reflect the perpetrator's intent on controlling all aspects of the victim's life regardless of the legal consequences.

When attempting to understand the unique needs and responses of child or adolescent victims of stalking, there are additional developmental considerations that must be observed. Basic patterns of victimization among children and adolescents vary as a function of age and social relationships. According to Tolan and Guerra (1998), children younger than age 12 are more frequently victimized by adults, whereas adolescents between ages 12 and 19 are less likely to be victimized by adults but are more likely to be victimized by other youths. More specifically, children younger than 12 are more likely to be the victims of child abuse, whereas adolescents are more often victims of a violent crime perpetrated by another teenager. As a group, however, children and adolescents are at an elevated risk for violence overall. According to data reported by Tolan and Guerra, children and adolescents constitute approximately 10% of the general population but make up about 23% of violent crime victims. As noted in the previous chapter, although most stalking offenders are not violent, there is a very high level of threatening behavior that is likely to cause severe emotional and psychological distress in victims.

Stalking research has only recently begun to address the issue of how victims are affected by chronic and repetitive forms of harassment. A very small portion of this research provides some insight into the impact that stalking can have on child and adolescent victims. For instance, victim response patterns have been examined in research samples that have included some adolescent victims. Additionally, research on victim responses to other forms of obsessional harassment, such as bullying and sexual harassment, provides insight into how young victims of stalking are likely to respond.

In this chapter, general principles on how stalking may affect child and adolescent victims are reviewed. The first topic to be discussed is a specific pattern of stalking in which an adult obsessionally follows a child or teenage victim. The issue of adults who stalk or sexually exploit children is a useful starting point because it introduces relevant issues related to the victimization of children and adolescents in criminal cases. This issue raises once again the need for proper terminology, as some of these cases call for stalking to be differentiated from predatory forms of behavior that may not necessarily meet the legal definition of stalking. A second general topic to be discussed is the psychological impact of stalking on child and adolescent victims. Specific research is reviewed on victim responses to stalking, and developmental considerations are outlined to highlight similarities and differences between adult and young stalking victims. Following this discussion, general assessment and treatment issues are presented to assist clinicians who provide mental health services to child and adolescent victims of stalking.

ADULTS WHO STALK CHILDREN AND ADOLESCENTS

Stalking cases may involve many different victim–perpetrator relationships, but one unique pattern consists of an adult who repeatedly harasses or follows a child victim. One well-publicized case from Michigan illustrates some of the challenges raised when an adult stalks a younger victim. In 1996, a 25-year-old man was accused of making numerous obscene and harassing telephone calls to high school girls whose pictures he had seen in the local newspaper (Fracassa, 1996a, 1996b). One victim had been stalked over a period of 2 years, and in another case the victim experienced extreme fear and her parents were outraged that the man was able to continue making obscene telephone calls to their daughter. The perpetrator had a prior conviction for misdemeanor stalking that had been omitted from his criminal record due to a clerical error; once the error was discovered, he faced more serious charges of aggravated stalking. What is particularly egregious in this case is that the perpetrator continued to make harassing telephone calls while incarcerated in the county jail, resulting in the suspension of his telephone privileges. He was ultimately sentenced to $2^{1}/_{2}$ to 5 years in prison after entering a plea of guilty to 6 counts of aggravated stalking. This case prompted the Michigan legislature to amend its stalking statute to make the stalking of a person younger than 18 a felony on the first offense (Pardo, 1997).

This case is a fairly clear example of stalking by an adult that is directed toward a teenage victim. Moreover, although stalking is a serious criminal behavior, there is likely to be a more rapid legal response when the victim is a minor because there tends to be a greater presumption of serious psychopathology on the part of the perpetrator in such cases. This presumption may be warranted, depending on the specific dynamics of the case. Some stalking cases in which both perpetrator and victim are adults involve very serious personality disturbances or clinical symptomatology in the perpetrator. Yet, when a stalking case involves an adult perpetrator and a child victim, the motivational basis for the stalking must be closely examined. Because many stalking offenders are motivated by a need to control, dominate, or exclusively possess the object, there are likely to be more serious social inadequacies and inappropriate sexual interests (e.g., paraphilias) that are cause for concern when the object of fixation is a child or adolescent. However, it is important to draw a distinction between those cases of stalking where an adult obsessionally follows a child and those cases involving a crime other than stalking that is perpetrated against the child by an adult.

The prototypic cases involving offenses other than stalking in which an adult victimizes a child, and yet in which the term *stalking* is often used to describe the behavior of the perpetrator, are those involving sexual offenses against children. On the heels of a wave of anti-stalking legislation that was passed in the United States in the early 1990s, significant legislation was passed that addressed the issue of sexual offenses directed against children. The first major type of legislation was sex offender registration and community notification laws that fall under the general rubric of "Megan's Law." In New York, for example, the state corrections law was amended in 1995 for the purpose of requiring convicted sex offenders to register and report changes of address to the New York State Division of Criminal Justice Services (Sex Offender Registration Act, 1995). The statute was not intended to be punitive to sex offenders; rather, it was implemented to regulate information on the whereabouts of sex offenders in the community (Greenberg, 1996). Nevertheless, the statute provides for varying levels of risk that may be assigned to sex offenders, and certain limited information about a sex offender may be released to the public when the offender is deemed to be a serious threat.

A second form of sex offender legislation stems from the U.S. Supreme Court decision outlined in *Kansas v. Hendricks* (1997). The issues in this case concerned the constitutionality of Kansas's Sexually Violent Predatory Law (1994) which established procedures whereby the state could civilly commit individuals who were deemed to have a mental abnormality or personality disorder that made it highly likely that the person would engage in predatory acts of sexual violence in the future. Most significant was the fact that the Kansas statute permitted individuals to be committed after they had served their entire criminal sentence. The offender in the case, Leroy Hendricks, had been convicted of sexual offenses involving two 13-year-old boys and had served almost 10 years in state prison. When the state sought to have him committed as a sexually violent predator, evidence was offered to support the state's position that he should be committed indefinitely. Even Hendricks testified at his hearing that he believed treatment would be worthless and that the only way to ensure that he would not continue sexually abusing children was if he were dead.

The Supreme Court ruled in *Hendricks* that individual states can establish civil commitment procedures for felons who have completed their criminal sentence. The court drew a distinction between criminal and civil procedures in that individuals facing commitment under such statutes had procedural safeguards, such as more frequent judicial reviews of their case, to protect their individual rights. This landmark decision has been the subject of much scholarly analysis, and the various competing interests have been debated, including the need for public safety and the civil rights of the individual offender (Cornwell, 1998; Janus, 1998; McAllister, 1998; Morse, 1998; Schopp, 1998). Regardless of the specific issues raised in this debate, the *Hendricks* decision is significant in that it points to a growing trend toward indefinitely confining potentially dangerous individuals .

Both community notification and dangerous sex offender commitment legislation are significant because they point to a growing legal movement to increase protections that are afforded children in society. The relevance of this legislation to the topic of adults who stalk children is that increased public awareness about adults who prey on children for sexual gratification has often included discussions on the various precautions that parents, teachers, and others responsible for the care of children can take to prevent sexual victimization of children. Consequently, it is not uncommon to hear about pedophiles who "stalk," or groom, children by using various manipulative ploys to gain the trust of a vulnerable child. It is possible that an adult who develops a disturbed fixation on a child may have pedophilic interests. However, it is also important to draw a distinction between stalking and predatory acts that are part of a *modus operandi* that precede a sexual assault. This distinction was discussed in chapter 1; *stalking* involves repetitive acts of threatening or harassing behavior that are intended to evoke fear in the victim, whereas *predatory aggression* is generally subtle or clandestine and seeks to heighten the element of surprise before an act of violence. With respect to adults who stalk children, a meaningful distinction appears to exist between those who stalk for the purpose of controlling the victim and those who manipulate their victims to gain a false sense of trust in order to commit a sexual assault. The former type of offender is likely to have strong narcissistic and obsessive personality features, whereas the latter is likely to harbor pedophilic sexual interests and avoidant or schizoid personality traits that reflect underlying social inadequacies. Although both types of offenders pose a danger to children, the underlying patterns and motives of victimization are different.

The personality dynamics of many adult stalking offenders who select children as their primary victim are likely to include prominent obsessive and narcissistic disturbances, extremely poor age-appropriate social skills, and strong needs for control and personal mastery. An obsessive preoccupation with a young victim represents an object fixation that provides an unusual and highly disturbed source of narcissistic gratification. The young victim tends to be viewed as an object to be possessed and in more serious cases, complete control or destruction of the object will be seen by the obsessional follower as the only way to truly possess it (Badcock, 1997). Selection of a younger victim who becomes the sole focus of the obsessional follower's thoughts and fantasies creates a strong and very serious bond with the victim from the perspective of the pursuer. Because children are often perceived as and frequently are more vulnerable, naive, and easily influenced by others in authority, young people may be prime targets for those obsessional followers who are particularly inept in social relationships and cannot relate well to other adults. Badcock (1997) noted that offenders who narrowly direct their fixation on a specific object are attempting to increase the level of their feelings of self-efficacy, which gives them a greater sense of purpose and self-assurance. He also cited a case study involving an adult male who stalked teenage boys as a way of restoring and maintaining a narcissistic equilibrium. In short, the adult stalking offender who targets young victims is likely to have severe personality disturbances with obsessive and narcissistic traits, as well as schizoid or avoidant features. Of course, psychosexual disturbances involving inappropriate or unusual sexual interests and arousal patterns should also be considered in these cases.

PSYCHOLOGICAL IMPACT OF STALKING

The adverse consequences of stalking can vary in intensity and severity as a function of many different factors. Specifically, the length of time the harassment endures, the nature of the threats that are made, and the personality traits or individual vulnerabilities of the victim are a few of the factors that determine the nature and extent of psychological injury. One study of stalking victims found that 37% met criteria for posttraumatic stress disorder (PTSD), and another 18% had diagnostic features of PTSD but did not meet formal criteria for the disorder (Pathe & Mullen, 1997). This study concluded that a significant social and psychological injury occurs in stalking victims and that current legal and mental health responses are inadequate. Additionally, in a national sample of stalking victims, Tjaden (1997) found that there were long-term psychological consequences. About one-third of victims reported having sought psychological treatment as a result of being stalked, and about 20% lost time from work, with 7% never returning to work. Despite the small number of studies on stalking victims, the preliminary results strongly suggest that there are long-term and very serious consequences of stalking.

Victims are likely to seek psychological treatment or legal intervention when there has been an escalation in the frequency or severity of stalking, when some emotional or physical injury has been sustained, or when some relationship or employment difficulties have resulted from being stalked (Roberts & Dziegielewski, 1996). In cases involving a child or adolescent victim, treatment or legal interventions are likely to be sought when harassing behavior escalates and causes concern among parents or school officials or results in significant impairment in the child's or teenager's school functioning.

A few studies have been conducted on samples of college undergraduates or primarily adult samples with a small portion of teenage victims.

In addition, child and adolescents and victims of other forms of obsessional harassment, such as bullying and sexual harassment, have been studied, and this work provides relevant information on how young people are apt to respond to repetitive forms of threatening or harassing behavior.

One of the largest studies of stalking victims is reported by D. M. Hall (1998). She solicited participants nationwide in an effort to better understand how victims are affected. Her sample consisted of 145 stalking victims, of whom 83% were female and 17% were male. Although the victims were primarily adults, 3% of the sample was younger than 18. A large portion of stalking victims reported being less friendly or outgoing and much more cautious and easily startled as a result of being stalked. In addition, stalking victims reported greater levels of suspiciousness and aggressive feelings as a consequence of being stalked:

> Respondents concur that the experience of being stalked for months and even years at a time is akin to psychological terrorism. Their entire lives change. Many move or quit jobs, some change their names, others have gone underground, leaving friends and family behind in order to escape the terror. Several stalking victims changed their appearance by dyeing their hair, gaining weight, and even getting a breast reduction in the hopes that their stalker would not recognize them. (pp. 133–134)

Indeed, these findings indicate that stalking takes a dramatic toll on and severely affects the lives of victims.

In another recent study on the psychological affects of stalking among female undergraduates, Westrup, Fremouw, and Thompson (1999) used objective measures of posttraumatic stress symptomatology, as well as general psychological distress, to measure the adverse effects of stalking. The study compared 36 female college students who reported being the victim of stalking with 43 young women who had been harassed and 48 young women who served as a control group. *Stalking* was defined as intentional and repetitive following, harassing, or threatening behavior directed toward the victim, which was also labeled as "being stalked."

Harassment was defined similarly to stalking, but victims did not label threatening behavior as being stalked. Those individuals who reported being stalked endorsed significantly more symptoms of PTSD, and they also reported more severe symptoms than did those undergraduates who were harassed or in the control group. Moreover, stalking victims reported significantly higher levels of psychological distress, including greater levels of interpersonal sensitivity, depression, and general distress. Results from this study are also interesting in that some participants who reported being the victims of stalking experienced more intrusive and threatening behaviors than did participants who were harassed, suggesting that there are important differences in victim response patterns between those who are stalked and those who are harassed.

Gallagher, Harmon, and Lingenfelter (1994) conducted a survey of chief student affairs officers from two- and four-year colleges in the United States and Canada. Results from their survey revealed that stalking is a growing problem on college campuses. During the 1991–1992 academic year, 57 students were physically injured by obsessional pursuers, and 5 students were killed by the individuals who were stalking them. These figures are difficult to interpret because the study did not report the total number of stalking cases during the academic year studied, and therefore base rates could not be calculated for stalking, physical violence to victims, and homicide. Nevertheless, the data reported by Gallagher and colleagues reveal that in college student populations, lethal violence is a significant concern in stalking cases.

McCreedy and Dennis (1996) provided another study on the effects of stalking in college students. They surveyed 760 students on a southern university campus about their personal experiences with crime. Of the students who reported being the victims of stalking (6.1% of the sample), almost half (46.7%) reported long-lasting effects. The adverse consequences of stalking included increased fears of being the victim of a crime and avoidance of night classes.

Studies of stalking victims that use college students as the primary sample have some relevance to adolescents because, as noted previously, the college years are a transitional period between late adolescence and adulthood. However, there are no studies on the effects of stalking on younger individuals. Some forms of interpersonal violence that are related to stalking, such as dating violence, bullying, and sexual harassment, have been studied and offer evidence that younger individuals are adversely affected by obsessional harassment. Children who are victims of bullying experience depression, helplessness, and lowered self-esteem (American Psychological Association, 1993; Kolko, 1998). Child victims of repetitive violence such as bullying and recurrent peer aggression may also experience suicidal ideation (Olweus, 1993), loneliness, and fewer stable peer relationships (Slaby, 1998).

The research on college students who report being victims of stalking and on younger individuals who are exposed to other forms of obsessional harassment suggests that a range of social and psychological difficulties result for all victims of stalking, regardless of age. Some social concerns include profound changes in one's lifestyle, such as altering the way one goes to school, and less satisfying peer relationships. Moreover, although adult victims report long-standing problems as a result of being stalked, children and adolescents also experience long-term effects from obsessional harassment that can continue into late adolescence and adulthood (Slaby, 1998). Also, children and adolescents experience psychological difficulties as a result of being harassed on a continuous or repetitive basis, including depression, anxiety, suicidal ideation, insecurity, and symptoms of posttraumatic stress. Parents, mental health professionals, teachers, and other individuals who work with or care for young individuals who have been exposed to obsessional forms of harassment must be cognizant of these adverse social and psychological effects and should seek appropriate treatment for the child.

ASSESSMENT AND TREATMENT OF YOUNG STALKING VICTIMS

The basis of any clinical intervention that seeks to reduce symptomatology is a thorough assessment and evaluation of the individual. Through the process of assessment, a clinician can identify specific symptoms that contributed to the person seeking treatment, as well as the personality traits and social factors that affect the person's level of functioning and individual response to specific stressors.

The most common psychological disturbances are likely to be those found in individuals exposed to severe stress or trauma. Emotional responses to being stalked are likely to include depression, anxiety, fear, and posttraumatic stress. More specifically, individuals exposed to severe stress often report sleep disturbances, social withdrawal, concentration difficulties, and other symptoms of general emotional distress. Clinical syndromes found in young stalking victims are likely to include mood, anxiety, and adjustment disorders as outlined in the *DSM-IV* (American Psychiatric Association, 1994). One diagnosis that must be considered, as suggested by research on the effects of stalking among college student populations (Westrup, Fremouw, & Thompson, 1999), is PTSD. It is important to keep in mind that the diagnosis of PTSD requires specific criteria, as stated in the *DSM-IV*, including exposure to an event "that involves actual or threatened death or serious injury, or other threat to one's physical integrity;. . . . The person's response to the event must involve intense fear, helplessness, or horror" (American Psychiatric Association, 1994, p. 424). In addition to this provision, the diagnosis of PTSD also requires that the person re-experience the event through recurrent and intrusive experiences (e.g., nightmares, flashbacks), avoid stimuli associated with the stressor (e.g., lack of memory for specific details, avoiding social situations that remind the person of the event), and exhibit hyper-arousal (e.g., exaggerated startle response, sleep disturbance). Therefore, stalking victims may be diagnosed with PTSD only if the threats to which they have been exposed or acts of violence perpetrated by the obsessional follower satisfy the criteria as outlined in the *DSM-IV*. In other words, mere knowledge that one is being stalked is not sufficient to support a diagnosis of PTSD.

On the other hand, the *DSM-IV* diagnostic criteria for PTSD do not always adequately capture the way in which victims of trauma may be affected. As noted by van der Kolk and McFarlane (1996), a fixation on the criteria of PTSD as laid out in the *DSM-IV* ignores the fact that victims of severe stress and trauma can experience psychological symptoms that overlap with, but may not meet formal criteria for PTSD. Some individuals exposed to a stressor that is chronic and severe but that is not appropriately characterized by the requirement in the *DSM-IV* that the stressor involve "threatened death or serious injury, or other threat to one's physical integrity" (American Psychiatric Association, 1994 p. 424) can still experience other symptoms of posttraumatic stress such as avoidance of stimuli associated with the stressor and hyper-arousal. Some stalking offenders use subtle threats that are intended to intimidate the victim but that do not involve a threat of death or serious bodily injury. Nevertheless, the chronicity of threatening behavior in stalking cases often takes a profound toll on the victim; posttraumatic stress symptoms, as opposed to the formal disorder, may be experienced by victims. Therefore, alternative diagnoses such as anxiety disorder not otherwise specified, adjustment disorder, acute stress disorder, or other similar diagnoses may be warranted. Proper assessment and diagnosis of young stalking victims must rely on close adherence to formal diagnostic criteria as outlined in the *DSM-IV*, as well as a broad approach to assessment that examines clinical symptoms, phenomenological experiences, interpersonal relationships, personality, and social supports of the young stalking victim.

Assessment Issues

The initial interview with a child or adolescent victim of stalking should generally be structured like any formal diagnostic interview. A detailed account of the circumstances that brought the child or adolescent to treatment should be obtained, and collateral information from parents is crucial for gathering information on their child's reaction to stressors and current functioning, as well as the adequacy of the child's social and family support network. In addition to general aspects of the child or adolescent's history (e.g., developmental, medical, school, family) and mental status, details about their exposure to stalking should be covered. Information specific to the stalking should include how the perpetrator and victim know each other, behaviors that have been used to stalk the victim, what actions the victim has taken to avoid or stop the obsessional harassment, and the perpetrator's response to preventive actions taken by the victim. Moreover, assessment of third-party interventions (e.g., school officials, teachers, parents) that have been attempted to stop or curb the stalking should also be assessed. The resources that are available to the victim, including access to an attorney, family and parental supports, and whether or not others have taken the stalking behavior seriously, should also be evaluated.

A comprehensive assessment of the child or adolescent stalking victim's clinical status is another important part of the initial phases of clinical intervention. The use of structured clinical interviews has received increased attention in recent years, and instruments specifically designed for children and adolescents may have some clinical utility. Among the major instruments for assessing childhood psychopathology that are likely to be most relevant to the types of problems found in young stalking victims are the Diagnostic Interview Schedule for Children (DISC), the Children's Assessment Schedule (CAS), and the Diagnostic Interview for Children and Adolescents (DICA); each of these instruments has been reviewed by Rogers (1995). The DISC has six modules measuring anxiety, affective, schizophrenic, disruptive behavior, substance abuse, and miscellaneous (e.g., tic) disorders. Rogers noted that this instrument is reliable and clinically useful primarily in outpatient settings. The CAS has two parallel forms, one for parents and one for the child, and is organized around 11 topic areas: school, friends, activities, family, fears, worries/anxieties, self-image, mood/behavior, physical complaints, acting out, and reality testing. Rogers noted that the CAS does not have strong validity support for differential diagnosis, but it may be useful clinically as a measure of dimensions of psychopathology rather than specific diagnoses. The DICA is a comprehensive structured interview for child and adolescent psychopathology that is applicable to a wide range of clinical settings and concerns.

The advantages to using structured interviews in clinical and forensic practice include comprehensive and reliable coverage of diagnostic criteria and useful algorithms for making differential diagnoses. Structured interviews also have limitations when they are used in clinical settings because they often control the interview process and individual or specific issues relevant in a particular case may be difficult to assess. Moreover, some protocols for these instruments have been developed for research purposes and are difficult to obtain commercially. Rogers (1995) has provided detailed information on the reliability, validity, and clinical applications of these and other structured diagnostic interviews, as well as information on how to obtain copies of the interview materials.

The only application that structured interviews, such as the DICA and CAS, might have in the routine clinical assessment of young stalking victims is evaluating anxiety and mood disturbances. The CAS may have some circumscribed applicability in evaluating related symptoms such as physical problems, peer relationships, school problems, family disruptions, and self-image disturbances. However, the time investment required for structured interviews is generally not worthwhile, and the limitations placed on the flow and pace of the interview often inhibit the interview process and impede rapport. Therefore, structured interviews for child and adolescent psychopathology are best suited for research settings or in forensic cases in which more extensive data are required; their routine clinical use tends to prove unwieldy and overly restrictive in the treatment process.

Another set of assessment instruments that may be useful in assessing the psychological status of victims of obsessional harassment include self-report instruments such as the Millon Adolescent Clinical Inventory (MACI; Millon, Millon, & Davis, 1993), the Minnesota Multiphasic Personality Inventory-Adolescent (MMPI–A; Butcher et al., 1992), and the Adolescent Psychopathology Scale (APS; Reynolds, 1998). The MACI, MMPI–A, and APS are general clinical assessment inventories that sample a variety of personal concerns, symptoms, and personality characteristics in adolescents. One advantage that these broad assessment instruments have is that they survey a wide range of potential problems among adolescents such as depression, anxiety, substance abuse, perceived family support, self-esteem, and similar issues that may be areas requiring attention in treatment. Another consideration when selecting an instrument for use in clinical settings is the nature of the diagnostic information that is needed and the practical utility of the instrument. For instance, the MACI assesses 12 distinct personality types, as well as specific concerns and clinical syndromes that are common among adolescents. However, the MACI does not have a scale specifically for measuring symptoms of posttraumatic stress, which may be needed in specific cases, whereas the APS has a scale specifically designed for measuring such symptoms. On the other hand, the MACI, which has 160 items, is briefer than either the MMPI–A or APS, which have 478 and 346 items, respectively. Because adolescents are often resistant to mental health assessment and treatment, presenting a challenge to the clinician, the MACI has distinct advantages over the more lengthy psychometric inventories (McCann, 1999).

Additional issues should be considered when evaluating the reactions of children and adolescents to traumatic experiences, particularly if the harassment of the victim has been aggressive or violent in nature. Nader (1997) noted that the timing of the assessment with respect to when the child or adolescent has been exposed to a severe stressor, age of the victim, and scaling that is used to quantify ratings of traumatic stress are important considerations. Toward this end, several instruments have been designed to measure childhood trauma. One such instrument that is commercially available is the Trauma Symptom Checklist for Children (TSCC; Briere, 1996), which is composed of 54 items that measure six general categories of traumatic stress, including anger, anxiety, depression, dissociation, posttraumatic stress, and sexual concerns. The TSCC has extensive normative data for children and adolescents ages 8 to 16. The commercial availability and extensive normative data for the TSCC make it a particularly useful instrument in forensic settings, where there is a need for reliable and valid data that can be documented and defended in court. Moreover, the TSCC is relatively brief and can be used in conjunction with other assessment instruments to provide information on the child or adolescent's emotional reactions to severe trauma or stress.

Nader (1997) also reviewed several other structured interviews and self-report instruments for assessing traumatic experiences in children and adolescents, including the Child Posttraumatic Stress Reaction Index, My Worst Experience Survey, My Worst School Experience Survey, When

Bad Things Happen Scale, and Children's Impact of Traumatic Events Scale. Most of these instruments have been developed for research purposes, and Nader provided a detailed review of the reliability, validity, and clinical uses of these instruments. For general clinical and forensic applications, however, the TSCC is particularly useful given its commercial availability and extensive normative data.

Treatment Issues

Several issues often arise in treatment of the stalking victim, including facilitating procedures that will stop the stalking behavior, assuring personal safety, supporting the victim, and reducing symptoms of psychological distress. One of the basic principles in clinical management of stalking cases is to strongly emphasize to the victim that there should be no initiated contact with the stalking offender. Meloy (1997) noted that "each victim contact is an intermittent positive reinforcement and predicts an increase in frequency of approach behavior" (p. 177). That is, a stalking offender who approaches, follows, or in other ways harasses the victim will continue or increase approach behavior if the victim initiates contact. Although the victim may intend to tell the stalker that his or her behavior is unwanted, any contact that is initiated by the victim sends a message to the obsessional follower that persistence, recurrent contact, and other forms of pursuit ultimately result in an interaction with the victim. Therefore, clinicians who work with young stalking victims should help the victim develop a strategy for making it known to the obsessional follower that his or her contact should stop. Although Roberts and Dziegielewski (1996) suggested that therapists work with the victim to develop a way of telling the stalker directly that contact is unwanted, a more cautious approach that is less likely to reinforce approach behavior is to have a third party communicate the victim's desire for no contact. A school administrator, family lawyer, or law enforcement officer would be the best choice, because these individuals are in positions of authority.

A contact that should be made by school or law enforcement officials, particularly when stalking cases involve a child or adolescent obsessional follower, is with the parents of the offender. This option is unique to stalking cases involving children and adolescents and may facilitate appropriate interventions being initiated by the offender's parents. Making the offender's parents recipients of any legal or court notifications potentially adds another source of influence over the stalking offender's behavior. However, notification of the offender's parents does not guarantee that they will be responsive or effective. Moreover, if the offender's parents attempt to impede the young obsessional follower's access to the object, it places them in a position of heightened risk for violence, and thus appropriate warnings should be made.

Other treatment issues involve encouraging the young stalking victim and his or her parents to take an active approach to managing the situation and to not expect the police or school officials to be completely effective. Meloy (1997) stated that stalking victims must be responsible for their personal safety; this implies that in cases involving young victims, the parents of the victim must also be responsible for the safety of their child. Therapists can provide needed guidance, such as directing the family to document and record all acts of stalking, including keeping recordings of telephone messages, notes and letters, bizarre or unusual gifts, and the like. Parents may be tempted to throw out offensive materials to protect their children in the same way that some adult victims, for example, may be tempted to erase threatening telephone messages. All acts of threatening and harassing behavior must be preserved, because these materials are the best way to prove a "course of conduct" of threatening behavior that can be used in legal proceedings.

Meloy (1997) also recommended that a team approach to managing stalking cases is preferred. In cases involving children and adolescents, multidisciplinary teams might include the victim, parents, school personnel, law enforcement officers, attorneys, and a mental health professional. The use of civil orders of protection is a method that is often sought in stalking cases, and this issue is discussed more fully in chapter 9.

With respect to providing psychotherapy to young stalking victims, a number of principles and approaches may be useful. Roberts and Dziegielewski (1996) suggested that treatment goals be short-term and realistic. For example, to expect the stalking behavior to cease perma-

THE IMPACT ON VICTIMS

nently when a civil order of protection is served may be appropriate in less severe cases, but this expectation is unrealistic in those cases in which the stalking has been chronic and pervasive. Specific treatment interventions that are active and aimed at symptom reduction should be considered, including relaxation training, cognitive–behavioral treatment for symptoms of anxiety and depression, and crisis intervention during those times when increased attention and precautions may be needed. For example, Meloy (1997) described "dramatic moments" when the stalking offender's humiliation and shame are more intense and the risk for aggression and violence is greater. These dramatic moments tend to occur when the obsessional follower has been shamed or humiliated, such as the first notice that his or her contact is unwanted, the issuance of a protective order, or perceived interference from third parties. At these times, the therapist will need to be available to the victim and his or her family for crisis intervention, support, or consultation either in person or by telephone.

Aside from the practical issues associated with reducing stalking behavior, young stalking victims also require support to affirm that they are not enduring the stalking alone and that there are others to whom they can turn for guidance. Treatment for symptoms of posttraumatic stress, depression, anxiety, and anger may also be part of the plan and consultation with medical and psychiatric colleagues may be warranted in those cases in which symptoms are severe and may respond to medication. Some recurring issues that may arise in treatment stem from personality dynamics of the victim, including a wish to please others, identity concerns, boundary concerns, and mistrust of adults. These issues often translate into problems that may arise when treating the young stalking victim. For example, a strong need to please others may result in the young stalking victim attempting to placate the stalking offender with the thought that the stalking will soon stop. This type of thinking should be confronted, as it risks initiated contact that will increase approach behavior. Likewise, young victims who have identity concerns that are more pronounced may be prone to develop an identification with the offender that resembles the "Stockholm Syndrome" in which victims will identify with their victimizers in an effort to reduce terror (Roberts & Dziegielewski, 1996). This behavior must also be addressed, as it can lead to initiated contact with the obsessional follower.

CONCLUSION

This chapter covers a range of issues that pertain to the effect stalking can have on its victims. Although there is virtually no research on the impact of stalking on younger victims, some research on older adolescents and college students suggests that a range of psychological effects occur as a result of being stalked. These adverse effects include anxiety, depression, symptoms of posttraumatic stress, and interpersonal difficulties. In addition, the term *stalking* is often used to describe the behavior of some adults who sexually abuse and victimize children; and recent sex offender legislation, such as community notification and violent sexual predator laws, are two examples of society's response to adults who victimize children. However, it is important to distinguish between those cases of sexual offending that involve actual stalking, in which there is a pattern or course of conduct that is intended to cause fear in the victim, and those cases of sexual victimization in which the offender engages in pre-offense behavior (e.g., loitering around parks) that is not immediately threatening or that is part of the offender's attempt to gain the child's trust. This distinction is similar to the one that was made earlier between stalking and predatory violence.

A number of issues pertaining to the assessment and treatment of young stalking victims were also covered in this chapter. Comprehensive assessment of the stalking behavior, the victim's social supports, and the psychological reaction to the stalking are necessary before an informed treatment plan can be developed and implemented. Many comprehensive structured interviews and self-report instruments are available for children and adolescents and can be used with stalking victims. Treatment interventions must include support for the victim, reduction of symptoms of psychological distress, referral to community support services, and education or advice on managing stalking that does not exacerbate or place the victim in a more vulnerable position. Among the critical guidance that should be given to young stalking victims is that they should not initiate any contact with the perpetrator. However, they should document all incidents of threat, save all evidence for possible prosecution, and consult with law enforcement or legal professionals. Many community resources are available, with additional information and resources available on the Internet (see chapter 8). The best approach to helping young stalking victims is one that is multidisciplinary and includes input from mental health professionals, law enforcement officials, school personnel, parents, and attorneys.

8

Interventions and Case Management

The recurrent threatening and harassing behaviors that constitute stalking present concerns as to whether or not victims will be subjected to violence. A parent would understandably be fearful if his or her child or teenager was the target of an obsessional follower. Although human nature leads us to fear many things that we do not clearly understand, stalking provokes additional fears because the very nature of the behavior involves implied or direct threats against the victim. What is most critical in cases of stalking involving children or adolescents is to intervene in a way that removes the threat and reduces the likelihood of violence.

Stalking represents a threat to the victim's health—significant adverse psychological consequences are what a victim of stalking endures and this threatens the victim's physical well-being. Thus, a critical question that must be answered is, "What are the factors in a child or adolescent's life that can protect him or her from harm?" A partial answer to this question comes from the National Longitudinal Study of Adolescent Health that examined the social context of threats to the health of students in grades 7 through 12 (Resnick et al. 1997). This study examined both risk-enhancing and protective factors at three levels (i.e., family, school, and individual) as they pertain to emotional health, violence, substance abuse, and sexuality in the lives of adolescents. Although this study did not address stalking or obsessional harassment directly, the problems of violence, emotional health, and sexuality all relate in some manner to stalking in juveniles. Therefore, this study provides some insight into the factors that reduce the level of harm to young people who experience various threats to their well-being.

Findings from this longitudinal study reveal three major factors that tend to protect adolescents from harm. First, family connectedness was consistently shown to act as a buffer for adolescents against threats to their physical and emotional health. Although parental expectations and presence at home during stressful times were moderately related to reduced risk against emotional distress, violence, and substance abuse, by far the most significant family protective factor was when teenagers felt warmth, love, and acceptance from their parents. Therefore, the quality of the relationship between children and their parents is a critical factor that protects against harm in a young person's life.

Second, the study found that school connectedness was also consistently related to reduced likelihood of harm to adolescents' health. Emphasis on policies governing school conduct were much less important than was a perception by students that teachers and administrators were caring and interested in students and had high expectations for their performance as students. Although these findings do not necessarily suggest that school policies and guidelines, such as those published in student handbooks, are not important, they indicate that young people are likely to experience less psychological and physical harm when they perceive that school officials and personnel are sensitive and invested in the well-being of their students.

Third, the study revealed several individual factors that were related to reduced risk of harm to teenagers' physical and emotional health. How students conducted themselves and scheduled or structured their lives was positively related to a greater sense of emotional well-being and reduced risk of violence. When students are able to have activities that bring them a sense of satisfaction and when their peer relationships are viewed as supportive, they are likely to experience less harm. Both the social environment, such as family and school relationships, and individual factors play a significant role in reducing the threat of emotional stress, violence, substance abuse, and sexual problems among adolescents.

Other research findings reveal that several factors contribute to a more favorable and healthy adaptation when children and adolescents experience stressful life situations. These factors include (a) active as opposed to passive attempts at coping (e.g., asking for help from adults); (b) feelings of self-efficacy; (c) a stable emotional relationship with at least one parent or adult attachment figure; (d) a supportive and open educational climate and positive parental role models; and (e) social supports from people outside of the family (Garbarino, Kostelny, & Barry, 1998). These factors are often associated with such concepts as resiliency or adaptability that are used to describe the effective coping strategies of many children and adolescents.

With respect to young stalking victims, both individual and environmental resources can be used to protect against threats of violence. Specific social supports include the role of family and school systems in taking action to protect the victim and intervene in preventing further harassment by the perpetrator. In this chapter, I outline the ways in which school systems, the juvenile justice system, mental health professionals, and parents can act to intervene in stalking cases to prevent aggression and violence. I also discuss some steps that children and adolescents can take to protect themselves, as well as supports and resources that are available to stalking victims and their families. These interventions and supports can be used to manage potentially violent cases, and they comprise multiple lines of attack that are often needed in these difficult cases.

THE ROLE OF THE SCHOOL SYSTEM

In school settings, there are a number of opportunities for students to tease and harass one another, and in recent years more attention has been given to preventing school-based harassment. The role of the school system in addressing the problem of stalking cannot be overstated because teachers, administrators, and support staff may often be in the best position to identify the beginning stages of obsessive forms of harassment, particularly when the perpetrator and the victim are peers. Moreover, it has been noted by McCann (1998c) that many cases of stalking that are ultimately referred for mental health intervention come from school officials who have observed stalking behavior in the classroom or hallways. In some cases, a student may have been suspended as a result of harassing or threatening behavior, and mental health assessment or treatment is required before the student will be permitted back into school.

Because school systems are in an excellent position to serve a major role in the prevention of stalking, it is important that strong measures are in place to confront school-based harassment. In fact, recent federal court rulings have held that school boards may be liable for damages under private civil suits for a teacher's sexual harassment of a student, as well as for student-on-student harassment. Although these cases deal with the issue of sexual harassment in the schools, their legal rulings are likely to apply to stalking cases, particularly when the harassment is of a sexual nature or if the school has notice that the harassment is occurring and fails to take appropriate action. Moreover, because a student's bonding to school is a factor that both protects against the risk for violence and facilitates adaptive coping to stress, it is important to remove all sources of harassment in the school environment, including that which occurs between teachers and students as well as between peers.

Two recent U.S. Supreme Court cases have addressed the issue of harassment in schools and have affirmed that private civil actions may be brought against school districts under Title IX of the Education Amendments of 1972, which states:

> No person in the United States shall, on the basis of sex, be excluded from participation in, be denied the benefits of, or be subjected to discrimination under any education program or activity receiving Federal financial assistance. (20 U.S.C §1681(a))

Therefore, school districts that receive federal funds must comply with the mandates of Title IX or will risk losing federal money to support educational programs.

In the case of *Gebser v. Lago Vista Independent School District* (1998), the Supreme Court considered the issue of whether a student could seek monetary damages for a teacher's sexual harassment of the student in a civil suit supported under Title IX. The case involved a girl in middle school who had a sexual relationship with a high school teacher who was employed by the school district. After the two were discovered having sexual relations, the teacher was arrested, and his employment was terminated by the school district. The student had not disclosed the relationship to school officials, but one of the central issues in the case was whether the school district was at fault for not distributing a formal grievance procedure for filing sexual harassment complaints and not having a policy on sexual harassment in place. After the student and her mother filed a civil suit, raising a claim under Title IX, the trial court judge in the Federal District Court for the Western District of Texas granted the school district's motion for summary judgment. In effect, this ruling dismissed the complaint because the court found that there was insufficient evidence that the school district had notice of the teacher's conduct, because there had been no previous complaints about the teacher. The Court of Appeals for the Fifth Circuit upheld the District Court's ruling.

On appeal, the Supreme Court held in *Gebser* that the lower courts had ruled correctly and that to sustain a private action for monetary damages under Title IX for teacher-on-student sexual harassment, there must be actual notice to the school district of the teacher's conduct, and there must also be evidence that the school district acted with deliberate indifference to the teacher's conduct once proper notice was received. Therefore, the ruling appears to leave open the possibility of a school district facing civil suits if a showing can be made that it received notice of a teacher's conduct and there is evidence that the school district acted with intentional indifference after being notified of the teacher's behavior.

Another recent Supreme Court case ruled on the issue of a school district's liability for student-on-student sexual harassment under Title IX. In *Davis v. Monroe County Board of Education* (1999), the victim was a fifth-grade girl who had been subjected to a lengthy course of sexual harassment by a male classmate. He had attempted to touch her breasts and genital area and made harassing comments such as "I want to get in bed with you" and "I want to feel your boobs." After the girl reported these incidents to her mother and to her classroom teacher, her mother was reassured that the school principal was aware of these incidents. However, the conduct continued for several months and the boy was subsequently charged with sexual battery for his conduct. The girl and her parents brought a civil action under Title IX seeking monetary damages and injunctive relief.

As the trial court did in *Gebser,* the District Court of Georgia in *Davis* dismissed the claim on the grounds that Title IX provides no legal basis for supporting a claim of student-on-student sexual harassment, and the Court of Appeals for the Eleventh Circuit affirmed. However, the Supreme Court held in a majority opinion by Justice Sandra Day O'Connor that a private action for damages is permissible under Title IX for student-on-student harassment only when the school district receiving funds under Title IX acts with deliberate indifference after being put on notice that the harassment is occurring. Moreover, the Supreme Court held further in *Davis* that liability could be established only if the harassment is so severe, pervasive, and offensive that it prevents the student's access to educational programs and opportunities. Moreover, the opinion in *Davis* comments further that courts must recognize that schools are different than adult workplaces in that children often interact with one another in ways that would be inappropriate or unacceptable for adults. In a dissenting opinion, Justice Anthony Kennedy noted that the ruling in *Davis* could cause an increase in litigation over student-on-student sexual harassment. He also argued that because the majority opinion offered no standards about what would constitute student-on-student sexual harassment, courts could have difficulty distinguishing harmless teasing from inappropriate harassment.

The rulings in *Gebser* and *Davis* indicate that school districts may be sued for monetary damages under Title IX if they have notice that a teacher or student is sexually harassing another student; that the harassment is severe, pervasive, and objectively offensive; and that the school district acts with deliberate indifference to the harassment. Because stalking overlaps with sexual harassment among children and adolescents, it appears that school districts will be required to take appropriate action when they are made aware of obsessive forms of harassment in their programs and activities. Therefore, not only are school personnel in a good position to make an intervention, they are legally required to do so when they receive notice of harassment that affects a student in their programs.

Nevertheless, there is much confusion about what specifically constitutes sexual harassment in schools. As a result, the U.S. Department of Education has attempted to provide guidance in the development of policies and procedures for handling sexual harassment in schools (Sexual Harassment Guidance, 1997). These guidelines note that for conduct to be sexually harassing, it must be unwelcome by the recipient and that acquiescence or failure to complain does not necessarily imply that the behavior is welcome. Also, the federal guidelines note that for conduct to be deemed severe, persistent, or pervasive, a number of factors must be taken into account. These factors include (a) the extent to which the education of one or more students is affected by the conduct; (b) the type, frequency, and duration of the conduct; (c) the relationship between the alleged harasser and the victim or victims of the harassment; (d) the number of individuals involved; (e) the age and gender of the alleged harasser and victim of the harassment; (f) the size of the school and location of the incidents; and (g) other factors such as gender-based harassment and acts of physical aggression in the school.

These guidelines also state that a school district may receive notice of harassment based on a number of responses by the recipient of the conduct, including complaints from the student or a parent. If a school employee or an agent of the school district witnesses the harassment, then notice may be effectively made. In addition, the guidelines offered by the Department of Education note that there should be some mechanism that allows the victims of school-based harassment to have their confidentiality protected while also providing for prompt and equitable grievance procedures in which the accused person has an opportunity to respond.

Many of these procedures can be applied to cases of school-based harassment that involve stalking or obsessional harassment; however, others may pose unique challenges. For example, because stalking often involves an intention to evoke fear in the victim, grievance procedures that permit the accused harasser to confront his or her victim may contribute to or exacerbate the pathological fixation on the victim. Rather than an opportunity to resolve the harassment, some grievance procedures may actually fuel the obsessional follower's fantasies about being unified with the victim. Therefore, cases of obsessional harassment in schools that involve stalking behavior need to be appraised differently than do cases of sexual harassment that do not involve stalking or obsessional following.

Overall, there are some ways in which schools can respond to stalking and obsessional following that can facilitate favorable outcomes. For instance, the Northwest Regional Educational Center (1998) has outlined strategies for preventing and responding to school-based harassment that can be adopted in stalking cases. Schools should have well-publicized policies and procedures for dealing with harassment in schools. Therefore, student handbooks and teacher's manuals should incorporate definitions of stalking that are adopted from the state code and provide examples of behaviors that constitute criminal stalking.

Many student handbooks classify misconduct into varying levels of severity; these levels dictate the nature of the intervention that should be taken by the school district. For instance, the lowest level of behavioral infractions are often minor offenses that interfere with classroom procedures, school functions, or extracurricular programs. Examples of low-level misconduct include abusive language, tardiness, and disruptive behavior, and typical administrative responses may include reprimands, withdrawal of privileges, or detention. Behavioral infractions that are of an intermediate level of severity are those involving repeated misconduct that does not seriously threaten the safety of others but that often requires more severe administrative interventions. For example, destruction of property, theft, and recurrent disregard for the school's dress or safety code often require a school's principal to intervene by contacting parents, giving a reprimand, or making in- or out-of-school suspensions. The most severe level of behavioral infractions involves major misconduct that may potentially result in criminal prosecution and includes threats to the safety and welfare of others. Examples of these severest forms of misconduct include making bomb threats, sexual harassment, assault, arson, or bringing a firearm to school. Schools generally have a zero tolerance policy for violence, and these more severe forms of misconduct generally result not only in parental contact and suspension, but also referral of the student to other alternative disciplinary programs or law enforcement agencies. Given the chronic and severe nature of stalking cases, schools should place obsessional following or stalking in the most severe category of behavioral misconduct in their student handbooks. In addition, provisions should be made for involving outside agencies if necessary, including youth diversion programs, the issuance of status offense petitions (e.g., Person in Need of Supervision), or referral to law enforcement agencies. However, consultation with the victim and his or her family should also occur prior to involving these outside agencies, because risks to the victim's safety may increase when the perpetrator is referred for possible criminal prosecution.

Another important part of a school district's policy is to ensure that teachers and other school personnel receive training on the dynamics of stalking and obsessional following, including the behaviors stalkers use to threaten and intimidate victims, the ways in which victims are affected, and the factors that increase the risk for violence. In addition, school curricula can be modified to include information and reading materials for students on the dynamics of obsessional following. Many of the national resource centers described later in this chapter provide information that can be adapted for classroom use.

One of the most important components of a school district's approach to dealing with stalking and obsessional harassment is the availability of properly designed grievance or complaint procedures. The

Northwest Regional Educational Center (1998) has recommended a number of factors for implementing such procedures in cases of sexual harassment that can be adapted for stalking cases. In particular, the formal complaint procedures in stalking cases would document the names of the victim and perpetrator, when and where the stalking occurred, what specifically the perpetrator did, how the victim responded, what the perpetrator's reaction was to the victim's behavior, whether or not any witnesses were present, and documentation of evidence (e.g., notes, tape recordings of messages, bizarre gifts). There should be some means for appealing the findings from any administrative hearing, and students and their families should be kept updated on the status of complaints.

The pathological nature of stalking and the persistent fixations that many perpetrators have make it an ill-advised policy to have the perpetrator and victim confront one another in a joint meeting with school officials. For example, well-intended, yet misguided, efforts to resolve the situation in a friendly or cordial manner by having the victim write a letter to the perpetrator in which she expresses her feelings about being victimized should be strongly discouraged or avoided. I was consulted by the parents of a girl who had been repeatedly followed and harassed by a male classmate who had maintained an obsessive sexual preoccupation on the girl for almost two years. His behavior escalated and involved his writing numerous letters and notes in which he first proclaimed his love. Later his notes became hostile and threatening when she did not reciprocate his feelings. She and her parents made it clear to the boy and to the school that she wanted no contact with the boy and that the letters were to stop. Despite warnings from the school and ongoing counseling, the harassment continued. The boy's school guidance counselor thought that it would help reduce his preoccupation by getting the two students together to help him "work through his feelings of rejection." Such interventions only tend to fuel the obsessional follower's fantasies and preoccupation with the object and should be avoided. If repeated warnings fail to stop the harassment, then negotiation in a counseling session in which the victim is present is unlikely to have any appreciable impact on the situation.

However, student victims of stalking should have some input into how their complaints are handled by school officials, because the act of giving notice to a stalking perpetrator that a complaint is being considered by the school may constitute a "dramatic moment" (Meloy, 1997), in which the perpetrator is narcissistically injured and the risk for violence increases. Therefore, school districts may also need to consider providing information on local resources and remedies that may be available, such as where to seek restraining orders, to students who make complaints of stalking behavior.

Another response by school districts is a requirement that the identified stalking perpetrator seek a mental health evaluation as a condition of remaining in school. This action has typically been encountered in cases in which the stalking behavior has been particularly disruptive to the school environment and has affected more than one student victim. Although issues of confidentiality are sometimes murky in these cases, in that the student engaging in stalking behavior and his or her parents may be reticent to permit mental health professionals to disclose unfavorable information to the schools, such mental health evaluations can provide valuable information on the level of risk for violence, treatment recommendations, and prognosis. Referral for mental health evaluation and treatment can be an extremely useful mechanism for school districts in managing harassment cases that involve stalking or obsessional following.

PERSONAL PROTECTION MEASURES

Another critical component in the management of cases involving children or adolescents who are the victims of stalking includes measures that must be taken to ensure the safety of the victim at home and in his or her personal life. Parents of victims, school personnel who are responsible for the safety and security of students, and mental health professionals who work with young stalking victims are often placed in a position in which they must take some action to protect the victim from further harassment or potential violence. The National Victim Center (1997) has set forth several guidelines that victims can follow in situations in which there is imminent or potential danger. Although many of these guidelines are generic and apply to most stalking victims, a few modifications are recommended below to account for some of the unique needs of younger victims.

According to the National Victim Center guidelines, situations that involve imminent danger or violence have the immediate safety of the victim as their primary goal. As such, stalking victims should be familiar with the locations of police stations, residences of family or friends who can provide shelter, and domestic violence shelters where support services can be obtained. For younger victims, this may entail parents and school officials instructing the victim on the location of these resources. In school settings, the offices of guidance counselors, principals, and other responsible adult staff are additional places to seek out when imminent danger is present. Younger victims should always carry emergency telephone numbers and instructions on how to contact the police, parents, or another responsible adult who can provide safety.

In situations in which the potential for violence or danger is not imminent, there are other protective measures that parents and victims can take. The filing of a civil order of protection, or restraining order, can be useful whereby stalking offenders must refrain from contacting or coming within a prescribed radius of the victim. Although such orders are not completely effective in all cases, research tends to support their efficacy in reducing the risk for potential violence; this research is reviewed in chapter 9. In addition, documentation of all stalking behavior is critical, including the saving of notes, letters, recorded telephone messages, and so forth. This documentation can later serve as evidence in criminal prosecution under anti-stalking laws.

The National Victim Center guidelines also offer a number of personal protective measures that stalking victims can institute at home. A few additional guidelines are included that specifically apply to younger stalking victims:

- Install adequate outside lighting around the victim's home.
- Maintain an unlisted telephone number and a call of origin visual display on the telephone. Parents can screen all calls if telephone harassment is a problem.

- Take all threats seriously, and report them to parents, school officials, and law enforcement.
- Provide school personnel with the name of the stalking perpetrator and notice of any court orders that are in effect. Also provide a picture of the stalker if he or she is not enrolled in the school.
- Vary travel routes to and from school, extracurricular activities, stores, and other routinely visited public places.
- Make sure that there is a contingency plan for transportation if a parent or other adult who is relied on for a ride is unavailable.
- Stay in small groups of friends who can provide support and who can serve as witnesses of continued stalking behavior.
- Make sure all doors, windows, and points of entry to the home are secure and locked.
- Keep emergency telephone numbers and the names of contact persons on hand.
- Maintain an open and supportive relationship between the victim and his or her family, including open communication about threats, stalking behavior, and concerns.

On a more practical level, de Becker (1999) offered a straight-forward rule that applies to unwanted pursuit as children enter adolescence and begin to date. He stated that teenagers, typically young girls, should not negotiate with someone with whom contact is no longer desired.

> Once a girl has made the decision that she doesn't want a relationship with a particular man, it needs to be said one time, explicitly. Almost any contact after that rejection will be seen as negotiation. If a woman tells a man over and over again that she doesn't want to talk to him, that is talking to him, and every time she does it, she betrays her resolve in the matter. If you tell someone ten times that you don't want to talk to him, you *are* talking to him–nine more times than you wanted to. (p. 203; emphasis in original)

Interestingly, de Becker also stated that although he supports anti-stalking laws, a more valuable approach to addressing the problem of stalking at younger ages would be to have all high school students take a course that would teach young men how to hear and accept a rejection from young women and for young women to learn that it is acceptable to clearly reject advances from men. This proposal may sound like an unattainable ideal; however, it is not unrealistic and could be readily incorporated into the curricula for sex education, health, or ethics classes that are taught in most schools.

In addition, de Becker (1999) noted seven basic "survival signals" that children and adolescents can be taught to recognize as a way of avoiding potentially dangerous situations. More specifically, he noted that in dating situations obsessional followers or predators seek to gain control over their potential victims. These "survival signals" are as follows:

1. *Forced teaming* — the person seeks to create premature trust by creating the illusion that the obsessional follower and victim have something in common.
2. *Charm and niceness* — the obsessional follower uses excessive charm to create an image of being likeable to lower the victim's defenses.
3. *Too many details* — the obsessional follower offers too many details about matters as a way of attempting to hide deception or to create an appearance of credibility.
4. *Typecasting* — the offering of a slight insult (e.g., "You're probably too shy to go out with me") that the victim may try to disprove.
5. *Loan-sharking* — making an offer or promise to create a feeling of obligation in the victim.
6. *Unsolicited promises* — the offer of a false sense of security that is not based on a true intent (e.g., "I promise we won't go anywhere unsafe.").
7. *Discounting "No"* — the obsessional follower ignores or fails to accept the victim's refusals.

According to de Becker, these behaviors are often evidence of potential problems and dangers when a pursuer or potential date exhibits them. For individuals who are interested in a very practical and highly readable guide to personal safety, de Becker's (1999) book *Protecting the Gift* is recommended.

As noted earlier, research suggests that children and adolescents are less likely to suffer adverse psychological and physical harm when they experience a feeling of connectedness to their family and school. In stalking cases, it is likely that those young victims who have supportive and responsive families will have more favorable outcomes. Similarly, young stalking victims who perceive that school officials, teachers, and guidance counselors are sensitive and willing to assist in protecting them both in and near the school are also likely to have more favorable outcomes. As such, it is important for parents, siblings, teachers, and school personnel to be aware of several details of the child or adolescent stalking victim's case, including who the perpetrator is, what stalking behaviors have occurred, the presence of any civil orders of protection, and the specific protective measures the victim has taken to deal with the stalking behavior.

INTERVENTIONS FOR THE YOUNG STALKING PERPETRATOR

A key component of any case management strategy is the sentencing and supervision of stalking offenders (Violence Against Women Grants Office, 1998). State stalking codes generally provide for sentencing options, including incarceration, community supervision, and referral to mental health treatment services in those cases in which it is believed that a stalking offender can benefit from such services. The sentencing strategies that are adopted in any stalking case are guided by a number of factors, including the number of previous stalking offenses a perpetrator has, the victim's relationship to the offender, and the type of behavior that is used to harass or threaten the victim. In many cases, particularly those involving stalking that occurs within the context of intimate partner violence, the perpetrator may receive probation with certain conditions that are mandated by the court, including substance abuse counseling, enrollment in a treatment program for batterers, or some other form of mental health intervention.

STALKING IN CHILDREN AND ADOLESCENTS

With cases that involve child or adolescent stalking perpetrators, two general considerations must be recognized with respect to sentencing and supervision. First, most states have special criminal provisions that permit individuals under the age of majority, which is usually ages 16 or 18, to be sentenced as youthful offenders. Second, the criminal justice system often recognizes that young offenders are at a stage of development that requires recognition of the psychological changes that occur between adolescence and adulthood. Therefore, young offenders are often afforded access to programs that are more treatment and rehabilitation oriented, as opposed to punitive forms of correctional placement. As such, young stalking offenders may be sentenced as youthful offenders and given probation with specific conditions such as attending mental health treatment. In this section, the issues surrounding youthful offender status and treatment issues for young stalking offenders are briefly reviewed.

Sentencing Issues

The manner in which youthful offenders are treated under the law is different than how adults are treated. Specifically, children who are under the age of 16 or 18, depending on state law, can have limitations placed on their behavior in ways that differ markedly from the types of prohibitions that can be placed on the behavior of adults. For instance, many legal jurisdictions have status offense legislation that permits courts to prohibit minors from staying out late, associating with certain peers, skipping school, or rejecting their parents' authority (McCann, 1998a; Mnookin & Weisberg, 1989). These status offenses are often referred to as Person in Need of Supervision (PINS), Child in Need of Supervision (CINS or CHINS), or other similarly named legal status. In addition, minors can be ruled to be delinquent and placed in the custody of a particular government agency, such as the state's youth authority, if he or she has engaged in an act that would be a crime if it had been committed by an adult (Grisso, 1998). However, in some cases a youth's conduct may be so egregious or violent that he or she may be transferred from youthful status and adjudicated as an adult. In these latter instances, the youth typically undergoes a waiver hearing in which evidence is presented to a judge, who then determines whether the youth should be tried as a juvenile or as an adult.

Grisso (1998) outlined many factors that are often considered in making the decision as to whether a minor is offered youthful status or is transferred to adult court. Among the various factors considered include (a) the youth's amenability to be rehabilitated; (b) the seriousness of the offense; (c) prior criminal charges; and (d) the potential for violence or further risk to the community. With respect to children and adolescents who engage in stalking behavior, it is clear, as discussed in chapter 9, that anti-stalking laws have been applied to youthful offenders and that minors can be held criminally responsible for stalking behavior. That is, the same behaviors that constitute criminal stalking among adults can also represent the crime of stalking if committed by a young person. Therefore, an important issue becomes how young stalking offenders should be managed within the criminal justice system.

There is no formal research on the adjudication of young stalking offenders. However, in all cases of stalking by a child or adolescent that I have observed or in which I have had direct involvement, the youthful offender was maintained in the juvenile justice system and sentenced as a minor. Although each case must be considered on an individual basis, there are some factors that support the adjudication of young obsessional followers as youthful offenders. Typically, adult stalking cases involve sentencing and supervision strategies that are unique to stalking cases (Violence Against Women Grants Office, 1998). More specifically, stalking offenders may be placed under strict supervision by probation offices, particularly for first-time offenses, with the goal being to redirect the obsessional follower's anger away from the victim and toward the criminal justice system. This strategy may not always be effective and may, in fact, exacerbate feelings of rage and anger directed at the victim as well as third parties.

However, the sentencing of stalking offenders also can consist of mandated mental health treatment, involuntary commitment in cases in which there is imminent risk of violence, and other strategies that are directed at modifying the obsessional follower's behavior. Because the juvenile justice system generally operates on a rehabilitation-oriented model rather than on a punitive or retribution model of incarceration, maintaining young stalking offenders in the juvenile justice system is likely to make treatment services more accessible. Therefore, it is recommended that the sentencing of young stalking offenders be retained in the jurisdiction of the juvenile or family courts, unless the stalking case involves egregious behavior (e.g., murder, serial sexual offenses) that mandates longer term-sentencing under adult court jurisdictions. The sentencing of young stalking offenders should include referral for comprehensive psychological or psychiatric examinations, mental health treatment if indicated, and periodic violence risk assessments.

Assessment and Treatment Issues

Although the research on stalking is beginning to provide some documentation of the various forms of psychopathology found in obsessional followers, there is almost no literature on the treatment of stalking offenders. Therefore, assessment and treatment of stalking offenders must be conceptualized on an individual-case basis, depending on the nature of the problems presented by any one offender.

Research on adult populations of stalking offenders has documented that there is a range of *DSM-IV* diagnoses (American Psychiatric Association, 1994) on Axis I and Axis II, including substance abuse disorders, mood disorders, psychotic disturbances, and personality disorders (Meloy, 1996, 1998b, 1999b). As discussed in chapter 3, there are many clinical syndromes and personality disturbances in children and adolescents who engage in stalking behavior. Although some forms of psychopathology found in adult samples have been observed in cases involving younger obsessional followers, such as substance abuse (McCann, 2000) and erotomania (Urbach, Khalily, & Mitchell, 1992), other conditions that have their onset in childhood or adolescence have also been identified in young obsessional followers, such as conduct disorder (McCann, 1998c) and attention deficit hyperactivity disorder (Johnson & Becker, 1997; McCann, 2000). As such, treatment of the child or adolescent obsessional follower will be guided by the diagnosis, similar to the manner in which treatment of adult cases is approached (Meloy, 1997).

The use of psychotropic medications with children and adolescents has been somewhat controversial, given concerns about the long-term effects of such agents. Some conditions in children and adolescents have shown favorable response to medication when diagnosed properly, including the use of stimulants for attention deficit hyperactivity disorder (Barkley, 1998; Gitlin, 1990) and benzodiazepines for sleep disturbances (Gitlin, 1990). Mood disorders and psychoses in children and adolescents are likely to show some improvement when they are treated with antidepressant and antipsychotic agents, respectively, but perhaps not as much as has been observed in adults (Campbell & Spencer, 1988; Gitlin, 1990). Nevertheless, in stalking cases in which the perpetrator has a diagnosis of erotomania, mood disorder, or schizophrenia, the use of psychotropic medication as an adjunct to psychotherapy should be considered.

In cases in which there are prominent personality disturbances, the focus of treatment should be on the interpersonal problems that are present. For instance, there is often intense interpersonal ambivalence noted in the personality dynamics of young obsessional followers. This ambivalence is sometimes manifest in schizoid and avoidant personality characteristics in which the youth has strong dependency needs that are unfulfilled due to feelings of isolation and detachment that are driven by fears of being teased or rejected. More specifically, the youth isolates from interpersonal relationships, has few friends or acquaintances, and has very poor social skills due to rejection, repeated teasing, or other negative experiences with others and yet longs for interpersonal contact and intimacy. Consequently, the youth develops obsessive fixations on strangers, unattainable love objects, or casual acquaintances that fuel fantasies of an idealized relationship. In other cases, interpersonal ambivalence is manifest in borderline personality dynamics in which the youth harbors strong dependency needs, yet strong projective identification operates in which there is an expectation of rejection or abandonment. Therefore, the youth is highly susceptible to rage and anger in response to real or perceived abandonment. Therefore, the youth may engage in desperate attempts to regain and restore the relationship through stalking or obsessional following. Therefore, the personality dynamics manifest in a specific case will guide the treatment process.

In chapter 4, the role of jealousy and envy were discussed with respect to their role in creating a heightened sensitivity to extreme emotional reactions in response to rejection or unreciprocated feelings by the love object. Guerrero and Andersen (1998) outlined how extreme emotional devastation can occur in response to jealousy, for example, in the form of confusion, fear, anxiety, depression, and insecurity. Likewise, envy often involves feelings of fear, anxiety, frustration, and resentment when the person focuses on his or her unfulfilled needs. The emotions of anxiety, depression, and anger may therefore be a major focus in psychotherapy with children and adolescents who engage in stalking.

Stalking that occurs within the context of the breakup of an intimate relationship is more likely to be motivated by feelings of fear, anger, and depression that are based in feelings of jealousy. The young obsessional follower is threatened by possible abandonment, depression, or sadness over actual or potential loss and feelings of betrayal. Consequently, the goal of the obsessional follower in treatment may be finding ways to restore the love object's positive feelings, whereas the realistic treatment goals may be to facilitate the young obsessional follower's successful resolution of loss and grief. Although strong resistance may be encountered, treatment techniques such as reframing, evoking positive imagery, and restoring positive self-object experiences are useful in working with resistance. Wexler (1991) outlined an approach to increasing the self-management strategies in adolescents using a combination of cognitive–behavioral and psychoanalytic self-psychology techniques. This approach may prove useful with adolescent obsessional followers with borderline personality disturbances who are jealous, angry, and fragile.

Stalking that occurs within the context of relationships with casual acquaintances or strangers is likely to be motivated by feelings of anxiety, anger, and depression that are based in feelings of envy. Specifically, the young stalking offender is likely to focus on feelings of resentment or anger toward rivals and anxiety over feelings of inferiority or insecurity.

Moreover, the young obsessional follower may experience depression or sadness when focusing on personal shortcomings, and there are often strong feelings of longing that are frustrated. In these cases, the focus of treatment may be best targeted at increasing feelings of competence, improving social skills through group work if the child or adolescent is capable of functioning socially in small groups, and developing strategies for improving social skills and self-competence. Again the youth may have treatment goals that differ from those that are realistically attainable. That is, the youth may see treatment as an opportunity to find strategies for getting the object to reciprocate. However, the treatment goals should be targeted on reducing feelings of resentment and insecurity and channeling behavior away from obsessional following and toward more socially accepted ways of developing relationships.

COMMUNITY PREVENTION PROGRAMS

One of the major characteristics of cases in which a person stalks or obsessionally follows another person is that there is a severe disruption in attachment and the manner in which relationships are initiated and/or maintained. In effect, stalking involves an attempt to create a power imbalance in which the object will either acquiesce to the demands of the obsessional follower or feel intimidated and fearful. Normal attachment behavior and the capacity to develop adaptive interpersonal relationships rely heavily on a stable and supportive parent–child relationship in the early years of life (cf. chapter 4). Therefore, community programs that are aimed at reducing partner abuse, domestic violence, and other forms of violence in intimate relationships, such as stalking, are likely to be most effective when they identify factors that place a person at risk for such violence and implement the program long before the violence emerges.

There are some examples of preventive programs that have been developed for various forms of violence among children and teenagers that overlap with stalking. These programs hold promise for reducing the incidence of stalking, although this promise is untested. For instance, programs aimed at reducing the severity and extent of bullying have been developed and implemented in various school districts (Kolko, 1998). These programs include classroom behavioral management training for teachers to provide them with immediate responses to situations when one or more students bully a peer. Other facets of these programs include teaching children at young ages about the adverse effect of bullying on others, empathy training, and adaptive problem-solving skills to offer alternatives to bullying or other forms of violence. Given the parallels between stalking and bullying, these programs may be useful for preventing future stalking behavior if they are implemented during the early school years.

Another example of a prevention-oriented program that holds promise for reducing stalking behavior is the Youth Relationships Project described by Wekerle and Wolfe (1998). This program is intended to "help at-risk youths understand the critical importance of the abuse of power and control to relationship violence" (p. 357). The goals of this program are to increase youths' understanding of issues related to healthy relationships (e.g., reducing negative gender stereotypes, providing accurate information on the effects of violence), developing skills for building healthy relationships (e.g., conflict resolution, communications skills), and encouraging the development of new attitudes and skills to increase feelings of community involvement and social action (e.g., community supports, role-playing). These programs can be implemented through community social services agencies (where children and youth exposed to domestic violence are often referred), school districts, and mental health agencies. Although such programs have not been examined with respect to stalking, they have much potential for reducing dating and relationship violence, including stalking or obsessional following, when implemented during the school years.

SUPPORTS AND RESOURCES FOR STALKING VICTIMS

The victims of stalking and their families may often find that dealing with the constant threats and harassment consumes an inordinate amount of time, energy, and resources. One major reason for having to cope with stalking on a seemingly continuous basis is that the perpetrator often intensifies feelings of fear in the victim by making threats at different times, in various contexts, and in unexpected situations. Consequently, the victim may feel as though the obsessional follower is controlling his or her life. Another reason that stalking consumes a great deal of the victim's time and resources is that agencies or individuals who are viewed as having the power to intervene, such as police, school officials, or other people in positions of authority, may be unresponsive to the victim's needs or state that they do not have the power to control the offender's behavior until the victim encounters more aggressive or violent behavior.

Although stalking has been recognized as a crime in all state and federal jurisdictions of the United States and in many other countries such as Canada and Great Britain, public awareness of the problem has only recently been raised. Likewise, there is inconsistency across legal jurisdictions as to the degree to which police agencies are knowledgeable about the crime of stalking and are willing to take appropriate action. For example, the Threat Management Unit of the Los Angeles Police Department (cf. Zona, Palarea, & Lane, 1998) is one of the most visible specialized law enforcement units devoted to investigating and managing stalking cases. However, the presence of many high-profile individuals in the Los Angeles area, such as celebrities who are targeted by stalkers, was likely a major factor that warranted a specialized threat management unit in that city's police department. In other parts of the country there are likely to be varying needs for such units, and in jurisdictions where no such unit exists and the incidence of stalking is lower, victims may find the response from law enforcement to be lacking.

For child and adolescent victims of stalking and their families, there may be even less information available to provide guidance on coping with and managing stalking behavior. Recent advances in technology and access to materials on the Internet have resulted in greater accessibility to information on a wide variety of topics. With respect to stalking, there are several web sites that provide very useful and valuable information on stalking that can be accessed by victims, their families, mental health professionals, lawyers, police agencies, and other helping professionals. Some of these web sites deal specifically with the topic of stalking, and others address problems related to stalking, such as sexual harassment, school violence, and other forms of obsessional harassment. Although a review of these web sites is beyond the scope of this book, an overview of the most relevant ones will provide interested readers with a guide for obtaining supportive information on the Internet.

The National Center for Victims of Crime provides a web site (http://www.ncvc.org) that has a number of documents that can be downloaded. A particularly useful feature of the web site is a search engine that allows individuals to identify materials using key words. There are documents on safety planning guidelines for stalking victims that provide risk factors suggesting when there is a heightened risk for violence or information for victims on how to handle threats. Overall, the National Center for Victims of Crime web site is comprehensive and provides valuable information to stalking victims and their families. Although the material available does not deal with young stalking victims in particular, much of the information is comprehensive and applicable to most victims of stalking, regardless of their age.

A web site that deals exclusively with the crime of stalking is the Antistalking Web Site (http://www.antistalking.com). This web site provides a range of information for stalking victims, including guidelines for handling threats, security precautions that one can take, risk factors for violence, and information on whether or not to obtain an order of protection. Although this site is a valuable resource for victims, it is also one of the best resources for professionals who work with victims or perpetrators or who provide case management and security services. There is a continuously updated list of published research studies on the crime of stalking, as well as an updated list of educational events and workshops. There are also links to other Internet resources for stalking victims.

Other Internet resources for stalking victims are available and although these sources do not provide information that is specific to child and adolescent victims of stalking, much of the information provided is applicable to victims who are younger. Survivors of Stalking (http://www.soshelp.org) provides workshops, cassette tapes, access to community support services in specific locations, and legal information that will assist victims of stalking obtain needed services. In addition, the Stalking Victims' Sanctuary (http://www.stalkingvictims.com) has a reading list of self-help and scholarly books on stalking as well as guidelines that victims can follow to protect themselves.

Other Internet resources provide information on a variety of problems that are related to stalking in children and adolescents. For example, the Justice Information Center sponsored by the National Institute of Justice (http://ncjrs.org/homepage.htm) has a number of government documents and research studies on school violence, stalking, domestic violence, and juvenile crime that provide useful information for professionals and scholars. The National School Safety Center (http://www.nsscl.org) also provides comprehensive information on school violence and safety. Materials from these Internet resources can be downloaded and given to school personnel, law enforcement officials, attorneys, and others who are in a position to intervene. Although there is no assurance that these individuals will use this information to manage stalking cases involving children and adolescents more effectively, increased public awareness and attempts to educate professionals about the problem is often most effective when it is implemented at the grassroots level. Connecting with other stalking victims and their families may facilitate increased awareness and responsiveness by schools, police agencies, and government officials.

Child and adolescent stalking victims and their families should be encouraged to seek out support from community agencies that are likely to be sensitive to the crime of stalking and can provide access to needed services. Although shelters for battered women and domestic violence agencies deal with a specific form of obsessional harassment, these resources can often provide direction to stalking victims and their families on such matters as how to go about obtaining an order of protection or which law enforcement agencies provide special protective services to stalking victims. Likewise, many communities have crime victims assistance agencies that provide supportive counseling, information on local support groups, and referrals for legal assistance. Parents, teachers, and other adults who provide support to young stalking victims should be encouraged to make use of these community resources.

CONCLUSION

The effective management of stalking cases involves an interdisciplinary approach in which individuals from various professions work together to reduce the risk for violence. In general, the task requires input from mental health professionals, law enforcement officers, personal and public safety professionals, and other skilled individuals. Moreover, the victim must also take an active part in case management and assume responsibility for his or her personal safety. When stalking cases involve a child or adolescent victim, there must be additional input from the school administration and the victim's family. Recent case law reveals that schools may be civilly sued for inaction if they receive notice of harassment that is of such severity it interferes with a student's access to an education. Although schools are not necessarily required to remain completely harassment free, they appear to have a duty to respond when they receive notice of harassment that interferes with a student's access to educational opportunities. Therefore, if stalking behavior creates such an impediment, schools may be required to address the problem. Many school-based programs should include training for teachers and staff on the dynamics of obsessional harassment among students and effective strategies for managing such behavior in the classroom. Moreover, school districts that respond in a supportive and accessible fashion in stalking cases will increase the chances of a favorable outcome for the victim.

Individual child and adolescent stalking victims and their families can also implement a number of personal safety measures that are likely to reduce the risk for violence. One critical factor that can contribute to a more favorable outcome is an open and supportive relationship between parent and child. In addition, mental health professionals who work with young stalking perpetrators are in a position to reduce obsessive preoccupations, treat psychological symptoms and disturbances that may contribute to or exacerbate obsessive fixations, and assess the potential for violent acting out. Preventive programs that are aimed at addressing various forms of obsessional harassment in children and adolescents, such as sexual harassment, dating violence, and bullying, also hold considerable promise for reducing future stalking behavior by giving young people effective coping strategies for starting and ending intimate relationships, enhancing self-efficacy, and solving interpersonal conflict adaptively. Some programs are currently being implemented, but they need to be studied more fully to examine their effectiveness for preventing stalking in young people.

9

Legal Responses

Professionals from various specialty areas generally agree that the effective management of stalking cases involves a combination of legal sanctions and mental health intervention. For instance, Meloy (1997) recommended a multidisciplinary approach to case management that involves both psychological treatment and criminal penalties for the obsessional follower as well as the use of civil orders of protection for the victim. Mullen, Pathe, Purcell, and Stuart (1999) noted that mental health treatment tends to be more effective for stalking offenders whose primary motivation is seeking intimacy with the object, as well as those who are socially incompetent. On the other hand, stalking offenders who are primarily predatory in their motives require criminal justice intervention, although treatment for paraphilic sexual behavior may be indicated. Mullen and his colleagues recommended a differential weighting of legal and mental health intervention depending on the primary motivation of the stalker. Likewise, the Violence Against Women Grants Office (1998) recommended in its *Third Annual Report to Congress under the Violence Against Women Act* that there be greater collaboration between the legal and mental health systems.

In previous chapters, discussions focused primarily on psychological concepts and theories related to stalking, research findings from the behavioral sciences, and issues related to the assessment and treatment of perpetrators and victims. Although legal issues were mentioned peripherally as they related to case management, this chapter provides more detailed discussions on the application of anti-stalking laws to young stalking offenders and victims as well as the efficacy of these laws in curbing stalking behavior. Moreover, the use of civil orders of protection as a means of protecting stalking victims is also discussed. Finally, various policy issues are covered that constitute avenues of further study that will clarify some of the more useful and effective ways for dealing with the social problem of stalking among young people.

The first formal legal response to the problem of stalking dates back to 1990 when California became the first state to pass anti-stalking legislation (Guy, 1993; Sohn, 1994). Most states followed with their own versions of anti-stalking laws, with some states patterning their laws after the California statute and others modifying existing harassment statutes. The National Institute of Justice (1993) developed a model anti-stalking code to help states draft felony-level anti-stalking laws. The intent was to reduce diversity in the way that stalking was defined across jurisdictions and to provide uniform guidelines for punishing and sentencing stalking offenders. Guy (1993) pointed out some of the significant variations that have occurred in the way stalking has been defined and conceptualized across different jurisdictions, and have resulted in serious limitations or omissions. For example, he noted that the 1992 West Virginia anti-stalking statute defined *stalking* only as conduct by a perpetrator that targeted a victim with whom there had been a prior live-in or intimate relationship. The law did not cover stalking in situations in which the perpetrator and victim were strangers or casual acquaintances. Therefore, model legislation proposals were intended to reduce variation in legislation and to prevent significant omissions that might affect how these laws are applied.

In 1996, the Interstate Stalking Punishment and Prevention Act was passed in the United States (Violence Against Women Grants Office, 1998). This statute prohibits people from crossing state boundaries with the intent to harm or harass another person or to place that person in fear of death or bodily injury. Thus, the United States currently has federal anti-stalking legislation in addition to the numerous state anti-stalking laws. Moreover, similar laws providing federal protection to stalking victims have been passed in other countries, including Canada, Australia, and the United Kingdom.

Although some anti-stalking laws include special provisions for the stalking of minors, these provisions typically involve making the stalking of a person younger than age 16 or 18 an aggravating factor that enhances the criminal penalties for the offender. However, the applicability of anti-stalking laws to young offenders and victims has not been addressed in any systematic way by considering the special challenges that exist when attempting to prove a stalking offense when the perpetrator or victim is a minor. In the sections that follow, some of these challenges are reviewed, and a general summary is provided on what changes, if any, need to be made in the way young stalking offenders and victims are viewed under current anti-stalking legislation.

ANTI-STALKING LAWS AND YOUNG
STALKING OFFENDERS

Although legal definitions of stalking vary across jurisdictions, the basic elements of the criminal offense of stalking include a pattern of repetitive threatening behavior or harassment and the intent to place the victim in reasonable fear of death or injury. In fact, a general legal definition provided by *Corpus Juris Secundum* (C.J.S.), a major legal encyclopedia, provides the following definition of *stalking*: "Any person who willfully, maliciously and repeatedly follows or harasses another person, and makes a credible threat with the intent to place that person in reasonable fear of death or bodily injury commits the offense of stalking" (86 C. J. S. §10, p. 528). In determining whether a child or adolescent can be charged under criminal statutes, a number of factors must be considered.

As noted in chapter 8, the juvenile justice system in most jurisdictions provides for individuals below a certain age, which is typically 18, to be adjudicated in family court or a specialized juvenile court if they commit an act that if performed by an adult would constitute a criminal offense. In some instances, however, the juvenile's conduct might be so egregious or severe that the law permits juvenile or family court jurisdiction to be waived so that the adolescent may be adjudicated as an adult. In this respect, a number of issues are significant in making determinations about the applicability of criminal and penal statutes to young offenders. These issues include whether a youth has the mental capacity or maturity to form the requisite intent to commit a crime, whether the youth can benefit from rehabilitation efforts available in the juvenile correctional system, and the presence of mitigating factors such as psychological disturbance that might be considered by courts during procedural hearings or sentencing.

With respect to the use of anti-stalking laws to prosecute children or adolescents who engage in obsessional following and other forms of harassment, the issue of intent is important. More specifically, most anti-stalking laws require that the perpetrator intend to create fear of death or injury in the victim. Thus, when establishing proof of legal guilt in cases of stalking perpetrated by a child or adolescent, one must be able to prove that the young offender intended to create such fear in the victim.

The case law reveals that challenges have been raised against the application of anti-stalking laws to juvenile offenders. Different legal arguments have been offered as to why anti-stalking laws should not be used in the prosecution of children or adolescents, but some courts have upheld the application of these laws to minors. For instance, one New York State Appellate Division court upheld a finding that a juvenile committed acts of stalking and harassment that were sufficient to meet the requirements of the *menacing* statute, which is the term used to describe criminal stalking in New York (*In the Matter of Luis A.,* 1996). An argument had been set forth by the youth's attorney that because the boy and his victim were in a dating relationship at the time the stalking occurred, a finding of the boy's guilt for menacing was not appropriate. The court stated "there is nothing in the statute itself to indicate a legislative intent to minimize stalkers who target persons familiar to them" (p. 375). In another case, an appellate court upheld without comment a family court ruling that a youth had committed several acts that would constitute the crime of harassment in the first degree as outlined by the state's anti-stalking law (*In the Matter of Jamar S.*, 1998).

These legal cases illustrate that arguments against applying anti-stalking laws to young offenders are not likely to meet with success, particularly if such arguments are based on the notion that harassment occurring while there is a dating relationship that exists between the stalker and his or her victim is somehow less severe. On the other hand, arguments that are based on whether the offender has the cognitive capacity to form the requisite intent to place the victim in fear may be more viable and acceptable, particularly when the offender is a child and has not yet developed the full cognitive skills required to appreciate the effects of his or her behavior on others. It is unclear how such arguments will be treated by the courts, but in stalking cases that involve younger children as perpetrators, the intellectual, cognitive, and psychological maturity of the child must be taken into account when making a determination of his or her capacity to form the intent to place the victim in fear of death or serious bodily injury, or the specific intent that is outlined in a particular anti-stalking law that applies in a given case.

There have been other legal challenges to state anti-stalking laws that have not addressed issues related to child or adolescent stalking perpetrators. However, a few of the issues raised in these legal cases may become relevant as more cases involving younger offenders are adjudicated. Bjerregaard (1996) analyzed 35 appellate court decisions that addressed the issue of vagueness or overbreadth in state anti-stalking laws. Vagueness challenges are based on the argument that language in the statutes is unclear and will likely lead to confusion, whereas overbreadth challenges are based on the argument that anti-stalking laws prohibit activities that are constitutionally protected or reach further than should be permitted by law. According to Bjerregaard's analysis, most challenges to the constitutionality of anti-stalking laws have been based on vagueness.

The two terms that have been the focus of most litigation are *repeatedly* and *without legitimate purpose.* Because stalking requires a course of conduct in which the perpetrator repeatedly engages in harassing or threatening behavior directed toward the victim, several state appellate courts have heard arguments that the term *repeatedly* is vague. However, most courts have ruled that this term is not vague and have held that it provides a specific intent and narrows the range of behaviors to those that involve a pattern of conduct that constitutes stalking. On the other hand, the term *without legitimate purpose* is included in many anti-stalking laws as a way of providing exceptions to conduct that is legally permissible or protected that would otherwise constitute stalking.

Bjerregaard noted that there is much greater diversity in court opinions on the vagueness of "without legitimate purpose." One opinion issued by the Oregon Court of Appeals held that the phrase was vague in a case in which there was an issue of the validity of a civil order of protection in one stalking case (*State v. Eccles*, 1995). However, the same court later reversed its prior holding and ruled that the phrase was not vague (*Foster v. Souders*, 1995). The Florida Court of Appeals has also held that the phrase is not vague (*Bouters v. State*, 1994). Although there is no consistent view on the issue of whether "without legitimate purpose" is inappropriately vague, the issue is likely to raise complex questions in cases involving child and adolescent stalking victims and perpetrators.

More specifically, it will be necessary to decide on a case-by-case basis what behaviors have a legitimate purpose and are thus protected by law. For example, if a court order of protection is issued that bars the perpetrator from coming within a certain distance of the victim and both the victim and perpetrator are students in the same school, it is foreseeable that the young stalking perpetrator could raise a legal challenge to the protective order on the basis that attending school, and thus gaining proximity to the victim, has a legitimate purpose. Consequently, courts may be presented with numerous challenges in drafting protective orders for young stalking victims that are more elaborate and outline those behaviors that constitute legitimate exceptions to the acts prohibited by the order. One way of circumventing these problems is to outline the behaviors that are proscribed in a protective order and provide school administrators with a copy of the order. In this way, some monitoring can take place to oversee the behavioral interaction between the perpetrator and victim in school while permitting a temporary exception to the requirement that the perpetrator maintain a specific distance from the victim when both are required to be in school.

It will be interesting to see what specific legal issues are raised in the future with respect to the applicability of anti-stalking laws to younger obsessional followers. In light of recent case law on sexual harassment in the schools, some guidance may emerge from the case law and legislation that arises from this related form of harassment, and this might provide direction on how the problem of stalking might be legally addressed.

ANTI-STALKING LAWS AND CHILD VICTIMS

The major impetus behind the passage of anti-stalking laws was the need to prevent various types of behaviors that constitute intentional, repetitive, and malicious following and harassment. It has been noted that prior to the passing of anti-stalking legislation, traditional laws, such as those proscribing harassment, were ineffective for curbing stalking (Rosen, 1993). Whereas harassment generally constitutes discrete episodes of threatening behavior, stalking involves repetitive and organized behavior that constitutes a course of conduct that disrupts the victim's life (Guy, 1993). Also, harassment statutes often require that perpetrators actually harm a victim before legal action, such as arrest, can take place.

The applicability and utility of anti-stalking laws as a means of preventing victimization of children is virtually untested. Most anti-stalking laws require that a credible threat be made against the victim by the perpetrator and that a victim respond with fear or threat of serious injury or death. With child victims, however, this statutory requirement may be difficult to satisfy, particularly with very young victims, because they often perceive threats and danger differently than do adults. Empirical findings show that younger children differ from older children and adolescents in terms of the kinds of events and circumstances they find threatening or

233

fear-inducing (Harter & Whitesall, 1989). In particular, younger children experience greater fear from a perceived threat of physical harm or death, such as a risk of being beaten up or kidnapped. These fears decrease between the ages of 3 and 11. Over this same age range, on the other hand, fear provoked by novel or unfamiliar situations increases gradually with age and there is also a slight increase in fear of social rejection. In addition, children tend to be more socially naive than adults and are less likely to perceive genuine threats of being kidnapped unless their parents instill these fears in the child (McCann, 1995).

These research findings are relevant to the application of anti-stalking laws to child and adolescent victims because credibility of a threat is a key element that is necessary to make stalking behavior a crime. Most anti-stalking laws require that the victim have some belief that a stalker is able to carry out a threat and whether or not a child victim believes the perpetrator can carry it out is an issue. As such, anti-stalking laws are generally ill-equipped to prevent the stalking of a child. There are, however, some exceptions that can serve as a model for state and federal jurisdictions.

One method for protecting children using anti-stalking laws is when legal elements of stalking statutes require the threats and course of conduct to be directed at someone who is a member of the victim's family. An example is the Arkansas anti-stalking law that extends the proscribed behavior to family members (Arkansas Code Annotated, 1993); the statute makes stalking a crime if threats are directed against the victim's family and the person has a reasonable fear that members of his or her family will be harmed. Although such provisions appear on their face to be useful, a problem with their application is that victims tend to be statutorily defined as the parent instead of the child. Moreover, there tends to be a gap in protective coverage of the child when children are threatened or stalked directly and the parent is not fully aware of the threat. Such familial provisions of anti-stalking laws generally fail to protect the child victim directly when the stalker's intent is to follow, threaten, or harass the child instead of using the threats against the child as a means to intimidate or harass the parent.

Another approach to using anti-stalking laws as a means of protecting children and adolescents is making special provisions for victims below the age of 16. In 1995, only four states (Alaska, Connecticut, South Dakota, and Vermont) had special provisions that made the stalking of a child an aggravating factor resulting in more severe criminal sanctions (McCann, 1995). According to a recent study reported in the *Third Annual Report to Congress under the Violence Against Women Act* submitted to Congress (Violence Against Women Grants Office, 1998), 10 states now make some mention of stalking or harassment of minors, but only 9 provide for enhanced penalties for those individuals who stalk or harass a child or adolescent. Five states (Alaska, Connecticut, Florida, New Mexico, and Vermont) have stiffer penalties for the stalking of a minor younger than 16, three states (Iowa, Michigan, and Minnesota) have more severe penalties for adults who stalk a minor younger than 18, and one state (Louisiana) uses 12 as the cut-off age. Furthermore, Missouri has created a special order of protection for children to protect them against stalking by a current or former member of the household.

These statutes represent some improvements in the legal response to the stalking of children, but there is considerable variability in how these laws address the problem. Some states make the stalking of a child or adolescent an aggravating condition that increases the perpetrator's potential sentence from 1 year to 5 years. Another state, Vermont, permits a monetary fine of up to $25,000 as well as a prison sentence for the stalking of a minor (Vermont Statutes Annotated, Title 13, §1063, 1994). Statutory provisions that permit stiffer penalties for people who stalk a child or adolescent rest on the assumption that harsher punishment will deter or incapacitate those who stalk children or adolescents. Although no empirical evidence currently exists that these provisions serve as a deterrent, a logical conclusion to draw is that lengthier sentences incapacitate those who stalk young people for the duration of their criminal sentence.

One state, South Dakota, is unique in that it has taken into account developmental differences between adults and children by defining the crime differently if victims are age 12 or younger (South Dakota Codified Laws Annotated, §22-19A-7, 1994). For victims that are older than 12, there must be a reasonable fear of death or great bodily injury, whereas for victims younger than 12 there need only be a reasonable fear for one's safety. Although the statute does not define what constitutes a reasonable fear, or even by what standard reasonableness is determined (i.e., reasonable person vs. reasonable person of similar age and maturity), there is a more liberal standard for proving the victim's fear when the victim is a pre-adolescent. As such, South Dakota appears to be the only state to consider developmental differences between child and adolescent victims when defining the standard for proving the nature of the victim's fear. Legislative changes in anti-stalking laws at the state and federal levels should follow the direction implemented by the South Dakota statute.

The success of any effort to change law and public policy is largely dependent on the underlying motivation for instituting change. When there is a great deal of public acceptance for a particular cause, the political ramifications for lawmakers is increased public support (and votes), and changes are more likely to occur. One example of popular political activity is the passage of public notification laws for convicted sex offenders who are released onto the community (Schopp, 1998). These laws are drafted with the stated intention of increasing public safety and the safety of children in particular. Another legal method for protecting children from victimization is anti-stalking laws. If society is to make a commitment to protecting children because they are resources for our future, one important step would be to protect them from the obsessional behavior of stalkers. A number of proposed changes in existing anti-stalking legislation are offered as a means for promoting protective measures for children who are victimized by stalkers.

One major change would be to increase the penalties for adults who are convicted of stalking children. Only nine states permit lengthier prison sentences for those who are convicted of stalking a minor (Violence Against Women Grants Office, 1998). Although it remains untested as to whether or not lengthier sentences will serve as a deterrent to stalking, lengthier incarceration will serve to incapacitate adults who stalk children so they cannot victimize the child or commit an act of violence.

A number of possibilities exist for using the age of the victim as a sentencing factor in stalking cases. For example, the age of the victim could be used to distinguish felony and misdemeanor stalking for first-time offenses. In other instances, the age of the victim could be used as an aggravating factor that distinguishes various classes of felonies. The ultimate goal would be to have longer prison sentences for adults who stalk children and teenagers, thus serving to incapacitate the perpetrator from committing offenses against younger victims.

Another method for reducing the victimization of children by stalkers is electronic monitoring of perpetrators with home-based detention devices. The use of these devices calls for law enforcement and parole officers to routinely monitor whether a paroled offender is adhering to prescribed release conditions. In northern California, for example, a program called the Sexual Habitual Offender Program (SHOP) identifies individuals paroled from prison who have been convicted of serial sexual crimes against children and who are believed to be the highest risk for repeat offenses (McCann, 1995). Other states use a central registry for convicted sex offenders in order to facilitate the location and identification of sex offenders. By collecting detailed information about unsolved assaults and crimes against children, electronic monitoring programs can be used effectively to assist police with linking similar cases across different jurisdictions.

Another method for reducing the stalking and victimization of children is by having courts order psychological or psychiatric evaluations of an alleged stalker. As noted in earlier chapters, the psychological stability, maturity, and potential for violence a stalking perpetrator poses are significant factors that must be considered when developing interventions and case management strategies. Toward this end, judges can use the option of referring a stalking perpetrator for psychological or psychiatric assessment and treatment to assist with legal disposition planning. A statutory provision mandating such examinations in stalking cases, particularly those involving children and adolescents, should be available in all legal jurisdictions. In the past, state and federal legislators have failed to recognize the importance of input from mental health professionals

(Violence Against Women Grants Office, 1998), most likely because of uncertainty or skepticism over the ability of mental health professionals to predict future violence or to treat certain groups of individuals who pose a threat to society, such as sex offenders.

Two states, Michigan and Hawaii, have written explicit provisions permitting judges to order psychological evaluations or treatment for suspected stalkers (McCann, 1995). In most cases, the decision of whether or not an obsessional follower receives mental health treatment is left to the discretion of the judge. Because individual judges vary in their willingness to refer a criminal defendant for evaluation or mandate treatment as a part of sentencing, there is likely to be considerable variability in the extent to which stalking offenders receive a mental health evaluation and treatment. Laws that make mental health assessment and treatment mandatory would improve the adjudication process and ultimately increase protective measures that are available to victims.

ARE ANTI-STALKING LAWS EFFECTIVE?

Although anti-stalking laws were drafted to provide protection to victims, there have been no systematic attempts to empirically measure their effectiveness. Nevertheless, there are several ways in which the worth of these laws can be appraised. One measure of their efficacy is whether or not they reduce the incidence and prevalence of stalking. Another measure of their effectiveness is whether they provide legal remedies for victims in situations where existing laws have failed to provide adequate protection (Sohn, 1994). Therefore, one must consider not only how anti-stalking laws affect the prevalence of stalking in society, but also how they compare with existing statutes that address related problems such as harassment, criminal contempt due to violation of a protective order, menacing, and similar forms of threatening behavior.

Before the passage of anti-stalking legislation, courts had to rely on the use of civil protection orders and the application of menacing and harassment statutes to address the problem of stalking. It has been generally recognized that these legal approaches were inadequate for dealing with the specific types of threatening and harassing behavior that occur in stalking cases (Bradfield, 1998; Sohn, 1994). Anti-stalking legislation was significant in that it provided a symbolic message that stalking would be taken seriously by the law enforcement and criminal justice systems, and it permitted the reasonableness of a victim's fear to be used to prove a stalker's intent (Violence Against Women Grants Office, 1998). Despite these positive efforts, several problems remain in the enforcement of these laws.

There is considerable diversity across legal jurisdictions as to whether or not crimes of stalking will be investigated and prosecuted. Sohn (1994) noted that the support of law enforcement agencies is largely dependent on whether or not there is a perception that stalking can be successfully prosecuted. In addition, there is often considerable variation among law enforcement agencies as to the training and knowledge that exists about stalking and how it differs from other forms of harassment. Likewise, many anti-stalking laws make it difficult for victims to seek protection with restraining orders because these laws often do not have specific provisions or protective orders, and courts must rely instead on statutes that govern general restraining orders which are not effective in every case (Violence Against Women Grants Office, 1998). This issue is significant because many civil orders of protection are drafted in such a way that it is often easy to avoid their authority on technical grounds (Sohn, 1994). That is, civil orders of protection must outline the specific behaviors from which an obsessional harasser must refrain; however, if the harasser engages in particular threatening or harassing behaviors that differ from those specified in the order, there is often no legal remedy other than to apply for a new or revised order. If all anti-stalking laws had provisions for protective orders that permitted a broader definition of threatening or harassing behavior, then courts would have greater authority to hold an obsessional follower in contempt if he or she violated the general parameters, rather than the specific provisions, of the order.

For example, an obsessional follower who is making threatening telephone calls and sending harassing letters to the victim could receive notice of a civil restraining order that must specify that he or she cannot telephone or send letters to the victim. If this case occurred in a legal juris-diction that permitted the issuance of a general restraining order, but no such order specific to stalking cases was available, the obsessional follow-er's legal counsel could be successful in getting the specific behaviors that are prohibited by the order to be individually listed. However, if the harassment then changes to the victim being physically followed and sent threatening e-mail messages, it could be argued that the original protec-tive order was not violated. In this way, the obsessional follower could continue to stalk the victim without violating a standing court order. If specialized protective orders are available under an anti-stalking law, then they could be drafted so that any behavior that represents the obsessional follower's course of conduct, which the victim reasonably perceives as threatening, could be considered a violation even if the behavior is not specifically listed in the order. By broadening the scope of behavior that would be prohibited by a protective order, there is an increased likelihood that the stalking offender would be unable to circumvent the order on technical grounds.

It is important when analyzing the effectiveness of anti-stalking legis-lation to recognize that some protective measures may exacerbate the stalking behavior. One example of a legal response to stalking that pro-vides a false sense of security for victims is a provision in some anti-stalk-ing laws that permit victims to file a civil suit for damages against the stalking offender (McCann, 1998b). Currently, four states (California, Oregon, Texas, and Wyoming) have specific provisions that permit a stalk-ing victim to bring a tort action against a stalking perpetrator (Violence Against Women Grants Office, 1998). Furthermore, it is feasible that in those states where no such provision exists in the anti-stalking statute that a tort action could still be based on an alternative legal theory, such as assault or intentional infliction of emotional distress.

Although civil actions in stalking cases might appear favorable at first glance, there are several problems with permitting victims to sue their obsessional followers. As noted by Meloy and Gothard (1995), for exam-ple, most stalking offenders are unemployed, and they are likely to have very few financial resources with which to pay prospective damages. With young stalking offenders, there is even less likelihood that they will have any financial resources to pay prospective damages because of unemployment or a lack of financial resources. Moreover, the extent to which parents may be held legally responsible for the actions of their children is a complicated legal issue. It is unclear as to whether or not parents of stalking offenders can and should be held accountable in a civil action for the behavior of their child or teenager. A second, and more important, reason that permitting stalking victims to sue their obsessional followers is ill-advised is that the process of pretrial discovery, including depositions and interrogatories, provide the obsessional follower with a legally sanctioned opportunity to continue stalking the victim (Meloy, as cited in McCann, 1998b). At depositions, for example, the defendant can sit face-to-face with the plaintiff victim and have his or her attorney ask questions of a very personal nature. Therefore, the filing of civil suits by stalking victims against their obsessional followers is not a course of action that should be encouraged.

On the other hand, there are other forms of legislation that provide stalking victims a measure of financial compensation without having to sue or directly confront the obsessional follower. For example, New York recently amended Chapter 443, Section 631(12) of its Executive Law (1998) to permit victims of stalking offenses such as menacing, harassment, aggravated harassment, and criminal contempt to receive financial payments from the Crime Victim's Board for lost wages and earnings, damage to personal property, costs for security devices, and counseling as a result of being stalked. The Crime Victim's Board in New York provides state financial assistance to the victims of crime. Similar programs could be funded with fines and court costs paid by stalking offenders as part of their sentence or contempt charges for violating protective orders. Again, however, the fact that many stalking offenders are either unemployed or underemployed (Meloy, 1996, 1998b; Meloy & Gothard, 1995) may limit the extent to which these fines could be collected. Nevertheless, by permitting money to be paid directly to the court, the victim is not placed in a position of having to obtain compensation directly from the stalking offender.

EFFICACY OF RESTRAINING ORDERS

One legal remedy for preventing harassing behavior in stalking cases is the use of civil orders of protection, or restraining orders. According to the Violence Against Women Grants Office's (1998) report to Congress, many states permit the issuance of restraining orders as part of their anti-stalking legislation, and the remaining states provide for such orders as part of general domestic violence or civil protective orders against abuse or harassment. The major purpose of protective or restraining orders is to prevent future harm to the victim, not to punish for past behavior (Meloy, Cowett, Parker, Hofland, & Friedland, 1997). Most anti-stalking laws make it a criminal offense to violate a protective order and in those states without a specific provision for such orders in their anti-stalking laws, violations of protective orders are punishable under the general contempt authority of the courts (Violence Against Women Grants Office, 1998). Whether these protective orders are effective depends on the stalking per-petrator's willingness to comply with the authority of the court. However, various opinions may be encountered as to whether a victim should obtain a protective order. One argument in support of restraining orders is that they provide a measure of legal protection and authority of the court ordering harassment to cease. An argument against restraining orders is that serving a stalking offender with an order may provoke him or her to commit further harassment and retaliatory violence (Hart, 1996). The validity of these arguments must be evaluated by looking at the empirical evidence on whether such orders are effective in preventing violence against the individuals they are designed to protect.

As noted in chapter 2, one study on dating violence among adoles-cents in Massachusetts found that 757 restraining orders were issued against teenagers over a 10-month period for threatening, stalking, and abusive behavior (National Victim Center, 1995). Moreover, the growing problem of dating violence and sexual harassment among younger individuals suggests that the use of restraining orders against individuals younger than age 18 will increase as a means of addressing relationship violence in younger people. Nevertheless, there appear to be no empirical studies that have examined the efficacy of restraining orders specifically among children and adolescents. Therefore, a survey of research on the effectiveness of these orders among adults may provide some useful insights and directions for future research on their application in cases of stalking involving younger individuals.

One study examined the effectiveness of restraining orders in domestic violence cases involving 355 women who had filed for temporary restraining orders against spouses, former spouses, or boyfriends (Harrell & Smith, 1996). This study is somewhat relevant in that the age range of the women was 16 to 60, and therefore adolescent victims of relationship abuse were included, although the exact percentage of teenagers in the sample is unclear. A range of abusive behaviors was also observed in the sample, including stalking and threatening communications. Overall, the results of the study by Harrell and Smith were equivocal in that 60% of the victims reported that their partners violated the order within a year, whereas 40% of the victims appear to have benefited from the issuance of a protective order.

There were other findings that offer some interesting observations about the efficacy of protective orders. For instance, Harrell and Smith (1996) found that when temporary protective orders were issued, the likelihood that a woman would return to court to seek a permanent order increased with age. This finding led Harrell and Smith to speculate that younger victims were more likely to expect that abuse would stop without further intervention from the courts. An alternative hypothesis would be that relationship abuse among younger individuals differs in that the victim and perpetrator are less likely to be married, and the abuse may end after a shorter period of time. Another finding by Harrell and Smith was that the issuance of a permanent order of protection did not significantly reduce the likelihood of contact with the perpetrator. The most common form of unwanted contact in such cases involved telephone calls; stalking behaviors were unaffected by the issuance of a permanent order of protection. Harrell and Smith noted a strong indication that abuse might continue in a given case was when the man strenuously objected to the issuance of a protective order.

A recent study by Carlson, Harris, and Holden (1999) demonstrated that protective orders are generally effective in reducing re-abuse in domestic violence cases. Using an extended 2-year period prior to and following issuance of the protective order, these researchers found a 66% decrease in police contact due to physical assaults following issuance of a protective order. However, several risk factors for re-abuse were observed, including lower socioeconomic status and greater investment in a long-term relationship for women of higher socioeconomic status. When couples shared biological children there was a greater risk for re-abuse, suggesting that strong emotional reactions surrounding parenting, visitation, and child custody may precipitate re-abuse in domestic violence cases. Although these findings are important in that they support the general efficacy of protective orders, they have limited applicability for determining whether such legal remedies are effective in cases of relationship violence, stalking, or harassment involving minors. This study is important in that it highlights the need to examine specific variables when conducting research on the efficacy of protective orders, such as the demographic characteristics of the parties, the nature of the relationship between victim and perpetrator, and the specific legal remedies (e.g., arrest) that are taken in response to violations of protective orders.

Another recent study also found support for the effectiveness of protective orders. Meloy and colleagues (1997) examined the validity of several variables in predicting arrest for criminal behavior and violence against individuals protected by a restraining order. This study used a reporting period that was more extensive than that used by Carlson and colleagues (1999) in that Meloy and his colleagues examined the three years prior to and the three years following issuance of an order. A major finding was that most individuals were not arrested for criminal or violent behavior toward the protectee following issuance of a protective order.

More importantly, Meloy and his colleagues examined specific variables that predicted subsequent criminal and violent behavior toward the protected individual, including one variable that had not been previously studied. Meloy and his colleagues examined whether the issuance of a mutual order of protection (i.e., one in which both victim and perpetrator have orders protecting each from the other) had a different effect on the rate of subsequent criminal and violent acting out toward the victim than a non-mutual order of protection (i.e., one in which the victim is protected from the perpetrator, but not vice versa). Interestingly, this study found that non-mutual protection orders increased the probability of subsequent arrest compared to mutual protective orders or no protective orders at all. In their discussion, Meloy and his colleagues offer some psychodynamic hypotheses that non-mutual orders of protection precipitate feelings of shame and humiliation because they represent public exposure of one's bad nature that are defended against with rage (Meloy et al., 1997). Also, mutual protective orders tend to offer the appearance of fairness and equity in legal proceedings that is likely to reduce the risk for subsequent violence or criminal acting out toward the victim. These research findings may have similar implications when applied in cases involving younger victims and perpetrators, because stalking is hypothesized to be a disturbance in attachment that has similar psychodynamics across all age groups (see chapter 4), and the appearance of fairness and avoidance of narcissistic injury in the perpetrator is likely to decrease the need for retaliation, regardless of the person's age.

Overall, the research generally supports the efficacy of protective orders for reducing subsequent abuse or violence against the protected individuals. The studies by Carlson and colleagues (1999) and Meloy and colleagues (1997) each reviewed the existing empirical literature and independently arrived at the same conclusion that protective orders are effective more often than not. However, the research also indicates that restraining orders are not uniformly effective, and specific variables may raise the risk of subsequent abuse or violence following issuance of a protective order. Certain demographic variables, such as age and socioeconomic status, and relationship variables, such as the presence of violence prior to issuance of the order or the sharing of biological children, serve as important risk factors. Also, the manner in which protective orders are issued and enforced, such as mutual versus non-mutual, appear to be important factors to consider. As such, research on the efficacy of restraining/protective orders in cases involving younger victims and perpetrators of interpersonal violence and harassment is very much needed. The effect of specific variables on the occurrence of violence subsequent to the issuance of a protective order needs to be studied in those cases involving child and adolescent perpetrators and victims.

POLICY ISSUES

A delicate balance exists between forces motivating the drafting of new legislation or reforming existing laws for the protection of stalking victims and the directions for reform that are frequently dictated by behavioral sciences research. On the one hand, legislation is needed to meet immediate safety demands or to placate political constituents. On the other hand, legal reforms that are made without input from the behavioral sciences may result in misguided or inappropriate legislation. For instance, the Violence Against Women Grants Office (1998), in its *Third Annual Report to Congress under the Violence Against Women Act,* outlined several recommendations for changing national policy and future directions for stalking research. The report concluded that "stalking is a much bigger problem than previously assumed and should be treated as a major criminal justice problem and public health concern" (p. 59). This conclusion is supported by the research of Tjaden (1997) from the National Violence Against Women Survey that found about 8% of women and 2% of men report having been stalked at some point in their lives.

However, the Violence Against Women Grants Office (1998) also concluded that "stalkers often do not threaten their victims verbally or in writing; therefore, credible threat requirements should be eliminated from anti-stalking statutes to make it easier to prosecute such cases" (p. 59). This policy recommendation is based on a conclusion that is not supported by the empirical research. In fact, studies of obsessional followers have shown that a majority of perpetrators explicitly threaten their victims. Meloy (1999) noted that 50%–75% of obsessional followers threaten their victims. In a recent Australian study using one of the largest samples of stalking offenders available, Mullen and his colleagues (1999) found that 58% of stalkers threatened their victims. Among child and adolescent obsessional followers, McCann (2000) found that the percentage of perpetrators who threatened their victims was just over 50%. Therefore, behavioral sciences research refutes the conclusion offered by the Violence Against Women Grants Office that most stalkers do not threaten their victims; on the contrary, most obsessional followers threaten their victims. Moreover, removal of the credible threat requirement in most anti-stalking laws would likely make prosecution more, not less, difficult because the prosecution would have to prove the perpetrator's intent to evoke fear in the victim, rather than the reasonableness of the victim's fear. That is, it would be more difficult to establish a stalker's intent when he or she is not required to testify in a criminal proceedings than it would be to have a victim testify that he or she was threatened by the offender's conduct and the judge or jury could determine the reasonableness of this fear.

The Violence Against Women Grants Office (1998) also made other suggestions in their report for reforming policy on stalking and directing future research. More specifically, the report suggested that because most stalking cases involve a perpetrator and victim who are either acquaintances or prior intimate partners, future research should focus on stalking between intimates and acquaintances rather than on the stalking of celebrities or politicians. Research generally supports this finding in that stalking between prior intimate partners is the prototypic stalking case. In cases involving children and adolescents, the typical case involves a perpetrator and victim who are acquaintances. However, very useful information has been obtained from research on the stalking of celebrities and politicians, such as the relationship between threatening communications and approach behavior (Dietz, Matthews, Martell, et al., 1991; Dietz, Matthews, van Duyne, et al., 1991), pre-offense behavior of lethal and near-lethal attackers (Fein & Vossekuil, 1999), and the differences between harmless and pathological celebrity fixations (Leets, de Becker, & Giles,

1995). Therefore, research on many different kinds of perpetrator–victim relationships is likely to produce useful information that can generalize to other settings and contexts. Therefore, diversity in research sampling and methodology should be encouraged.

In addition, the Violence Against Women Grants Office (1998) recommended that law enforcement agencies, lawyers, judges, parole and probation officers, and mental health professionals receive comprehensive training on stalking, the relationship between threats and violence, and appropriate interventions for both victims and perpetrators. Such training is likely to increase the responsiveness of professionals across all disciplines to the unique challenges raised by stalking cases.

Another important policy issue that must be addressed in the future is the extent to which findings from behavioral sciences literature will be incorporated into the drafting of legislation aimed at reducing stalking and harassment. For instance, the study by Meloy and colleagues (1997) on the efficacy of protective orders indicated that non-mutual orders of protection increase the risk for subsequent criminal and violent behavior toward the victim. Moreover, they suggest that mutual service of protective orders may serve to satisfy certain angry and retaliatory impulses in the perpetrator and reduce the risk for subsequent violence. This finding must be reconciled with conflicting legal standards in many jurisdictions. For example, in New York, the issuance of mutual orders of protection is not permitted unless each individual petitions the court for such an order. The underlying principle is that the court cannot independently institute a legal remedy that has not been brought before it because reasonable notice must be given to the parties and proper motions must be made prior to the implementation of an order. Therefore, although mutual orders of protection may be a useful remedy in many cases involving recurrent harassment and stalking to reduce the risk for subsequent violence, the laws in certain jurisdictions may not allow such selective use of remedies. This provides one example of how discrepancies between our understanding of social problems through behavioral sciences research and the principle of law must be reconciled as efforts are sought to improve the legal responses to stalking and obsessional harassment.

CONCLUSION

Although stalking is an old behavior, the laws making it a crime are fairly new (Meloy, 1999b). There is some diversity in the way stalking is defined across various jurisdictions and in the severity of criminal sanctions for stalking offenses. Anti-stalking laws have been the principle legal response to the social problem of persistent and repetitive harassing behavior, and these laws currently exist in all 50 states in the United States as well as in federal jurisdictions. The rapidity with which anti-stalking legislation has been implemented is a reflection of the significant need for legal responsiveness and interventions that are accessible to victims. However, little recognition has been given to how these laws can be applied to child and adolescent perpetrators and victims of stalking. Some case law reveals that young stalking offenders have been held legally accountable for stalking behavior. However, several issues are likely to create challenges in the application of anti-stalking laws to youthful offenders such as what behavior may be exempt from these laws due to a legitimate, legally protected purpose. In addition, a few states have special provisions that provide greater protection for young stalking victims such as more severe penalties for the stalking of a child or more liberal definitions of the type of fear a stalking victim must experience in order to prove stalking. These special provisions are the exception, rather than the norm, and considerable progress needs to be made in getting more state and federal laws to implement additional protections against the stalking of children and adolescents.

Effective legal responses to stalking can be examined in several ways. For instance, comparative legal studies are needed to determine which specific aspects of anti-stalking laws are most effective and how these laws can be drafted to provide specific protections for young victims. In addition, there is empirical evidence that supports the use of restraining orders as a generally effective means of protecting victims of stalking and harassment, although these orders are not effective in every case. Research on the efficacy of civil orders of protection needs to be replicated on samples of children and adolescents to determine their overall effectiveness for protecting younger victims of interpersonal violence. Recommendations for policy and changes in the legal response to stalking must be guided by the practical needs of victims as well as behavioral sciences theory and research.

EPILOGUE

In the wake of several highly publicized school shootings around the country, a number of proposals have been offered for combating the problem of school violence. Among the various changes in policy that have been either suggested or implemented include mandatory criminal sentencing for certain offenses (e.g., automatic suspension or expulsion for making a threatening statement), the use of metal detectors at school entrances, and so forth. Some suggestions, such as holding parents criminally liable for the actions of their children, are more punitive and provide intervention only after an act of violence has occurred. Many of these proposals reveal a strong desire to make schools, communities, and homes safe for children. It is important to implement policies and programs that have a high likelihood of success and are preventive, rather than ones that merely placate a demand for revenge or institute action only after violence has occurred.

Traditional methods for evaluating and identifying patterns of violence among children and adolescents are likely to be of limited use in managing threatening communications in school settings. For instance, the use of psychological profiles of violent students is useful for providing information on the characteristics and dynamics of those who have acted violently (e.g., McGee & DeBernardo, 1999), but such profiles are of limited use in predicting who will and who will not become violent. Moreover, traditional risk assessment models for identifying variables that are associated with violent behavior are again useful for providing insight into variables that contribute to the incidence of violence, but research has not provided useful actuarial equations that can be used to predict violent behavior by children or adolescents. An alternative approach to evaluating violent behavior, particularly targeted violence in which a person or group of people poses a threat to others, is the threat assessment model that has been developed and refined by the U.S. Secret Service (Borum, Fein, Vossekuil, & Bergulund, 1999; Pynchon & Borum, 1999).

Threat assessment differs from traditional risk assessment in that it seeks to identify the motives of the person making a threat, how the threat is communicated, factors that may raise the likelihood of someone posing a threat even if no direct threat has been made, types of obsessional harassment by the person posing the threat, and the thinking and behavioral patterns of the person that increase or decrease the likelihood of carrying out a violent act. Threat assessment is a preventive approach to evaluating and managing threats that can be applied to children and adolescents in school settings. By developing interdisciplinary teams comprised of mental health professionals, school personnel, law enforcement officials, and other trained professionals, potential threats can be assessed and managed before violence occurs. The hope is that students can be educated with minimal disruption to their lives, and individuals who have been identified as making or posing threats can receive proper services that will reduce the likelihood of violence and will be less punitive in nature.

This book outlines a specific form of violence and aggression among children and adolescents that consists of obsessive harassing and threatening behavior by one individual that is directed toward another person. As noted at the beginning of this book, stalking is an old behavior but a new crime and is an even newer area of behavioral sciences research. Although the primary focus of research has been on adult samples of obsessional followers, this book has provided evidence that stalking occurs in younger age groups. Moreover, even though research on adult samples has revealed that stalking offenders tend to be men in their late 30s, the study of stalking in populations of young people can reveal important insights into early manifestations and developmental dynamics of this disturbed form of behavior.

Because stalking has been conceptualized by some researchers as a disturbance in attachment (Kienlen, 1998), one would expect that stalking can be observed across the life span to the extent that disturbances in attachment are manifest across many different age groups. In fact, the research and case reports discussed in this book support the notion that stalking can be identified in some children or adolescents during the developmental phase when a person is beginning to explore close attachments outside of the family with peers and acquaintances. Although empirical data are very limited at this point, I have proposed that the earliest stage at which stalking is developmentally feasible is during late latency or early adolescence. Moreover, case reports and research on small sample sizes reveal that the modal stalking case in young people is between acquaintances, rather than prior intimate partners, although the latter form of stalking also occurs in young people.

As people move through pre-adolescence into the teenage years, they not only experience a change in the primary focus of their attachments from family to peers, they also begin to meet the challenge of developing a cohesive and stable identity. Adolescence is a period in which the person integrates values and ideals about who he or she is and what is important in life. Some of these principles come from early life experiences within the family, but they also develop from interactions with peers and experiences in social groups. In the same way that attachment experiences change through pre-adolescence into adolescence, changes in identity also occur. Stalking can be conceptualized as a disturbance in identity as well as attachment. Even adult stalking offenders manifest various signs of identity disturbance, including feelings of inadequacy, susceptibility to narcissistic injury, social ineptness that leads to clinging behavior, and an inability to manage or tolerate feelings of jealousy or envy.

Despite the fact that stalking can be identified as a form of obsessional harassment among young people, it remains unclear as to whether this is a common or very rare phenomenon. Indeed, there is considerable need for research on the prevalence of stalking among children and adolescents. Some forms of obsessional harassment among young people are well known, such as bullying, and other forms of obsessional harassment have been the focus of recent research, such as sexual harassment and dating violence. Both bullying (Kaufman et al., 1998) and sexual harassment (American Association of University Women Educational Foundation,

1993) are quite prevalent among school-age children, and there is collateral evidence presented in this book that these problems overlap with stalking. Specifically, bullying and stalking have similar definitions, and the psychological dynamics of bullies and obsessional followers parallel one another. In addition, stalking behavior appears to be a subset of sexually harassing behavior in schools.

This book also reviewed several issues related to the problem of stalking in young people, including factors associated with a risk for violence, assessment and treatment issues for stalking victims and perpetrators, and personal protection measures that can be followed in specific cases. A major point raised herein is the fact that effective management of stalking cases involving children or adolescents must be multidisciplinary and must include input from mental health professionals, school personnel and administrators, parents, the victim, law enforcement officials, and legal professionals. In general, stalking cases are likely to be managed most effectively when there are both legal and mental health interventions available (Meloy, 1997).

Much of the stalking research that was reviewed in this book focused on adult offenders and provided a context within with to explore some of the dynamics of stalking in younger populations. Other research that was discussed focused on problems that overlap with stalking but that are also unique in some respects. Very little research currently exists on the specific problem of stalking or obsessional following in children or adolescents, and much of the data presented consisted of individual case studies or anecdotal evidence. There is a need for more systematic study of the problem of stalking in younger populations, and one goal of this book is to heighten awareness of the problem and to sensitize researchers and clinicians to the need for more work in this area. As such, this book is intended to serve as a guide for clinicians, researchers, school officials, law enforcement professionals, parents, and other interested individuals for understanding what is currently known about the phenomenon of stalking in young people. In addition, the book may serve as a source of hypotheses that can be tested in research studies.

Among the various issues that require further study include the prevalence of stalking among children and adolescents, factors associated with an increased risk for violence, psychiatric diagnoses that are found in young stalking perpetrators, developmental course of stalking behaviors from adolescence through adulthood, and long-term outcome of young stalking offenders. The empirical study of these issues will require greater attention to the problem of stalking or obsessional following among school-age children, systematic gathering and studying of larger samples of young stalking offenders, and long-term monitoring of young stalking offenders as they mature into adulthood. The topic of stalking in children and adolescents clearly deserves greater attention, and like any scholarly pursuit that is based on both theoretical principles and empirical research, the subject matter will evolve as we learn more about this unusual but important problem.

References

Adams, G. R., Ryan, J. H., Hoffman, J. J., Dobson, W. R., & Nielson, E. C. (1985). Ego-identity status, conformity behavior and personality in late adolescence. *Journal of Personality and Social Psychology, 47,* 1091–1104.

Ainsworth, M. D. S. (1989). Attachments beyond infancy. *American Psychologist, 44,* 709–716.

Ainsworth, M. D. S., Blehar, M. C., Waters, E., & Wall, S. (1978). *Patterns of attachment: A psychological study of the strange situation.* Hillsdale, NJ: Lawrence Erlbaum.

Allen, J. P., Hauser, S. T., & Borman-Spurrell, E. (1996). Attachment theory as a framework for understanding sequelae of severe adolescent psychopathology: An 11-year follow-up study. *Journal of Consulting and Clinical Psychology, 64,* 254–263.

American Association of University Women Educational Foundation. (1993). *Hostile hallways: The AAUW survey on sexual harassment in America's schools.* Washington, DC: Author.

American Psychiatric Association. (1994). *Diagnostic and statistical manual of mental disorders* (4th ed.). Washington, DC: Author.

American Psychological Association. (1993). *Violence and youth: Psychology's response. Vol. 1: Summary of the American Psychological Association Commission on Violence and Youth.* Washington, DC: Author.

Anderson, S. C. (1993). Anti-stalking laws: Will they curb the erotomanic's obsessive pursuit? *Law and Psychology Review, 17,* 171–191.

Araji, S. K. (1997). *Sexually aggressive children: Coming to understand them.* Thousand Oaks, CA: Sage.

Arkansas Code Annotated § 5-71-229 (Michie 1993).

Arizona v. Laird, 186 Ariz. 203; 920 P2d 769 (Ariz. 1996).

Badcock, R. J. (1997). Developmental and clinical issues in relation to offending in the individual. In J. L. Jackson & D. A. Bekerian (Eds.), *Offender profiling: Theory research and practice* (pp. 9–41). Chichester, England; John Wiley & Sons.

Balint, M. (1969). *The basic fault.* London: Tavistock Publications Ltd.

Barbaree, H. E., Marshall, W. L., & Hudson, S. M. (Ed.). (1993). *The juvenile sex offender.* New York: Guilford Press.

Barkley, R. A. (1997). *ADHD and the nature of self control.* New York: Guilford Press.

Barkley, R. A. (1998). *Attention-deficit hyperactivity disorder: A handbook for diagnosis and treatment (2nd ed.).* New York: Guilford Press.

Bartholomew, K. (1990). Avoidance of intimacy: An attachment perspective. *Journal of Social and Personal Relationships, 7,* 147–178.

Bennett, L., & Fineran, S. (1998). Sexual and severe physical violence among high school students: Power beliefs, gender, and relationship. *American Journal of Orthopsychiatry, 68,* 645–652.

Bergman, L. (1992). Dating violence among high school students. *Social Work, 37,* 21–27.

Bjerregaard, B. (1996). Stalking and the first amendment: A constitutional analysis of state stalking laws. *Criminal Law Bulletin, 32,* 307–341.

Boer, D. P., Hart, S. D., Kropp, P. R., & Webster, C. D. (1997). *Manual for the sexual violence risk—20: Professional guidelines for assessing risk of sexual violence.* Burnaby, British Columbia, Canada: Mental Health, Law, and Policy Institute.

Boer, D. P., Wilson, R. J., Gauthier, C. M., & Hart, S. D. (1997). Assessing risk of sexual violence: Guidelines for clinical practice. In C. D. Webster & M. A. Jackson (Eds.), *Impulsivity: Theory, assessment, and treatment* (pp. 326–342). New York: Guilford Press.

Borum, R. (1996). Improving the clinical practice of violence risk assessment: Technology, guidelines, and training. *American Psychologist, 51,* 945–956.

Borum, R., Fein, R., Vossekuil, B., & Berglund, J. (1999). Threat assessment: Defining an approach for evaluating risk for targeted violence. *Behavioral Sciences and the Law, 17,* 323–337.

Borum, R., Swartz, M., & Swanson, J. (1996). Assessing and managing violence risk in clinical practice. *Journal of Practice in Psychiatry and Behavioral Health, 4,* 205–215.

Bouters v. State, 634 So2d 246 (Fla. App. 5 Dist. 1994).

Bowcott, O. (1998, April 28). Three boys convicted of bullying neighbours. *The Guardian,* p. 9.

Bowlby, J. (1973). *Attachment and loss: Vol. 2. separation: Anxiety and anger.* New York: Basic Books.

Bowlby, J. (1980). *Attachment and loss: Vol. 3. loss: Sadness and depression.* New York: Basic Books.

Bowlby, J. (1982). *Attachment and loss: Vol. 1. attachment (2nd ed.).* New York: Basic Books.

Bradfield, J. L. (1998). Anti-stalking laws: Do they adequately protect stalking victims? *Harvard Women's Law Journal, 21,* 229–266.

Briere, J. (1996). *Trauma symptom checklist for children (TSCC) professional manual.* Odessa, FL: Psychological Assessment Resources.

Burgess, A. W., Baker, T., Greening, D., Hartman, C. R., Burgess, A. G., Douglas, J. E., & Halloran, R. (1997). Stalking behaviors within domestic violence. *Journal of Family Violence, 12,* 389–403.

Buss, D. M. (1994). *The evolution of desire.* New York: Basic Books.

Buss, D. M., Larsen, R. J., Westen, D., & Semmelroth, J. (1992). Sex differences in jealousy: Evolution, physiology, and psychology. *Psychological Science, 3,* 251–255.

Butcher, J. N., Williams, C. L., Graham, J. R., Archer, R. P., Tellegen, A., Ben-Porath, Y. S., & Kaemmer, B. (1992). *MMPI-A manual for administration, scoring, and interpretation.* Minneapolis: University of Minnesota Press.

Cal. Penal Code § 646.9(a) (1993).

Campbell, M., & Spencer, E. K. (1988). Psychopharmacology in child and adolescent psychiatry: A review of the past five years. *Journal of the American Academy of Child and Adolescent Psychiatry, 27,* 269–279.

Carlson, M. J., Harris, S. D., & Holden, G. W. (1999). Protective orders and domestic violence: Risk factors for re-abuse. *Journal of Family Violence, 14,* 205–226.

Coggins, M. H., Pynchon, M. R., & Dvoskin, J. A. (1998). Integrating research and practice in federal law enforcement: Secret service application of behavior science expertise to protect the president. *Behavioral Sciences and the Law, 16,* 51–70.

Cornell, D. G. (1993). Juvenile homicide: A growing national problem. *Behavioral Sciences and the Law, 11,* 389–396.

Cornell, D. G., Benedek, E. P., & Benedek, D. M. (1987a). Characteristics of adolescents charged with homicide: Review of 72 cases. *Behavioral Sciences and the Law, 5,* 11–23.

Cornell, D. G., Benedek, E. P., & Benedek, D. M. (1987b). Juvenile homicide: Prior adjustment and a proposed typology. *American Journal of Orthopsychiatry, 57,* 383–393.

Cornwell, J. K. (1998). Understanding the role of the police and parens patriae powers in involuntary civil commitment before and after Hendricks. *Psychology, Public Policy, and Law, 4,* 377–413.

Corpus Juris Secondum, 86 C. J. S. § 10 (1996).

Cowan, P. A., Cohn, D. A., Cowan, C. P., & Pearson, J. L. (1996). Parents' attachment histories and children's externalizing and internalizing behaviors: Exploring family systems models of linkage. *Journal of Consulting and Clinical Psychology, 64,* 53–63.

Cupach, W. R., & Spitzberg, B. H. (Eds.). (1994). *The dark side of interpersonal communication.* Hillsdale, NJ: Lawrence Erlbaum.

Cupach, W. R., & Spitzberg, B. H. (1998). Obsessive relational intrusions and stalking. In B. H. Spitzberg & W. R. Cupach (Eds.), *The dark side of close relationships* (pp. 233–263). Mahwah, NJ: Lawrence Erlbaum.

Davis v. Monroe County Board of Education, 119 SCt 1661 (1999).

Dawes, R. M. (1989). Experience and validity of clinical judgment: The illusory correlation. *Behavioral Sciences and the Law, 7,* 457–467.

Dawes, R. M., Faust, D., & Meehl, P. E. (1989). Clinical versus actuarial judgment. *Science, 243,* 1668–1674.

de Becker, G. (1997). *The gift of fear: Survival signals that protect us from violence.* Boston: Little, Brown & Company.

de Becker, G. (1999). *Protecting the gift: keeping children and teenagers safe (and parents sane).* New York: Dial Press.

Dietz, P., Matthews, D., Martell, D., Stewart, T., Hrouda, D., & Warren, J. (1991). Threatening and otherwise inappropriate letters to members of the United States Congress. *Journal of Forensic Sciences, 36,* 1445–1468.

Dietz, P., Matthews, D., van Duyne, C., Martell, D., Parry, C., Stewart, T., Warren, J., & Crowder, D. (1991). Threatening and otherwise inappropriate letters to Hollywood celebrities. *Journal of Forensic Sciences, 36,* 185–209.

Dill, K. E., & Dill, J. C. (1998). Video game violence: A review of the empirical literature. *Aggression and Violent Behavior, 3,* 407–428.

Douglas, J. E., Burgess, A. W., Burgess, A. G., & Ressler, R. K. (1992). *Crime classification manual: A standard system for investigating and classifying violent crimes.* New York: Lexington.

Duncan, R. D. (1999). Peer and sibling aggression: An investigation of intra- and extra-familial bullying. *Journal of Interpersonal Violence, 14,* 871–886.

Dutton, D. G. (1998). The abusive personality: *Violence and control in intimate relationships.* New York: Guilford Press.

Education Amendments of 1972, 20 U. S. C. §§ 1681 *et seq.* (1997).

Elliott, D., Huizinga, D., & Morse, B. (1986). Self-reported violent offending: A descriptive analysis of juvenile violent offenders and their offending careers. *Journal of Interpersonal Violence, 1,* 472–514.

English, H. B., & English, A. C. (1958). *A comprehensive dictionary of psychological and psychoanalytic terms: A guide to usage.* New York: David McKay.

Erikson, E. H. (1968). *Identity: Youth and crisis.* New York: Norton.

Ewing, C. P. (1990). *When children kill: The dynamics of juvenile homicide.* Lexington, MA: Lexington.

Farnham, F. R., James, D. V., & Cantrell, P. (2000). Association between violence, psychosis, and relationship to victim in stalkers. *The Lancet, 355,* 199.

Farrington, D. P. (1989). Early predictors of adolescent aggression and adult violence. *Violence and Victims, 4,* 79–100.

Farrington, D. P., & Loeber, R. (1998). Major aims of this book. In R. Loeber & D. P. Farrington (Eds.), *Serious and violent juvenile offenders: Risk factors and successful interventions* (pp. 1–10). Thousand Oaks, CA: Sage.

Faust, D., & Ziskin, J. (1988). The expert witness in psychology and psychiatry. *Science, 241,* 31–35.

Fein, R. A., & Vossekuil, B. (1999). Assassination in the United States: An operational study of recent assassins, attackers, and near-lethal approachers. *Journal of Forensic Sciences, 44,* 321–333.

Fielkow, C. C. (1997). Bullies, words, and wounds: One state's approach in controlling aggressive expression between children. *Depaul Law Review, 46,* 1057–1110.

Fineran, S., & Bennett, L. (1999). Gender and power issues of peer sexual harassment among teenagers. *Journal of Interpersonal Violence, 14,* 626–641.

Forth, A., Hart, S., & Hare, R. (1990). Assessment of psychopathy in male young offenders. *Psychological Assessment, 2,* 342–344.

Foster v. Souders, 399 P2d 733 (Or. App. 1995).

Fracassa, H. (1996a, July 18). Warren man is jailed in stalkings. *The Detroit News,* p. B1.

261

Fracassa, H. (1996b, July 26). Suspect charged with stalking teen swimmer faces fifth felony. *The Detroit News*, p. B1.

Fremouw, W. J., Westrup, D., & Pennypacker, J. (1997). Stalking on campus: The prevalence and strategies for coping with stalking. *Journal of Forensic Sciences, 42*, 666–669.

Freund, K., Scher, H., & Hucker, S. (1983). The courtship disorders. *Archives of Sexual Behavior, 12*, 369–379.

Frick, P., O'Brien, H., Wootton, J., & McBurnett, K. (1994). Psychopathy and conduct problems in children. *Journal of Abnormal Psychology, 103*, 700–707.

Gagne, M. H., & Lavoie, F. (1993). Young people's views on the causes of violence in adolescents' romantic relationships. *Canada's Mental Health, 41*, 11–15.

Gallagher, R. P., Harmon, W. W., & Lingenfelter, C. O. (1994). CSAO's perception of the changing incidence of problematic college student behavior. *NASPA Journal, 32(1)*, 37–45.

Garb, H. N. (1998). *Studying the clinician: Judgment research and psychological assessment.* Washington, DC: American Psychological Association.

Garbarino, J., Kostelny, K., & Barry, F. (1998). Neighborhood-based programs. In P. K. Trickett & C. J. Schellenbach (Eds.). *Violence against children in the family and the community* (pp. 287–314). Washington, DC: American Psychological Association.

Gebser v. Lago Vista Independent School District, 118 SCt 1989 (1998).

Gilligan, M. J. (1992). Stalking the stalker: Developing new laws to thwart those who terrorize others. *Georgia Law Review, 27*, 285–342.

Gitlin, M. J. (1990). *The psychotherapist's guide to psychopharmacology.* New York: Free Press.

Gray, A. S., & Pithers, W. D. (1993). Relapse prevention with sexually aggressive adolescents and children: Expanding treatment and supervision. In H. E. Barbaree, W. L. Marshall, & S. Hudson (Eds.), *The juvenile sex offender* (pp. 289–319). New York: Guilford Press.

Greenberg, R. A. (Ed.). (1996). *New York criminal law.* St. Paul, MN: West.

Greenberger, E., & McLaughlin, C. S. (1998). Attachment, coping, and explanatory style in late adolescence. *Journal of Youth and Adolescence, 27*, 121–139.

Grisso, T. (1998). *Forensic evaluation of juveniles.* Sarasota, FL: Professional Resource Press.

Grove, W. M., & Meehl, P. E. (1996). Comparative efficiency of informal (subjective, impressionistic) and formal (mechanical, algorithmic) prediction procedures:

The clinical-statistical controversy. *Psychology, Public Policy, and Law, 2,* 293–323.

Guerrero, L. K., & Andersen, P. A. (1998). The dark side of jealousy and envy: Desire, delusion, desperation, and destructive communication. In B. H. Spitzberg & W. R. Cupach (Eds.), *The dark side of close relationships* (pp. 33–70). Mahwah, NJ: Lawrence Erlbaum.

Guralnick, D. B. (1987). *Webster's new world dictionary of the American language.* New York: Warner.

Guy, R. A. (1993). The nature and constitutionality of stalking laws. *Vanderbilt Law Review, 46,* 991–1029.

Hall, D. M. (1998). The victims of stalking. In J. R. Meloy (Ed.), *The psychology of stalking: Clinical and forensic perspectives* (pp. 113–137). San Diego, CA: Academic Press.

Hall. H. V. (1998). Violent groups and institutions in the United States. In H. V. Hall & L. C. Whitaker (Eds.), *Collective violence: Effective strategies for assessing and interviewing in fatal group and institutional aggression* (pp. 3–80). St. Lucie, FL: CRC Press.

Hare, R. (1991). *The Hare psychopathy checklist—Revised manual.* Tonawanda, NY: Multi-Health Systems.

Harmon, R., Rosner, R., & Owens, H. (1995). Obsessional harassment and erotomania in a criminal court population. *Journal of Forensic Sciences, 40,* 188–196.

Harmon, R. B., Rosner, R., & Owens, H. (1998). Sex and violence in a forensic population of obsessional harassers. *Psychology, Public Policy, & Law, 4,* 236–249.

Harrell, A., & Smith, B. E. (1996). Effects of restraining orders on domestic violence victims. In E. S. Buzawa & C. G. Buzawa (Eds.), *Do arrests and restraining orders work?* (pp. 214–242). Thousand Oaks, CA: Sage.

Harris, G. T., Rice, M. E., & Quinsey, V. L. (1993). Violent recidivism of mentally disordered offenders: The development of a statistical prediction instrument. *Criminal Justice and Behavior, 20,* 315–335.

Hart, B. (1996). Battered women and the criminal justice system. In E. S. Buzawa & C. G. Buzawa (Eds.), *Do arrests and restraining orders work?* (pp. 98–114). Thousand Oaks, CA: Sage.

Harter, S., & Whitesall, N. R. (1989). Developmental changes in children's understanding of single, multiple, and blended emotion concepts. In C. Saarni & P. L. Harris (Eds.), *Children's understanding of emotions* (pp. 81–116). New York: Cambridge University Press.

Hawkins, J. D., Herrenkohl, T., Farrington, D. P., Brewer, D., Catalano, R. F., & Harachi, T. W. (1998). A review of predictors of youth violence. In R. Loeber & D. P. Farrington (Eds.), *Serious and violent juvenile offenders: Risk factors and successful interventions* (pp. 106–146). Thousand Oaks, CA: Sage.

Hawkins, D. F., Laub, J. H., & Lauritsen, J. L. (1998). Race, ethnicity, and serious juvenile offending. In R. Loeber & D. P. Farrington (Eds.), *Serious and violent juvenile offenders: Risk factors and successful interventions* (pp. 30–46). Thousand Oaks, CA: Sage.

Hazan, C., & Shaver, P. R. (1994). Attachment as an organizational framework for research on close relationships. *Psychological Inquiry, 5,* 1–22.

Hazler, R. J. (1996). *Breaking the cycle of violence: Interventions for bullying and victimization.* Washington, DC: Accelerated Development.

Heide, K. M. (1993). Weapons used by juveniles and adults to kill parents. *Behavioral Sciences and the Law, 11,* 397–405.

Heide, K. M. (1999). *Young killers: The challenge of juvenile homicide.* Thousand Oaks, CA: Sage.

Heilbrun, K. (1997). Prediction versus management models relevant to risk assessment: The importance of legal decision-making context. *Law and Human Behavior, 21,* 347–359.

Heilbrun, K., O'Neill, M. L., Strohman, K. L., Bowman, Q., & Philipson, J. (2000). Expert approaches to communicating violence risk. *Law and Human Behavior, 24,* 137–148.

Holt, R. R. (1986). Clinical and statistical prediction: A retrospective and would-be integrative perspective. *Journal of Personality Assessment, 50,* 376–386.

Hoover, J. H., Oliver, R. L., & Hazler, R. J. (1992). Bullying: Perceptions of adolescent victims in the midwestern U.S.A. *School Psychology International, 13,* 5–16.

In re Paul G., 1992 LEXIS 2304 (Conn. Super. Ct. 1992).

In the Matter of Jamar S., 672 NYS2d 793 (A.D. 2 Dept. 1998).

In the Matter of Luis A., 637 NYS2d 375 (A.D. 1 Dept. 1996).

In the Matter of Robert D. Hall, 1997 LEXIS 532 (Minn. Ct. App. 1997).

Janus, E. S. (1998). Hendricks and the moral terrain of police power civil commitment. *Psychology, Public Policy, and Law, 4,* 297–322.

Jobes, D. A., Berman, A. L., O'Carroll, P. W., Eastgard, S., & Knickmeyer, S. (1996). The Kurt Cobain suicide crisis: Perspectives from research, public health, and the news media. *Suicide & Life Threatening Behavior, 26,* 260–271.

Johnson, B. A., Brent, D. A., Connolly, J., Bridge, J., Matta, J., Constantine, D., Rather, C., & White, T. (1995). Familial aggregation of adolescent personality disorders. *Journal of the American Academy of Child and Adolescent Psychiatry, 34,* 798–804.

Johnson, B. R., & Becker, J. V. (1997). Natural born killers?: The development of the sexually sadistic killer. *Journal of the American Academy of Psychiatry and the Law, 25,* 335–348.

Jones, J. (1992). *Let me take you down: Inside the mind of Mark David Chapman, the man who killed John Lennon.* New York: Villard.

Kansas v. Hendricks, 117 SCt 2072 (1997).

Kansas Sexually Violent Predator Law, Kan. Stat. Ann. §§ 59-29a01 et seq. (1994).

Karen, R. (1994). *Becoming attached: First relationships and how they shape our capacity to love.* New York: Oxford University Press.

Kaufman, P., Chen, X., Choy, S. P., Chandler, K. A., Chapman, C. D., Rand, M. R., & Ringel, C. (1998). *Indicators of school crime and safety, 1998.* Washington, DC: U.S. Department of Education and U.S. Department of Justice.

Kazdin, A. E. (1996). *Conduct disorders in children and adolescents (2nd ed.).* Thousand Oaks, CA: Sage.

Kernberg, O. F. (1984). *Severe personality disorders: Psychotherapeutic strategies.* New Haven, CT: Yale University Press.

Kernberg, O. F. (1992). *Aggression in personality disorders and perversions.* New Haven, CT: Yale University Press.

Kernberg, P. F., & Chazan, S. E. (1991). *Children with conduct disorders: A psychotherapy manual.* New York: Basic Books.

Khan, M. R. (1974). *The privacy of the self.* New York: International Universities Press.

Kienlen, K. K. (1998). Developmental and social antecedents of stalking. In J. R. Meloy (Ed.), *The psychology of stalking: Clinical and forensic perspectives* (pp. 51–67). San Diego, CA: Academic Press.

Kienlen, K. K., Birmingham, D. L., Solberg, K. B., O'Regan, J. T., & Meloy, J. R. (1997). A comparative study of psychotic and nonpsychotic stalking. *Journal of the American Academy of Psychiatry and the Law, 25,* 317–334.

Kingery, P. M., Coggeshall, M. B., & Alford, A. A. (1998). Violence at school: Recent evidence from four national surveys. *Psychology in the Schools, 35,* 247–258.

Klaczynski, P. A., Fauth, J. M., & Swanger, A. (1998). Adolescent identity: Rational vs.

experiential processing, formal operations, and critical thinking beliefs. *Journal of Youth and Adolescence, 27,* 185–207.

Klassen, D., & O'Connor, W. A. (1994). Demographic and case history variables for risk assessment. In J. Monahan & H. J. Steadman (Eds.), *Violence and mental disorder: Developments in risk assessment* (pp. 229–258). Chicago: University of Chicago Press.

Klassen, D., & O'Connor, W. A. (1989). Assessing the risk of violence in released mental patients: A cross-validation study. *Psychological Assessment, 1,* 75–81.

Klein, M., & Riviere, J. (1964). *Love, hate, and reparation.* New York: Norton.

Kolko, D. (1998). Treatment and intervention for child victims of violence. In P. K. Trickett & C. J. Schellengach (Eds.), *Violence against children in the family and the community* (pp. 213–249). Washington, DC: American Psychological Association.

Kropp, P. R., & Hart, S. D. (1997). Assessing risk of violence in wife assaulters: The spousal assault risk assessment guide. In C. D. Webster & M. A. Jackson (Eds.), *Impulsivity: Theory, assessment, and treatment* (pp. 302–325). New York: Guilford Press.

Kumpulainen, K., Rasanen, E., Henttonen, I., Almqvist, F., Kresanov, K., Linna, S. L., Moilanen, I., Piha, J., Puura, K., & Tamminen, T. (1998). Bullying and psychiatric symptoms among elementary school-age children. *Child Abuse & Neglect, 22,* 705–717.

Laner, M. R. (1990). Violence or its precipitation: Which is more likely to be identified as a dating problem? *Deviant Behavior, 11,* 319–329.

Leets, L., de Becker, G., & Giles, H. (1995). Fans: Exploring expressed motivations for contacting celebrities. *Journal of Language and Social Psychology, 14,* 102–123.

Lewis, D. O. (1992). From abuse to violence: Psychophysiological consequences of maltreatment. *Journal of the American Academy of Child and Adolescent Psychiatry, 31,* 383–391.

Litwack, T. R., & Schlesinger, L. B. (1999). Dangerousness risk assessments: Research, legal, and clinical considerations. In A. K. Hess & I. B. Weiner (Eds.), *The handbook of forensic psychology (2nd ed.)* (pp. 171–217). New York: John Wiley & Sons.

Loeber, R. (1990). Development and risk factors of juvenile antisocial behavior and delinquency. *Clinical Psychology Review, 10,* 1–41.

Loeber, R., & Dishion, T. J. (1983). Early predictors of male delinquency: A review. *Psychological Bulletin, 94,* 68–98.

Loeber, R., Farrington, D. P., & Waschbusch, D. A. (1998). Serious and violent juvenile offenders. In R. Loeber & D. P. Farrington (Eds.), *Serious & violent juvenile offenders: Risk factors and successful interventions* (pp. 13–29). Thousand Oaks, CA: Sage.

Longman, J. (1998, December 1). Gymnast Moceanu gets order of protection against father. *The New York Times,* p. D1.

Lyons-Ruth, D. (1996). Attachment relationships among children with aggressive behavior problems: The role of disorganized early attachment patterns. *Journal of Consulting and Clinical Psychology, 64,* 64–73.

Magdol, L., Moffitt, T. E., Caspi, A., & Silva, P. A. (1998). Developmental antecedents of partner abuse: A prospective-longitudinal study. *Journal of Abnormal Psychology, 107,* 375–389.

Mahler, M. S., Pine, F., & Bergman, A. (1975). *The psychological birth of the human infant.* New York: Basic Books.

Main, M., & Solomon, J. (1990). Procedures for identifying infants as disorganized/disoriented during the Ainsworth strange situation. In M. T. Greenberg, D. Cicchetti, & E. M. Cummings (Eds.), *Attachment in the preschool years* (pp. 121–160). Chicago: University of Chicago Press.

Markman, R., & Labrecque, R. (1994). *Obsessed: The stalking of Theresa Saldana.* New York: William Morrow.

Martello, J., & Balsly, E. (1996, December 4). Yes, they're serious about this . . .; More than 100 teens take part in the latest round of a stalking game. *The Kansas City Star,* p. A1.

Marton, P., Korenblum, M., Kutchner, S., Stein, B., Kennedy, B., & Pakes, J. (1989). Personality dysfunction in depressed adolescents. *Canadian Journal of Psychiatry, 34,* 810–813.

Masterson, J. F. (1981). *The narcissistic and borderline disorders: An integrated developmental approach.* New York: Brunner/Mazel.

Mattanah, J. J. F., Becker, D. F., Levy, K. N., Edell, W. S., & McGlashan, T. H. (1995). Diagnostic stability in adolescents followed up 2 years after hospitalization. *American Journal of Psychiatry, 152,* 889–894.

McAllister, S. R. (1998). Sex offenders and mental illness: A lesson in federalism and the separation of powers. *Psychology, Public Policy, and Law, 4,* 268–296.

267

McAnaney, K. G., Curliss, L. A., & Abeyta-Price, C. E. (1993). From imprudence to crime: Anti-stalking laws. *Notre Dame Law Review, 68,* 819–909.

McCann, J. T. (1995). Obsessive attachment and the victimization of children: Can antistalking legislation provide protection? *Law and Psychology Review, 19,* 93–112.

McCann, J. T. (1998a). *Malingering and deception in adolescents: Assessing credibility in clinical and forensic settings.* Washington, DC: American Psychological Association.

McCann, J. T. (1998b). Risk of violence in stalking cases and legal case management. *Pennsylvania Bar Association Quarterly, 69*(3), 115–119.

McCann, J. T. (1998c). Subtypes of stalking/obsessional following in adolescents. *Journal of Adolescence, 21,* 667–675.

McCann, J. T. (1999). *Assessing adolescents with the MACI: Using the Millon adolescent clinical inventory.* New York: John Wiley & Sons.

McCann, J. T. (2000). A descriptive study of child and adolescent obsessional followers. *Journal Forensic Sciences, 45,* 195–199.

McCreedy, K. R., & Dennis, B. G. (1996). Sex-related offenses and fear of crime on campus. *Journal of Contemporary Criminal Justice, 12,* 69–80.

McGee, J. P., & DeBernardo, C. R. (1999). The classroom avenger: A behavioral profile of school based shootings. *The Forensic Examiner, 8*(5&6), 16–18.

Meehl, P. E. (1954). *Clinical versus statistical prediction: A theoretical analaysis and a review of the evidence.* Minneapolis: University of Minnesota Press.

Meissner, W. W. (1985). Theories of personality and psychopathology: Classical psychoanalysis. In H. I. Kaplan & B. J. Sadock (Eds.), *Comprehensive textbook of psychiatry/IV (4th ed.)* (pp. 337–418). Baltimore: Williams & Wilkins.

Meloy, J. R. (1988). *The psychopathic mind: Origins, dynamics, and treatment.* Northvale, NJ: Jason Aronson.

Meloy, J. R. (1989). Unrequited love and the wish to kill: Diagnosis and treatment of borderline erotomania. *Bulletin of the Menninger Clinic, 53,* 477–492.

Meloy, J. R. (1992). *Violent attachments.* Northvale, NJ: Jason Aronson.

Meloy, J. R. (1996). Stalking (obsessional following): A review of some preliminary studies. *Aggression and Violent Behavior, 1,* 147–162.

Meloy, J. R. (1997). The clinical risk management of stalking: "Someone is watching over me. . . ." *American Journal of Psychotherapy, 51,* 174–184.

Meloy, J. R. (Ed.). (1998a). *The psychology of stalking: Clinical and forensic perspectives.* San Diego, CA: Academic Press.

Meloy, J. R. (1998b). The psychology of stalking. In J. R. Meloy (Ed.), *The psychology of stalking: Clinical and forensic perspectives* (pp. 1–23). San Diego, CA: Academic Press.

Meloy, J. R. (1999a). Erotomania, triangulation, and homicide. *Journal of Forensic Sciences, 44,* 421–424.

Meloy, J. R. (1999b). Stalking: An old behavior, a new crime. *Psychiatric Clinics of North America, 22,* 85–99.

Meloy, J. R. (in press). Threats, stalking, and criminal harassment. In G. Pinard & L. Pagani (Eds.), *Clinical assessment of dangerousness: Empirical contributions.* New York: Cambridge University Press.

Meloy, J. R., Cowett, P. Y., Parker, S. B., Hofland, B., & Friedland, A. (1997). Domestic protection orders and the prediction of subsequent criminality and violence toward protectees. *Psychotherapy, 34,* 447–458.

Meloy, J. R., Davis, B., & Lovette, J. (in press). Risk factors for violence among stalkers. *Journal of Threat Assessment.*

Meloy, J. R., & Gothard, S. (1995). A demographic and clinical comparison of obsessional followers and offenders with mental disorders. *American Journal of Psychiatry, 152,* 258–263.

Meloy, J. R., Rivers, L., Siegel, L., Gothard, S., Naimark, D., & Nicolini, R. (2000). A replication study of obsessional followers and offenders with mental disorders. *Journal of Forensic Sciences, 45,* 189–194.

Menzies, R., Fedoroff, J. P., Green, C., & Isaacson, K. (1995). Prediction of dangerous behavior in male erotomania. *British Journal of Psychiatry, 166,* 529–536.

Meyers, J. (1998). Cultural factors in erotomania and obsessional following. In J. R. Meloy (Ed.), *The psychology of stalking: Clinical and forensic perspectives* (pp. 213–224). San Diego, CA: Academic Press.

Meyers, J., & Meloy, J. R. (1994). Discussion of "A comparative study of erotomania and obsessional subjects in a forensic sample" [Letter to the editor]. *Journal of Forensic Sciences, 39,* 906–907.

Miller, M., & Hemenway, D. (1999). The relationship between firearms and suicide: A review of the literature. *Aggression and Violent Behavior, 4,* 59–75.

Millon, T., & Davis, R. D. (1996). *Disorders of personality: DSM-IV and beyond.* New York: Wiley.

Millon, T., Millon, C., & Davis, R. (1993). *Millon adolescent clinical inventory manual.* Minneapolis, MN: National Computer Systems.

Mnookin, R. H., & Weisberg, D. K. (1989). *Child, family and state: Problems and materials on children and the law (2nd ed.).* Boston: Little, Brown & Company.

Moffitt, T. E. (1993). Adolescence-limited and life-course persistent antisocial behavior: A developmental taxonomy. *Psychological Review, 100,* 674–701.

Monahan, J. (1984). The prediction of violent behaviors: Toward a second generation of theory and policy. *American Journal of Psychiatry, 141,* 10–15.

Monahan, J. (1992). Mental disorder and violent behavior: Perceptions and evidence. *American Psychologist, 47,* 511–521.

Monahan, J. (1995). *The clinical prediction of violent behavior.* Washington, DC: Northvale, NJ: Jason Aronson. (Original published in 1981)

Monahan, J., & Steadman, H. J. (Eds.). (1994). *Violence and mental disorder: Developments in risk assessment.* Chicago: University of Chicago Press.

Monahan, J., & Steadman, H. J. (1996). Violent storms and violent people: How meteorology can inform risk communication in mental health law. *American Psychologist, 51,* 931–938.

Morse, S. J. (1998). Fear of danger, flight from culpability. *Psychology, Public Policy, and Law, 4,* 250–267.

Mossman, D. (1994). Assessing prediction of violence: Being accurate about accuracy. *Journal of Consulting and Clinical Psychology, 62,* 783–792.

Mullen, P. E. (1991). Jealousy: The pathology of passion. *British Journal of Psychiatry, 158,* 593–601.

Mullen, P. E., & Pathe, M. (1994a). Stalking and the pathologies of love. *Australian and New Zealand Journal of Psychiatry, 28,* 469–477.

Mullen, P. E., & Pathe, M. (1994b). The pathological extensions of love. *British Journal of Psychiatry, 165,* 614–623.

Mullen, P. E., Pathe, M., Purcell, R., & Stuart, G. W. (1999). Study of stalkers. *American Journal of Psychiatry, 156,* 1244–1249.

Myers, W. C. (1994). Sexual homicide by adolescents. *Journal of the American Academy of Child and Adolescent Psychiatry, 33,* 962–969.

Myers, W. C., Burgess, A. W., & Nelson, J. A. (1998). Criminal and behavioral aspects of juvenile sexual homicide. *Journal of Forensic Sciences, 43,* 340–347.

Myers, W. C., & Mutch, P. J. (1992). Language disorders in disruptive behavior disordered homicidal youth. *Journal of Forensic Sciences, 37,* 919–922.

Myers, W. C., Scott, K., Burgess, A. W., & Burgess, A. G. (1995). Psychopathology, biopsychosocial factors, crime characteristics and classification of 25 homicidal youths. *Journal of the American Academy of Child and Adolescent Psychiatry, 34,* 1483–1489.

Nader, K. O. (1997). Assessing traumatic experiences in children. In J. P. Wilson & T. M. Keane (Eds.), *Assessing psychological trauma and PTSD* (pp. 291–348). New York: Guilford Press.

National Institute of Justice. (1993). *Project to develop a model anti-stalking code for states* (NIJ Publication No. NCJ 144477). Washington, DC: U.S. Government Printing Office.

National Victim Center. (1995). *School crime: K-12.* Arlington, VA: Author.

National Victim Center. (1997). *Stalking: Safety plan guidelines.* Arlington, VA: Author.

9-year-old accused of stalking schoolmate. (1996, March 8). *The New York Times,* p. A21.

Nelson, R. O., & Hayes, S. C. (1986). The nature of behavioral assessment. In R. O. Nelson & S. C. Hayes (Eds.), *Conceptual foundations of behavioral assessment* (pp. 1–41). New York: Guilford Press.

New York Executive Law, § 631 (12) (Supp. 1998).

Northwest Regional Educational Center. (1998). *Strategies for preventing and responding to school-based harassment.* Portland, OR: Author.

O'Keeffe, N. K., Brockopp, K., & Chew, E. (1986). Teen dating violence. *Social Work, 31,* 465–468.

Oliver, R., Hoover, J. H., & Hazler, R. (1994). The perceived roles of bullying in small-town midwestern schools. *Journal of Counseling & Development, 72,* 416–420.

Olweus, D. (1993). *Bullying at school: What we know and what we can do.* Cambridge, MA: Blackwell.

Otto, R. K. (1992). Prediction of dangerous behaviors: A review and analysis of "second-generation" research. *Forensic Reports, 5,* 103–133.

Palerea, R. E., Zona, M. A., Lane, J. C., & Langhinrichsen-Rohling, J. (1999). The dangerous nature of intimate relationship stalking: Threats, violence, and associated risk factors. *Behavioral Sciences & the Law, 17,* 269–283.

Pardo, S. (1997, June 26). Legislators boost penalty for stalking. *The Detroit News,* p. B1.

Pathe, M., & Mullen, P. E. (1997). The impact of stalkers on their victims. *British Journal of Psychiatry, 170,* 12–17.

Peretti, P. O., & Pudowski, B. C. (1997). Influence of jealousy on male and female college daters. *Social Behavior and Personality, 25,* 155–160.

Person, E. S. (1995). *By force of fantasy: How we make our lives.* New York: Basic Books.

Pithers, W. D., & Gray, A. (1998). The other half of the story: Children with sexual behavior problems. *Psychology, Public Policy, and Law, 4,* 200–217.

Pithers, W. D., Gray, A. S., Cunningham, C., & Lane, S. (1993). *From trauma to understanding.* Brandon, VT: Safer Society Program & Press.

Pynchon, M. R., & Borum, R. (1999). Assessing threats of targeted group violence: Contributions from social psychology. *Behavioral Sciences and the Law, 17,* 339–355.

Quinsey, V. L., Harris, G. T., Rice, M. E., & Cormier, C. A. (1998). *Violent offenders: Appraising and managing risk.* Washington, DC: American Psychological Association.

Raboin, S. (1998, December 9). A family torn apart after the Olympic gold medal, love and loathing collide. *USA Today,* p. 1C.

Raine, A. (1993). *The psychopathology of crime.* New York: Academic Press.

Resnick, M. D., Bearman, P. S., Blum, R. W., Bauman, K. E., Harris, K. M., Jones, J., Tabor, J., Beuhring, T., Siering, R. E., Shew, M., Ireland, M., Bearinger, L. H., & Udry, R. (1997). Protecting adolescents from harm: Findings from the national longitudinal study on adolescent health. *Journal of the American Medical Association, 278,* 823–832.

Ressler, R. K., Burgess, A. W., & Douglas, J. E. (1988). *Sexual homicide: Patterns and motives.* New York: Lexington.

Rey, J. M., Morris-Yates, A., Singh, M., Andrews, G., & Stewart, G. W. (1995). Continuities between psychiatric disorders in adolescents and personality disorders in young adults. *American Journal of Psychiatry 152,* 895–900.

Reynolds, W. M. (1998). *Adolescent psychopathology scale.* Odessa, FL: Psychological Assessment Resources.

Rice, M. E. (1997). Violent offender research and implications for the criminal justice system. *American Psychologist, 52,* 414–423.

Ritter, K., & Cole, C. L. (1999, October 18). Nashua killer detailed his intent on Internet. *The Boston Globe,* pp. A1, A9.

Roberts, A. R., & Dziegielewski, S. F. (1996). Assessment typology and intervention with the survivors of stalking. *Aggression and Violent Behavior, 1,* 359–368.

Rogers, R. (1995). *Diagnostic and structured interviewing: A handbook for psychologists.* Odessa, FL: Psychological Assessment Resources.

Roscoe, B., & Callahan, J. E. (1985). Adolescents' self-report of violence in families and dating relations. *Adolescence, 20,* 545–553.

Roscoe, B., Strouse, J. S., & Goodwin, M. P. (1994). Sexual harassment: Early adolescents' self-reports of experiences and acceptance. *Adolescence, 29,* 515–523.

Rosen, R. A. (1993). On self-defense, imminence, and women who kill their batterers. *North Carolina Law Review, 71,* 371–411.

Rosenstein, D. S., & Horowitz, H. A. (1996). Adolescent attachment and psychopathology. *Journal of Consulting and Clinical Psychology, 64,* 244–253.

Rygaard, N. P. (1998). Psychopathic children: Indicators of organic dysfunction. In T. Millon, E. Simonsen, M. Birket-Smit, & R. D. Davis (Eds.), *Psychopathy: Antisocial, criminal, and violent behavior* (pp. 247–259). New York: Guilford Press.

Saunders, R. (1998). The legal perspective on stalking. In J. R. Meloy (Ed.), *The psychology of stalking: Clinical and forensic perspectives* (pp. 25–49). San Diego, CA: Academic Press.

Schopp, R. F. (1998). Civil commitment and sexual predators: Competence and condemnation. *Psychology, Public Policy, and Law, 4,* 323–376.

Schwartz-Watts, D., Morgan, D. W., & Barnes, C. J. (1997). Stalkers: The South Carolina experience. *Journal of the American Academy of Psychiatry and the Law, 25,* 541–545.

Schwartz, D., McFadyen-Ketchum, S. A., Dodge, K. A., Pettit, G. S., & Bates, J. E. (1998). Peer group victimization as a predictor of children's behavior problems at home and in school. *Development and Psychopathology, 10,* 87–99.

Sex Offender Registration Act, N.Y. Correction Law §168 *et seq.* (McKinney, 1995).

Sexual Harassment Guidance: Harassment of Students by School Employees, Other Students, or Third Parties, 62 Fed. Reg. 12034 (1997).

Silver, E., Mulvey, E. P., & Monahan, J. (1999). Assessing violence risk among discharged psychiatric patients: Toward an ecological approach. *Law and Human Behavior, 23,* 237–255.

Skoler, G. (1998). The archetypes and psychodynamics of stalking. In J. R. Meloy (Ed.), *The psychology of stalking: Clinical and forensic perspectives* (pp. 85–112). San Diego, CA: Academic Press.

Slaby, R. G. (1998). Preventing youth violence through research-guided intervention. In P. K. Trickett & C. J. Schellenbach (Eds.), *Violence against children in the family and community* (pp. 371–399). Washington, DC: American Psychological Association.

Snow, R. L. (1998). *Stopping a stalker: A cop's guide to making the system work for you.* New York: Plenum.

Sohn, E. F. (1994). Antistalking statutes: Do they actually protect victims? *Criminal Law Bulletin, 30,* 203–241.

South Dakota Codified Laws Annotated § 22-19A-9 (Supp. 1994).

Spielman, P. M. (1971). Envy and jealousy: An attempt at clarification. *Psychoanalytic Quarterly, 40,* 59–82.

Spitzberg, B. H., & Cupach, W. R. (Eds.). (1998). *The dark side of close relationships.* Mahwah, NJ: Lawrence Erlbaum.

Spitzberg, B. H., Nicastro, A. M., & Cousins, A. V. (1998). Exploring the interactional phenomenon of stalking and obsessive relational intrusion. *Communication Reports, 11,* 33–47.

Spitzberg, B. H., & Rhea, J. (1999). Obsessive relational intrusions and sexual coercion victimization. *Journal of Interpersonal Violence, 14,* 3–20.

State v. Eccles, 136 Or App 30 (1995).

State v. Jensen, 1998 SD 52, 579 NW2d 613 (S.D. 1998).

State v. Laird, 186 Ariz. 203, 920 P2d 769 (Ariz. 1996).

Stets, J. E. & Pirog Good, M. A. (1987). Violence in dating relationships. *Social Psychology Quarterly, 50,* 237–246.

Svedberg v. Stamness, 525 NW2d 678 (N.D. 1994).

Suarez, K. E. (1994). Teenage dating violence: The need for expanded awareness and legislation. *California Law Review, 82,* 423–471.

Tharp, M. (1992, February 17). In the mind of a stalker. *U.S. News & World Report,* pp. 28–30.

Thomas, K. R. (1993). How to stop the stalker: State antistalking laws. *Criminal Law Bulletin, 29,* 124–136.

Tjaden, P. (1997). *The crime of stalking: How big is the problem?* (NIJ Research in Brief No. NCJ 163921). Washington, DC: U.S. Department of Justice.

Tolan, P. H., & Gorman-Smith, D. (1998). Development of serious and violent offending careers. In R. Loeber & D. P. Farrington (Eds.), *Serious and violent juvenile offenders: Risk factors and successful interventions* (pp. 68–85). Thousand Oaks, CA: Sage.

Tolan, P. H., & Guerra, N. (1998). Societal causes of violence against children. In P. K. Trickett & C. J. Schellenbach (Eds.), *Violence against children in the family and the community* (pp. 195–209). Washington, DC: American Psychological Association.

Trudell, J. (1999, October 17). Web pages show killer's fascination with victim, murder. *The Telegraph*, p. A1, A9.

Urbach, J. T., Khalily, C., & Mitchell, P. P. (1992). Erotomania in an adolescent: Clinical and theoretical considerations. *Journal of Adolescence, 15*, 231–240.

van der Kolk, B. A., & McFarlane, A. C. (1996). The black hole of trauma. In B. A. van der Kolk, A. C. McFarlane, & L. Weisaeth (Eds.), *Traumatic stress: The effects of overwhelming experience on mind, body, and society* (pp. 3–23). New York: Guilford Press.

Verlinden, S., Hersen, M., & Thomas, J. (2000). Risk factors in school shootings. *Clinical Psychology Review, 20*, 3–56.

Vermont Statutes Annotated, Title 13, § 1063 (Supp. 1994).

Violence Against Women Grants Office. (1998). *Stalking and domestic violence: The third annual report to Congress under the violence against women act* (NCJ Publication No. 172204). Washington, DC: U.S. Department of Justice.

Walker, L. E., & Meloy, J. R. (1998). Stalking and domestic violence. In J. R. Meloy (Ed.), *The psychology of stalking: Clinical and forensic perspectives* (pp. 139–161). San Diego, CA: Academic Press.

Webster, C. D., Douglas, K. S., Eaves, D., & Hart, S. D. (1997a). Assessing risk of violence to others. In C. D. Webster & M. A. Jackson (Eds.), *Impulsivity: Theory, assessment, and treatment* (pp. 251–277). New York: Guilford Press.

Webster, C. D., Douglas, K. S., Eaves, D., & Hart, S. D. (1997b). *HCR-20: Assessing risk for violence: Version 2*. Burnaby, British Columbia, Canada: Mental Health, Law, and Policy Institute.

Wekerle, C., & Wolfe, D. A. (1998). Windows for preventing child and partner abuse: Early childhood and adolescence. In P. K. Trickett & C. J. Schellenbach (Eds.), *Violence against children in the family and the community* (pp. 339–369). Washington, DC: American Psychological Association.

Westrup, D., & Fremouw, W. J. (1998). Stalking behavior: A literature review and suggested functional analytic assessment technology. *Aggression and Violent Behavior, 3*, 255–274.

Westrup, D., Fremouw, W. J., & Thompson, N. (1999). The psychological impact of stalking on female undergraduates. *Journal of Forensic Sciences, 44*, 554–557.

Wexler, D. B. (1991). *The adolescent self: Strategies for self-management, self-soothing, and self-esteem in adolescents*. New York: W. W. Norton & Co.

Widiger, T. A., & Trull, T. J. (1994). Personality disorders and violence. In J. Monahan & H. J. Steadman (Eds.), *Violence and mental disorder: Developments in risk assessment* (pp. 203–226). Chicago: University of Chicago Press.

Wiebush, R. G., Baird, C., Krisberg, B., & Onek, D. (1995). Risk assessment and classification for serious, violent, and chronic juvenile offenders. In J. C. Howell, B. Krisberg, J. D. Hawkins, & J. J. Wilson (Eds.), *Serious, violent, and chronic juvenile offenders: A sourcebook* (pp. 171–212). Thousand Oaks, CA: Sage.

Witt, P. H., & Dyer, F. J. (1997). Juvenile transfer cases: Risk assessment and risk management. *Journal of Psychiatry & Law, 25,* 581–614.

Wolfe, A. (1999, October 16). Two dead in murder, suicide. *The Telegraph,* p. A1, A17.

Zona, M. A., Palarea, R. E., & Lane, J. C. (1998). Psychiatric diagnosis and the offender-victim typology of stalking. In J. R. Meloy (Ed.), *The psychology of stalking: Clinical and forensic perspectives* (pp. 69–84). San Diego, CA: Academic Press.

Zona, M. A., Sharma, K. K., & Lane, J. (1993). A comparative study of erotomanic and obsessional subjects in a forensic sample. *Journal of Forensic Sciences, 38,* 894–903.

Author Index

Subject Index

ABOUT THE AUTHOR

Joseph T. McCann, PsyD, JD, is a psychologist and attorney in Binghamton, New York. He is the author of several books, including *Malingering and Deception in Adolescents* (American Psychological Association, 1998) and the forthcoming *Threats in Schools: A Practical Guide for Managing Violence*. Dr. McCann has published and lectured widely in the area of personality disorders, personality assessment, and forensic psychology, and he is founding editor of the *Journal of Threat Assessment*. He is a clinical psychologist at United Health Services Hospitals and a private forensic psychological consultant in criminal and civil cases. In addition, Dr. McCann is a Fellow of the American Psychological Association (Division 41), the Society for Personality Assessment, and the American College of Forensic Examiners.